Natural Resource and Environmental
POLICY ANALYSIS

About the Book and Editors

As natural resources have become scarcer, issues of environmental policy have become more vital and subject to debate in global as well as local arenas. Through the use of case studies especially developed for this book, the authors analyze the wide range of institutional contexts in which natural resource and environmental policy issues arise and the processes by which they are resolved. The first chapter provides a theoretical framework of key resource and environmental economics concepts—an overview that gradually broadens as the student is exposed to alternative methods of analysis, including market-oriented analysis, institutional analysis, and modeling. The case studies all begin with discussions of the pertinent biological, physical, social, and institutional issues before economic analysis is applied and policy conclusions are drawn. Suggested readings and study questions follow each chapter.

This book is designed for use in upper-level college courses in natural resource and environmental economics and graduate courses in resource management. It can be used either as a primary text in conjunction with theoretical readings or as a supplemental source of case study readings. The cases will also be valuable for natural resource, environmental, and community development economists.

George M. Johnston is an associate economist with Planning and Development Collaborative International (PADCO). **David Freshwater** is a senior economist with the Joint Economic Committee of the United States Congress. **Philip Favero** is an associate professor and extension economist at the University of Maryland.

Natural Resource and Environmental
POLICY ANALYSIS

Cases in Applied Economics

George M. Johnston
David Freshwater
Philip Favero

EDITORS

WESTVIEW PRESS
Boulder & London

Copyright © 1988 by Westview Press, Inc.

Published in 1988 in the United States of America by Westview Press, Inc.; Frederick A. Praeger, Publisher; 5500 Central Avenue, Boulder, Colorado 80301

Library of Congress Cataloging-in-Publication Data
Natural resource and environmental policy analysis.
  Bibliography: p.
  Includes index.
  1. Environmental policy—Case studies. 2. Natural
resources—Management—Case studies. I. Johnston,
George M. II. Freshwater, David. III. Favero,
Philip.
HC79.E5N355 1988   333.7   87-31601
ISBN 0-8133-0388-5
ISBN 0-8133-0389-3 (pbk.)

Printed and bound in the United States of America

The paper used in this publication meets the requirements of the American National
Standard for Permanence of Paper for Printed Library Materials Z39.48-1984.

10   9   8   7   6   5   4   3   2   1

Contents

Tables and Figures

Preface for Teachers

As teachers we have often had difficulty finding readings for classroom use that contain adequate and readily understandable information on natural resource and environmental problems and policies. It has been particularly difficult to find readings that provide a case study approach emphasizing the application of economics to these problems. Very little of the applied work developed by economists in these areas finds its way into a format that students can easily obtain and understand. This book addresses these needs by supplying original, self-contained case studies covering resource and environmental issues of regional, national, and international concern. All of the readings in this volume were written expressly for this purpose by economists with particular expertise in the area on which they are writing.

Each case study covers the physical, social, and economic aspects of a significant issue. Chapter 1 reviews the economic concepts that are applied in the various case studies. Policy choices and their consequences are the primary focus; the process of developing and analyzing these choices requires the application of economic principles. Our purpose is to offer the reader an understanding of an important group of natural resource and environmental problems and policies and the role that economists can play in addressing and resolving these issues.

There are two primary classroom uses for this textbook. The text can serve as a collection of supplemental readings to complement a core text in a junior or senior level resource or environmental economics course. In this instance the main text would provide greater depth in the development of key concepts of economic theory that are reviewed here in Chapter 1. The book can also be used as a primary text for the growing number of resource and environmental management courses. In these classes the typical student has a background in a discipline other than economics but requires exposure to how economists analyze problems. If the course is oriented around the issues and policy questions set out in each chapter rather than focused on the approach used for analysis, the book will be particularly useful.

Chapter 1 includes the bulk of the refresher information on economic concepts that a student needs before the rest of the chapters are tackled. The other chapters of the book contain information on the application of economic concepts to current resource and environmental problems. Instead of a general discussion of these problems, the focused, case study approach provides an opportunity to examine an issue in detail. Each of the cases is designed as an introduction to an issue by describing the nature of biological, physical, and social characteristics that set up the policy problem. The core economic concepts used in the analysis are elaborated and applied to the issues and policies at hand. Finally, each chapter concludes with the author's comments on what can be generalized and applied to related issues as a result of the economic analysis.

An important function of the book is to encourage an appreciation of the diversity in economics through the use of case studies. The authors were invited by the editors to contribute chapters on the basis of two criteria: first, the author's understanding of the technical material in the chapter and second, his or her grasp of a particular approach or methodology. Our intent was to compile a book of readings that surveys important issues in resource and environmental economics and also provides students with a feel for the range of approaches employed by economists in dealing with policy issues.

We believe that these case studies constitute a powerful teaching tool. For the instructor who favors a different approach to any of the problems studied, an opportunity is created to apply a different methodology to the same problem and compare the results. Alternatively, if the instructor wishes to develop the problem in greater depth, the student has received an introduction that should simplify the process of understanding more advanced readings.

The studies are organized into three groups linked by methodological approaches. Introductory comments for each part guide the student on the material and linkages within the group. Each chapter begins with an abstract and ends with notes, references, and study questions.

We make no claim that the particular organization of the book is necessarily the best. Individual instructors may choose to cover chapters in a different order that is more compatible with their core text or personal preference for introducing issues. The self-contained nature of each study facilitates this process. Irrespective of how the instructor chooses to present the material we believe that students will find this book informative on the physical, social, institutional, and economic issues underlying current resource and environmental problems and they will also develop an appreciation of how economists approach these problems.

The Contributors

Dr. Louise M. Arthur, University of Manitoba, Winnipeg

Dr. Richard Barrows, University of Wisconsin, Madison

Dr. Roy R. Carriker, University of Florida, Gainesville

Dr. Ronald C. Faas, Washington State University, Pullman

Dr. Philip Favero, University of Maryland, College Park

Dr. David Freshwater, Joint Economic Committee, U.S. Congress

Dr. George M. Johnston, Planning and Development Collaborative International, Washington, DC

Dr. Karen Klonsky, University of California, Davis

Douglas J. Krieger, Michigan State University, East Lansing

Dr. Michael LeBlanc, U.S. Department of Agriculture, Washington, DC

Dr. David G. Pitt, University of Minnesota, St. Paul

Dr. John Reilly, U.S. Department of Agriculture, Washington, DC

Dr. Ivar E. Strand, Jr., University of Maryland, College Park

Dr. Dean F. Tuthill, Edgerton College, Njoro, Kenya

Dr. Philip Wandschneider, Washington State University, Pullman

Chapter One

The Role of Economics in Natural Resource and Environmental Policy Analysis

George M. Johnston

Natural resources are broadly defined as specific attributes of the environment that are valued or have proven useful to humans. The space we occupy, air we breathe, and water we drink are essential life-supporting natural resources. Energy and raw materials support human production and consumption. In judging the human condition, we must consider (both qualitatively and quantitatively) our use of environmental elements such as sea coasts, mountains, and wild species of plants and animals.

Problems

The two primary sources of global pressure on natural resources are increasing human population and the increasing per capita consumption of resources by that population. These problems exist in both industrialized and industrializing economies. Industrialized economies consume a dwindling and finite stock of oil, while the use of timber for fuel in the industrializing economies of Africa, Asia, and South America is leading to deforestation and seriously exhausting that renewable resource. Relatively affluent societies will be able to cope better with increasing scarcity, but the need for careful choices is critically important to poor societies where unrestrained population growth often strains the resource base.

Exhaustion of resources, destruction of environments and ecosystems, and the effects of residuals (air and water pollution) are neither new phenomena nor insurmountable problems. Nevertheless, concern over these issues has grown considerably in the last several decades. One reason for this change is that knowledge and understanding of the interdependence between various life-forms and other natural resources have multiplied within the biological and earth sciences, especially ecology. Although scientists have known about acid rain and the greenhouse effect for some time, there are now efforts to measure these relationships and show causality. As a result of this burgeoning knowledge as well as expanding public awareness, the preferences and, hence, the demand for preserving or improving natural environments has dramatically increased. Preferences for environmentally sensitive policies also have grown because more affluent communities are better able to change production modes and consumption patterns as a means to protect the environment.

Policy Questions

A common element of resource use decisions is their long-term effects. The policymaking issue is usually not one of hoarding resources but one of deciding upon the rate of resource use—the intertemporal dimension. How much do we use now and how much do we leave for future use? At what rate do we exhaust depletable resources, thereby affecting the endowment for future generations? In what condition do we leave the environment? What current actions have irreversible effects on resource availability and the assimilative ability of the environment? The intertemporal element permeates economic analyses of natural resource and environmental issues. This preoccupation with present and future outcomes of resource use includes concerns with efficiency, equity, conservation, preservation, environmental quality, and economic growth.

This chapter will explore a conceptual model of natural resource policy analysis. Ultimately the process of determining the boundaries of a conceptual model and defining concepts therein is one of individual choice. My view of how the pieces fit together should not necessarily be interpreted as either the best view or as the only view. I have made an effort to define commonly used economic concepts in a way acceptable to many, but no claim to universality is made or is even possible.

THE TASK OF ECONOMIC ANALYSIS

Economic and Scarcity Defined

Economics is a social science whose central focus is the process and institutions involved in weighing alternative uses of scarce resources. A resource is considered scarce when demand exceeds supply at zero price. Scarcity forms the basis of human interdependence concerning natural resources and the environment; scarcity involves both the amount available and how society allocates that amount.

The concept of opportunity cost—the value of a forgone alternative— follows directly from the assumption of resource scarcity: Every choice has an alternative and a cost reflecting the value of the opportunity sacrificed. Much of economic analysis, including benefit-cost analysis, is an extension of this concept. As the quantity of resources or the quality of the environment decreases, their opportunity cost increases, other things being equal.

A Framework for Policy Analysis

Broadly speaking, analysis involves the resolution of a complex issue into its parts in order to clarify the nature of the issue and to facilitate problem solving. The application of economics to resource policy analysis requires that the analysis proceed by identifying (1) key characteristics of the resource; (2) realistic policy constraints; (3) relevant participants and institutions; (4) behavioral responses of participants under different institutional arrangements and policy structures; and (5) current and future outcomes affected by policy options.

Natural systems have physical characteristics that affect the kinds of institutions likely to be useful in coping with or changing undesired outcomes. Socioeconomic characteristics such as the degree of excludability also affect resource use. Institutions, in turn, affect human production, consumption, and land use behavior. The outcomes or consequences of policy choices affected by institutions and behavior include residuals, resource availability now and in the future, the quality of life, and other concerns. From this core knowledge, the economist identifies behavioral results that suggest how policy alternatives affect various outcomes. Economists pursue the problem-solving nature of policy analyses with various degrees of theoretical abstraction and empirical evaluation, but these five steps are common elements in much of their work.

RESOURCE CHARACTERISTICS

Economists depend upon the physical and life sciences to provide information on physical traits of resources: rate of exhaustion of a depletable resource; capacity and extraction limits for a renewable resource; kind and rate of waste discharge; and other physical and biological traits of relevance to a particular policy issue. Changes in characteristics also become, in effect, outcomes—intentional or unintentional, direct or indirect—of policy decisions.

Some resource characteristics shape the policy debate over their use. The stock of specific natural resources can be classified as either depletable or renewable within a humanly relevant time period (McInerney, 1981). Some resources are depletable; their quantity is finite, and their current use reduces that quantity in the future. Oil, virgin natural habitat, natural gas, and minerals are all examples of depletable resources. The quantity of other resources is renewable at biological or biochemical rates, mostly out of human control. Timber, fish, wildlife, and most groundwater are examples of renewable resources. The current stock of both depletable and renewable resources may be consumed; renewable resources, however, have the potential of adding to their stock by a measurable amount if consumption does not exceed depletion. Issues associated with depletable resources center on intergenerational allocation and possible substitutes for these finite stocks; issues associated with renewable resources center on maintaining a sustainable flow of the resource. At the limit, the maximum physical flow of the resource that can be maintained in perpetuity is called the maximum sustainable yield. Both depletable and renewable resources can be exhausted through human use. There is thus an intrinsic issue of intertemporal allocation and distribution of such resources between current use and use by future generations.

Resources must be used for investments that will produce goods for future generations. But the use of natural resources can also alter or destroy environmental and ecological systems, thereby threatening future generations. Destruction of wetlands, for example, has dramatically affected a large number of wild species and the genetic foundation of many animal and plant resources. Such resource issues often arise when we make decisions about the use of land. Land use decisions are important because of the varied and interdependent attributes of land. The most important of these attributes is land's unique spatial and geographic features. The use and value of land often depends upon proximity to cities and towns; land close to or in urban areas is geographically unique and commands location or economic rents. Rents are defined as returns above costs of production resulting from natural limitations of supply.

Other attributes of land include soil productivity, mineral deposits, wildlife habitat, and scenic amenities. There are many cases of complementary land uses—forestry and some recreational and wildlife uses, for example—but land use decisions often involve choices between incompatible uses. Land can be used for urban housing *or* for agriculture. In some cases, land may have unique scenic, geographic, or biological traits whose loss, as a result of incompatible uses, would be irreversible.

Using natural resources for human production and consumption has physical consequences deriving from the principles of thermodynamics. Extraction and transformation of natural resources leads to conversion from a concentrated to a dispersed form or a residual that is then deposited back into the environment. These residuals can either overload the absorptive capacity of the environment or be of such an exotic nature as to cause severe long-term harm. Common examples of such residuals are air and water pollution from energy and mineral use. The alarming effect of residuals on the environment ultimately focuses our attention on natural resource use and results in public debates about the trade-offs between various forms of energy, soil conservation practices, and the use of pesticides and fertilizers, to name a few of the many questions to be addressed.

In addition to the physical characteristics of resources just discussed, there are social and economic characteristics that influence how society controls any resource. Four of these characteristics are incompatible use, joint impact, exclusion traits, and group size (Schmid, 1978).[1] These characteristics exist in various degrees in many natural resource and environmental issues.

Assuming scarcity, when a resource has two or more potential uses that are incompatible, one person's use means that the resource is unavailable to another. In the main, resource ownership determines resource use, buttressed by common, trespass, and nuisance law. In Western societies, private ownership and the market are the principal institutions used to determine resource use, but land use regulations and public ownership of land, energy sources, and minerals are also common. Further government concern with incompatible uses centers on maintaining a degree of competition in order to prevent monopoly conditions. Incompatible use also applies across generations. Current use of depletable resources, renewable resources being used beyond their carrying capacity, and permanent changes in environmental and ecological systems all create incompatible use between current and future peoples.

Within limits, some resources can be shared by two or more compatible users without subtracting utility from any one user. In economic terms, the marginal cost of an additional user is zero or close to zero. These are called joint-impact goods.[2] In terms of access to users, clean air, clean water, abundant wildlife, and other factors contributing to the quality of human life, have, in effect, a marginal cost of zero. These are joint-impact goods up to the point a threshold for the absorptive or replacement rate is exceeded. A central institutional issue associated with joint-impact traits is how the costs of providing these resources are shared. Providing good water quality or an electrical grid system will often be hindered if the cost-sharing issues are not resolved. Thus issues often arise about who will pay for these goods.

Regardless of whether a resource has incompatible-use or joint-impact traits, the ease of access or, conversely, the difficulty of excluding others from access or exposure to the good affects resource use and provision decisions. When exclusion costs are low, the control of access allows the resource owner to charge for the use of the resource. This is the case for an incompatible-use good such as land or a joint-impact good like electrical lines.

When exclusion costs are high, the access or exposure to the resource will be difficult to police or, in some cases, avoid. Nominal private ownership of incompatible-use resources such as migratory wildlife or some ocean fisheries would be of little value because access by nonowners is relatively easy and therefore difficult to police. Joint-impact goods with high-exclusion costs abound in the environment; air, water, and other qualitative features affected by residuals are prime examples. When a few individuals are affected and wish to change the situation, organizational possibilities exist to have this group engage in strategic bargaining within the market because the group can perceive its gains from involvement. When many are affected, which is often the case with air and water quality problems, the "free rider" situation arises. In this case, each air or water user knows that if these resources are made cleaner, no one can be excluded, even if they as individuals make no contribution to help clean up the resource. Pure market institutions are thus unlikely to provide these goods. Even should the good be provided, the joint-impact, cost-sharing issue would still exist with many goods. How would you charge a price for the good? Who would pay?

Group size can affect the ease or difficulty in dealing with high-exclusion cost situations. Individuals in a large group are less likely to perceive an ability to affect an outcome such as improving air or water quality. All affected individuals in a small group, in contrast, may be able to perceive the returns from collective action. For example, smaller, inshore fisheries are more often successfully managed than international fisheries because a smaller group with more uniform interests is involved.

Incompatible-use, joint-impact, exclusion, and group size traits do not exhaust the list of resource characteristics shaping human interdependence and resource use. These traits, however, combined with physical information relating to resource depletion, carrying capacity (the population that an area will support without deteriorating), and the incidence of residuals, provide a basis for predicting the effects of various institutional arrangements on the outcomes of the policy alternatives.

INSTITUTIONS AND TRANSACTIONS

Institutions include both formal and informal rules and procedures governing behavior (Wandschneider, 1986) and include the range of laws, administrative codes, customs, organizations, traditions, and their interactions as they affect the way in which society deals with complex resource issues (Buse and Bromley, 1975). Property rights refer to that subset of institutions that specify the rules and procedures governing the relationships among individuals with respect to their access to, and control over, resources. "Rules-of-the-game" connotes a specific set of institutions and property rights relevant to a particular problem and is the focus of policy analysis. Institutions establish the particular rights and rules that affect market, administrative, and traditional transactions. Institutions guide and condition the behavior of individuals and groups and ultimately affect resource outcomes. But this process requires the recognition of the complexity and subtlety of the relationship between resource characteristics and institutions.

Three institutional subsets often discussed by economists exhibit different types of transactions. Briefly, markets involve exchanges between legal equals, administrative transactions are between a superior and inferior, and traditional transactions are internalized standards of behavior or customs (Schmid, 1978). Natural resource and environmental problems often involve a complex mixture of transactions.

Market Transactions

Analysis of market institutions is central to resource and environmental issues because such institutions often determine the use of resources. Prices, mirroring supply-and-demand conditions, and substitutes play a critical role in natural resource use decisions. Market prices reflect the processing of large quantities of information about production and consumption while also serving as incentives to produce, consume, or conserve. For example, if a natural resource becomes scarcer, either as a result of diminishing supply relative to constant demand or to increasing demand relative to a constant supply, its price is likely to rise. The opportunity cost of the resource increases, and behavioral responses could include conservation, substitution of other resources, greater exploration for the now more valuable resource, increased research and development in search of technological changes, and recycling, among other responses.

Economists often prescribe rules that affect prices and the costs and returns available to firms as policies to avoid environmentally harmful residuals. Examples of such policies include emission charges, taxes, penalties, and tradable emission rights. Charges, taxes, or penalties are applied to actual levels of pollution, an action that increases the production cost to the firm and hence provides an incentive to reduce emissions. These policies, as well as other market approaches to resolving environmental issues, including marginal cost-price and tradable emission rights, while popular with economists, are much less in evidence than administrative rules and regulations.

Administrative Transactions

Legal, administrative, or regulatory systems of control are the general institutional devices that govern the environment in which individuals exchange goods and services. Through changes in laws, regulations, administrative procedures, adjustments are made in the nature of ownership of resources. For example, although market transactions and institutions predominate in land use decisions, administrative transactions are also involved via zoning, taxes, and the provision of public services. There are also many resources in the United States and Canada, including extensive land, timber, and mineral resources, that are owned by the federal governments. Furthermore, marine resources are now publicly regulated within 200 nautical miles of the coast.

Environmental residuals are managed by means of a predominant set of rules that include standards. These set rules regulate behavior by designating acceptable levels of ambient or effluent discharge or for specific technologies required of those companies discharging residuals. Many economists favor charges over standards because of perceived cost-effectiveness and ease of policing. Standards, nevertheless, are the most common form of transactions imposed because they are a more easily understood control device and because they allow the regulator to be more specific in determining the admissible level of emissions.

Traditional Transactions

Internalized standards of behavior or prescribed social and family obligations can have a major effect on natural resource use. Examples of such behavior are land stewardship, altriusm in provision of high-exclusion and joint-impact goods, and grants for posterity by the present generation. When a person contributes or donates land for a public park, the returns to that individual in terms of personal benefits are exceeded by the value of the gift to others. Many individuals are involved in group efforts such as the Nature Conservancy and the World Wildlife Fund, where the same process is at work. Provision for posterity at either the individual, group, community, or government level also reflects internalized beliefs of social obligations or stewardship. This type of action reflects the divergence that often exists between private or individual returns and benefits that accrue to the larger community.

Transaction Costs and the Boundary Issue

Regardless of the type of transactions, there are costs associated with changing or attempting to change resource use. Transaction costs arise both from resource characteristics and property rights. When there are large groups and high-exclusion costs, organizing either a market bid or even an administrative transaction will be difficult. Those affected by widely dispersed air pollution will find it difficult to organize to change the situation. In this case, assembling individuals into a cohesive group and assessing the magnitude of the total injury is an expensive proposition. Information and uncertainty affect the ease or difficulty in making a transaction or decision. Political activity and class action suits provide a means for short-circuiting this process. The ability to acquire information, to influence the flow of information, or to cope with uncertainty are unevenly distributed among the population and, therefore, affects resource use.

In order to understand resource use decisions, it is critical to examine the relationship between the physical, social, and economic boundaries of environmental problems and the political boundaries of the jurisdictions responsible for addressing those problems. Political jurisdictions and the resource/environmental decisions made by those jurisdictions seldom match the boundaries of those affected by the decisions. The "boundary issue" arises when the costs and benefits of an activity or decision affecting resource use are not contained solely within the jurisdiction making the decision. Solutions to problems arising from such a situation, if such solutions are to consider all parties affected, will require transactions between political entities. A few examples of boundary issues involving jurisdictions both within countries and between countries are river basin management; migratory wildlife management; marine fisheries management, particularly of migratory species such as tuna and salmon; and ambient air quality problems such as acid rain.

BEHAVIOR

Behavior that affects resource use is defined as the calculated and noncalculated response to resource, environmental, and institutional situations. These responses incorporate both current values and habits as well as the learning process, which results in changes in those values and habits. Wellposed problems with clear value choices, objectives, and expected outcomes can be aided by static economic analyses. Economists have provided a rich literature on market, production, and consumption behavior. This behavior includes accepting "reasonable" but not optimal criteria—"satisficing"—as well as accepting behavioral rules such as standard operating procedures. The insights of economists are brought to bear in various aspects of resource and environmental analyses: for example, the role played by the market and prices in the resource substitution process; the impact of uncertainty, expectations, and options on our behavior; time preferences and interest rates, which affect future generations; and the role played by social traps and common property. The following discussion addresses the behavioral issues that impact resource and environmental issues.

Substitution, Exploration, and Technological Change

Prices play an important role in determining resource use and chages in use. Prices result from and affect behavior through the interaction of supply and demand. Thus, as in other forms of incentives, humans are influenced by the consequences of their own behavior.

Substitution implies shifts to other resources as well as recycling (Howe, 1979). As relative prices increase (or decrease), there will be a shift to (or from) other resources. The ease and rate of this process will depend upon the availability of substitutes and preferences for those substitutes. A small change in relative prices can trigger a significant change in resource use if substitution is easy. If substitution is not easy, then it will take a larger change in relative prices to trigger the shift to other resources.

Price changes can also result in reuse of some resources. However, recycling of materials, primarily minerals, will not save the materials ad infinitum. Minerals are ultimately, in an economic sense, depletable because following each round of use some quantity is not recoverable. The costs of recycling, especially transportation, limit its application, and some rules, such as depletion allowances, favor the use of raw materials rather than recycling. Property rights also often favor disposal of residuals from production and consumption as the cost of disposal to the resource user is zero or subsidized (Pearce and Walter, 1977).

Prices or other factors that improve the returns to a resource can stimulate increased exploration for new resource sources. From the point of view of the firm, an increase in marginal revenue may provide the incentive to bear the larger marginal costs involved in exploration and discovery of the resource. The firm will find that expanding exploration is profitable whenever expected marginal revenue is greater than marginal cost, and the firm will continue to expand until marginal revenue equals marginal cost. The relative ease of exploration, discovery, and extraction will determine how much of a price increase will be needed to trigger such a response. Rapid increases in oil prices in the early 1970s resulted in greater investments in exploration and extraction of less accessible deposits. In other cases, exploration and discovery have become easier as a result of technological changes that have made locating and quantifying both depletable and renewable resources easier.

Improved technology can reduce the cost of extracting, transporting, processing, and using resourses. A search for such technology can be a purposeful response to increased extraction costs or improved revenues. Technological improvements can increase output per resource unit through new resource discoveries, utilization of lower grade resources that are easily accessed, or greater use of substitute resources (Baumol, 1986). Technology can also lead to more uses of a depletable resource or the possibility of exceeding the carrying capacity of a renewable resource. Technological change, triggered by competition for an open access resource, has, for example, allowed per unit costs of harvesting some marine fisheries to drop dramatically to the point of near destruction of the fishery. On the other hand, as the cost of pumping groundwater has increased because of declines in the water table, technology in agricultural uses has increased the productive efficiency of the water.

Uncertainty, Expectations, and Option Values

Uncertainty "is the gap between what is known and what needs to be known" in decisionmaking (Mack, 1971). Uncertainty permeates economic issues. It may be relatively small, when total knowledge is not quite possible, as is the case in many land use decisions. It may be extensive, when the type or direction of results, such as the greenhouse effect, is unknown.

Uncertainty exists over the following range of issues: the stock of depletable resources; the stock and carrying capacity of renewable resources; the short- and long-term effects of residuals; and the future demand for natural resources, a clean environment, and natural environments that have been lost due to irreversibilities in current decisions. The scope and nature of uncertainty will vary from issue to issue. The behavioral responses to uncertainty will depend upon the relative situation of the individual or group. Some may respond to uncertainty with a conservative approach, limiting the number of alternatives considered. Others may ignore the issue. For example, if there is no certainty about the cumulative effects of pesticides or the rate of groundwater pollution, their effects are easier to ignore.

We deal with the "gap" between the known and unknown by forming expectations. What one thinks about the likelihood of a future outcome depends upon many factors including the quality of information, past experience, the current situation, and one's mood on a particular day. Although expectations can change quickly, if acted upon, they can also have enduring, profound effects. For example, expectations of increasing farmland prices accentuated the increase in those prices in the 1960s and 1970s. The decline in farmland prices in the early and mid-1980s was also accentuated by expectations of continued price declines.

Expectations can also lead to a conservative attitude. Expectations on the success of exploration may affect the rate of depletion of the known resources. Fewer chances for success in exploration lead to slower depletion of known reserves. Thus, nonoptimizing concepts of behavior, including seeking satisfactory versus optimal outcomes, will be likely to predominate in the face of greater degrees of uncertainty. Finally, because future demands are uncertain, the present generation may perceive a value to maintaining an option for future uses of the resource (Krutilla and Fisher, 1975). Whether altruistic or self-serving, this behavior, especially directed at potentially irreversible resource losses, has affected resource decisions.

Time Preferences and Interest Rates

The current generation makes resource choices for future generations, like it or not. Current use of resources affects opportunities in the future by changing what will be available and, among other things, by improving knowledge of how to use resources. But extraction of depletable resources also represents a forgone future output, and use of a renewable resource can exceed the replacement rate. These are in effect intergenerational opportunity costs.

Time preferences gauge the degree to which concern for future generations is taken into account by the present generation. Uncertainty about the future results in a bias toward current use because the latter is more certain. Other factors affecting time choices are present and expected future income, perceived needs, age, education, and altriusm. For example, people with high incomes are able to defer some consumption more often than poorer people, who may lack even the most basic items and who therefore cannot defer consumption. Communities and governments are able to take a longer view. The degree to which they do also depends upon their relative income, uncertainty, and so on.

Interest or discount rates provide a means for comparing different streams of benefits and costs through time. The rates provide a means for weighting outcomes that occur at different points in time so that they have present value equivalents. Lower interest rates put greater weight on future outcomes; higher interest rates favor current consumption. With a lower interest rate, the opportunity cost of waiting is reduced. Clearly, there is a great deal of variety in time preferences and, hence, interest rates among individuals, groups, and societies. Interest rates chosen for appraising the benefits and costs of public projects are a value-weighting device and as such are subject to debate among groups holding different time preferences. The choice of interest rates will affect the choice of projects to be undertaken. A higher interest rate will restrict projects to those having fairly rapid recovery costs.

Social Traps and Common Property

Social traps (Platt, 1973; Schmid, 1978) exist when individuals or groups do something for their individual, marginal advantage that is collectively damaging to themselves, and/or the group as a whole, in the long term. Although individuals might be aware of the long-term consequences of their actions, they, of need, are trapped into responding to short-term situations and constraints. Even if individuals try to act differently, the outcome will not change unless there is collective action by all of the resource users. Social traps are often intractable but certainly not insolvable. Common property institutions will serve as an example of social traps and also provide an example of a method of analysis for breaking the trap.

As population growth and increased economic activity lead to greater resource scarcity, existing institutional arrangements like common property may induce behavior that can destroy that resource. Common property problems exist when the following conditions are present (Ostrom and Ostrom, 1977):

1. Property rights to the resource are unclear or held in common.
2. A large number of users have unrestricted access.
3. Collective action is needed to solve the problem.
4. Total demands upon the resource exceed the supply or carrying capacity.

Common property is an institutional arrangement that can coincide with a large variety of both physical and socioeconomic resource characteristics. Common property resources often represent incompatible uses because the marginal cost of an additional user is not zero. But common property can have either high- or low-exclusion costs, and its use can be affected by small or large groups. Examples of common property include international fisheries, fugitive wildlife resources, some underground oil and water pools, and ambient air and water systems. Adverse effects of human activity include exhausting the resource or polluting it with residuals.

An examination of international fisheries and issues of the freedom of the seas demonstrates the social-trap characteristics of common property institutions. Freedom of the seas permits unrestricted access to international fisheries. The number of users of a given fishery can, therefore, be quite large. In some cases, the demands placed upon the fishery have exceeded its production capacity and diminished or destroyed the fishery. As the fishery resource becomes smaller, the resource users will increase their effort to catch fish and/or invest in improved fishing gear in order to maintain the quantity of their catch. There will be no individual incentive to conserve because the bulk of the benefits of this behavior would pass to others. Everyone else will be in the same position unless some sort of collective action is undertaken to relieve the social trap. In the case of international fisheries, territorial limits have been either unilaterally or multilaterally extended as an effort to remedy some of the depletion problems. Other institutional solutions will depend upon the resource traits such as exclusion, group size, and international boundaries.

OUTCOMES

Outcomes are the consequences resulting from the interaction of resource characteristics, institutions, and human behavior. As such, they are the indicators of the impacts of institutions on resources and humans. They become defined within specific issues and problems. Outcomes may be measured by physical units, monetary units, or both, and can be defined for the individual, group, or government. Three broad categories of economic concepts relevant to understanding and judging outcomes are externalities, efficiency, and equity.

Externalities

In the broadest sense, externalities are the outcomes or effects of an action that are not accounted for by the actor and that therefore do not influence his or her decisions (Heyne, 1973). They can be either positive or negative. Three kinds of externalities are discussed here: technological, pecuniary, and political.

Technological externalities, called simply externalities by most economists, are the unaccounted-for physical consequences of a decision or resource use. Off-site effects of pollution on air and water, soil erosion, and losses and gains in wildlife habitat are physical effects caused by an individual or group not bearing the full costs or benefits of the act.

Pecuniary externalities are the unaccounted-for positive or negative monetary effects of an action. They are changes in relative prices that work their way through the market to enhance or detract from the value of assets held by others. Responses to technological externalities often create pecuniary externalities and vice versa (Baumol and Oates, 1975). If a steel mill's pollution is abated by regulations, thus "internalizing" the technological externality, the resulting pecuniary externalities can include higher prices for steel or lower profits for the steel firms. Similarly, efforts to change relative prices lead to changes in resources used in production or consumption activities.

Political externalities arise when the actions of a governmental unit affect citizens of other units of government. The boundary issue is an example of a political externality. However, the effects of political choices on those outside the choice process are measured by technological and/or pecuniary effects. The land-use zoning decisions of one jurisdiction can affect the housing demands made on other jurisdictions: Restrictive zoning to preserve agricultural uses will force housing developers to look and bid in other, more receptive jurisdictions and will raise the price of housing by limiting supply.

Technological, pecuniary, and political externalities provide concepts for categorizing the outcomes of given institutions on resource use and the environment. They also help to isolate the effects of market, administrative, and traditional transactions on resources. Externalities, as used here, become a way of tracking human interdependence in resource use decisions.

Efficiency

Efficiency measures how well inputs are combined in the process of making outputs. It is used by economists as a social norm, based upon the perfectly competitive model, to judge resource use. As with all outcome measures, the type of efficiency considered depends upon the units of measurement. Four kinds of efficiency are explained here—technical, price, allocative, and intertemporal (Freshwater and Appin Associates, 1985).

In technical efficiency, the physical combination of inputs to outputs is such that no greater output can be produced with the given inputs. Further, "technical efficiency is concerned with the physical determinants of 'ideal' output" (Bromley, 1984). This includes, for example, the physical relationship between grazing and watershed protection or timber production and grazing.

Price or private economic efficiency is measured by looking at how an individual or firm adjusts the ratio of inputs to outputs depending upon their relative prices. Prices serve as indicators of value derived from market transactions. They adjust to reflect changing tastes, levels of income, resource availability, and so on, when markets work well. Prices signal a set of production decisions that equate selling prices to their marginal production cost, assuming profit maximizing behavior.

Allocative efficiency is defined as the maximum consumption of goods and services given the available amount of resources. Prices provide the link between the production decisions of the firm and individual consumption decisions. It implies an allocation of resources, at the societal level, to produce a collection and allocation of goods and services that results in a situation where no individual can be made better off without another being made worse off. Allocative efficiency requires that individuals equate the marginal benefit of the last unit of every type of good obtained by that individual. In this sense, it is a measure of the opportunity cost of consumption of a particular good. For the individual, maximum welfare is achieved if the ratio of prices paid for the goods equals the ratio of the marginal utility provided by the goods. From the production side, the output mix is such that the social values between any two products are equal to the rate at which one is sacrificed for the other (Bromley, 1984).

Intertemporal efficiency conceptually applies the Pareto Optimality through time, acknowledging that a particular set of goods produced and distributed at one point in time will change in the future. As particular resources become scarcer, population grows, and consumption patterns change, efficient outcomes will change.

Economic calculations of efficiency assume, indeed require, that the conditions necessary for a perfectly competitive market be met. Efficiency also assumes a status quo distribution. When there are significant technological externalities, high-exclusion and joint-impact traits, or intertemporal depletion effects (Page, 1981), a perfectly competitive market does not exist, and, therefore, resources are not efficiently allocated by markets. In cases where there are many deviations from the perfect competition requirements, partial policy measures that eliminate some but not all deviations do not necessarily improve "social welfare." Efficiency, however, in a less technical sense, is still used as a rough measure of opportunity costs, focusing on the "reasonable" trade-offs involved in policy choices.

Equity

Equity in access and use of resources is an important, if not transcendent, policy determinant. Indeed, policy prescriptions based solely on economic efficiency criteria, which assume the status quo distribution, may receive little attention if they do not coincide with the values of the decisionmakers (Shabman, 1984; Bromley, 1984). Policy analysis, therefore, usually entails a description of the distributional consequences of choices being considered.

Equity or fairness issues have been discussed largely in an intertemporal dimension, but in practice, intratemporal distributions of wealth and access to resources often dominate the policymaking process. The policies adopted and institutions considered depend to a considerable extent upon who is involved in the decisions. As in the case of political externalities and the boundary issue, if you are not involved in the decisionmaking, your interests may not be considered even if you are affected by the decisions.

The distribution of resources also significantly affects the behavior and potential options open to various segments of society. We are not equal in our abilities to respond to price changes, use technological changes, respond to uncertainties, and save for the future. Policy issues are therefore often focused on changing the access to resources by various groups. Distributional issues also arise because of the joint-impact nature of many environmental issues. The marginal cost of additional users is effectively zero once clear air and water are provided. The issue then becomes allocating the cost in an "equitable" manner. Additionally, as previously mentioned, regulating pollution, a technological externality, has monetary effects on the value of assets associated with the pollution.

As no universal criteria for equity exists, economic policy analysts can only incorporate the distributional effects of policy choices into their analysis, eschewing a declaration of the "best" distribution. Because natural resource and environmental issues have inherent intertemporal choices, current economic analysis often reports, in some form, the effect of choices made today on resource availability and environmental conditions for the future.

Evaluating Outcomes

Externalities, efficiency, and equity are central to natural resource and environmental problems. Resolving a problem invariably involves choosing among policy prescriptions that are not value neutral and may result in the creation of an externality. Incorporating these issues into the analysis of a problem is often the major task for an economist involved in applied work.

Nevertheless, for many economists efficiency is the key criterion used to judge the desirability of outcomes. A more efficient solution is one that increases the aggregate quantity of output available to the consumer. In a perfectly competitive world it follows that equating marginal revenue with marginal cost will result in a distribution of goods and services in which nobody can be made better off without someone else being made worse off. Although this is a powerful result, it is restricted in it legitimate applications.

If the requirements of perfect competition are not met, making changes that lead to equating marginal revenue with marginal cost in individual markets will not necessarily lead to improved social welfare. Thus, in the presence of technological externalities, for example, moving a single market to a point where marginal conditions are satisfied need not improve our collective well-being. Further, the perfectly competitive model is silent on issues of distribution. If more is produced or less inputs are consumed this is a desirable outcome. Thus, making the wealthy even richer, providing that no poor people are made worse off, is just as desirable in a competitive model as making the poor wealthier and leaving the rich no poorer. As noted in the discussion on equity, more than efficiency enters the determination of which outcomes are the most desirable.

Despite these limitations, efficiency can be a useful criterion for economists. In many cases the gains from a more efficient solution are such that losers are compensated for the change, and thereby a clear benefit results. When this is the case, an argument for a more efficient solution is hard to refute, providing compensation takes place.

Even in cases that are less clear it may be useful for an economist to advance the case for efficient solutions, particularly if, in developing the argument, allowance has been made for the presence of externalities. In such cases economists must recognize that they are now advocates of particular outcomes and cannot claim that their position represents a value-neutral argument. Efficiency arguments may not be germane in all cases, but they may improve the discussion leading to the ultimate decision.

CONCLUSION

In analyzing the interaction of resource characteristics, policy constraints, institutions, human behavior, as well as the outcomes of policy options, economics can make a significant contribution to natural resource and environmental policymaking. This chapter has presented a framework used in various degrees by economists for analyzing natural resource and environmental issues. Many economic and physical concepts have been defined. Although most of the definitions should be acceptable to most economists, the points emphasized and the groupings of concepts reflect my perception of how the tools of economics can be applied to resource policy issues. The authors of the chapters that follow will expand, elaborate, or adjust this framework as befits their needs and approaches. The intent of this chapter is to provide an overview of important concepts; the diverse approaches to economic analysis represented in the case studies should provide the reader with a more specific understanding of how economics can be usefully applied to natural resource and environmental issues.

NOTES

1. The terminology used in this section is taken from Schmid (1978) because it allows greater precision in analysis. This terminology is not widely used among economists but other terms are less clear. For example, see Randall (1981).

2. In economics literature, high-exclusion cost, joint-impact goods are often called public goods. However, public goods are at various times defined as either high-

exclusion, joint-impact, or goods that the public should provide. Given this confusion in the literature, the term is not used here.

REFERENCES

Baumol, William J. (1986). "On the Possibility of Continuing Expansion of Finite Resources" *KYKLOS* 39:176–179.

Baumol, William J., and Wallace E. Oates (1975). *The Theory of Environmental Policy.* Englewood Cliffs, N.J.: Prentice-Hall, Inc.

Bromley, Daniel W. (1984). "Public and Private Interests in the Federal Lands: Toward Conciliation" in George M. Johnston, and Peter M. Emerson, eds., *Public Lands and the U.S. Economy: Balancing Conservation and Development.* Boulder, Colo.: Westview Press.

Buse, Reuben C., and Daniel W. Bromley (1975). *Applied Economics: Resource Allocation in Rural America.* Ames: Iowa State University Press.

Freshwater, David, and Appin Associates (1985). *Pesticide Regulation and Technological Change: A Discussion of the Issues.* Agriculture Canada Working Paper, 85–93. Ottawa: Agriculture Canada.

Heyne, Paul T. (1973). *The Economic Way of Thinking.* Chicago: Science Research Associates, Inc.

Howe, Charles (1979). *Natural Resource Economics: Issues, Analyses, and Policy.* New York: John Wiley and Sons.

Krutilla, John V., and Anthony C. Fisher (1975). *The Economics of Natural Environments.* Baltimore: Johns Hopkins University Press.

Mack, Ruth (1971). *Planning on Uncertainty.* New York: Wiley-Interscience.

McInerney, J. P. (1981). "Natural Resource Economics: The Basic Analytical Principles" in J. A. Butlin, ed., *Economics and Resources Policy.* Boulder, Colo.: Westview Press.

Ostrom, Vincent, and Elenor Ostrom (1977). "A Theory for Institutional Analysis of Common Pool Problems" in Garrett Hardin, and John Baden, eds. *Managing the Commons.* San Francisco: W. H. Freeman and Company.

Page, Talbot (1981). "Economics of a Throwaway Society" in J. A. Butlin, ed., *Economics and Resources Policy.* Boulder, Colo.: Westview Press.

Pearce, David W., and Ingo Walter (1977). *Resource Conservation: Social and Economic Dimensions of Recycling.* New York: New York University Press.

Platt, John (1973). "Social Traps." *American Psychologist,* no. 8 (August) 28(8):641–651.

Randall, Alan (1981). *Resource Economics: An Economic Approach to Natural Resource and Environmental Policy.* Columbus, Ohio: Grid Publishing, Inc.

Schmid, A. Allan (1978). *Property, Power, and Public Choice: An Inquiry into Law and Economics.* New York: Praeger Publishers.

Shabman, Leonard (1984). "Benefit-Cost Measurement in Policy Decision Processes: A Sceptical View." Paper presented at Symposium on Benefit-Cost Analysis and the Public Policy Process, Ithaca, N.Y.: American Agricultural Economics Association.

Wandschneider, Philip R. (1986). "Neoclassical and Institutionalist Explanations of Changes in Northwest Water Institutions." *Journal of Economic Issues,* 20 (March):87–107.

SUGGESTED READINGS

Butlin, John A., ed. (1981). *The Economics of Environmental and Natural Resources Policy.* Boulder, Colo.: Westview Press.

Twelve well-written chapters by separate contributors that explore the major economic theory and policy themes in natural resource and environmental issues.

Herfindahl, Orris C., and Allen V. Kneese (1974). *Economic Theory of Natural Resources.* Columbus, Ohio: Charles E. Merrill Publishing Co.
A solid presentation of economic theory for advanced students.

Schmid, A. Allan (1978). *Property, Power, and Public Choice.* New York: Praeger Publishers.
The analysis in this book presents the institutional theory from which many of the concepts in this chapter are taken.

Tietenberg, Tom (1984). *Environmental and Natural Resource Economics.* Glenview, Ill.: Scott, Foresman, and Company.
This textbook provides an excellent survey of both the theory and subject matter of the field.

Part One

Political Institutions and Economic Outcomes

Land and water are basic natural resources; their uses have major effects on the quality of life in every society. In the four chapters of Part 1 the authors explore policy issues in agricultural land use, water management, land use/water quality, and nuclear waste disposal, using similar methods of analysis. Each chapter follows a process of defining the characteristics of the natural resource, examining the behavior of resource users, considering consequences for affected groups, and describing institutions that guide the use of the resource. The authors discuss the interdependence of physical, economic, and institutional elements, illustrating how institutions and the "rules-of-the-game" affect the equity, efficiency, and externality outcomes of environmental issues. All factors are considered within the political context that constrains land and water issues and influences outcomes of the policy process.

In addition, the chapters explain and apply basic concepts of natural resource and environmental economics, many of which were introduced in Chapter 1. Externalities, free rider situations, irreversibilities, joint-impact goods, and the boundary issue are all applied to current policy issues. Later chapters draw implicitly on these core concepts while shifting the analytical focus to additional resource issues.

Chapter Two

Institutions, Incentives, and Agricultural Land Policy
A Case Study of a Wisconsin Law

Richard Barrows

*Land use conflicts, especially conflicts surrounding agricultural land pres-
ervation, are the focus of much public debate at the state and local levels
of government. This chapter examines market and political incentives
established by Wisconsin's Farmland Preservation Law (FPL) and reviews
a range of policy options from which the FPL was formed. The options
discussed include financial incentives to land owners, such as use value
assessment, and public regulation—strict zoning, for example. Effects on
the behavior of specific interest groups are reviewed. We learn that small
changes in the institutional rules-of-the-game for a natural resource/
environmental issue can have significant effects on the substantive policy
outcomes—that is, who gets what.*

The interaction of market incentives, publicly induced economic incentives,
and governmental regulation can produce a subtle but very profound influence
on natural resource use. The agricultural land use policy adopted by the
state of Wisconsin, the Farmland Preservation Law (FPL), offers an excellent
case study of those interactions. This case study also illustrates the interdependence of private economic incentives, the behavior of individuals in
the political system, and the rules governing natural resource use.

This chapter demonstrates how an economist, employed by a public
agency or private firm, analyzes a natural resource policy issue, develops
some policy alternatives, and identifies the likely results of each alternative.
The economist analyzing natural resource policy typically begins with a
simple study and description of the current uses of the resource and conflicts
over resource use that have led to the policy debate. Usually the economist
then applies economic theory to identify the key resource characteristics
and institutions that are the basis for the policy issues. This application of
theory allows the economist to analyze the incentives governing the behavior

of different groups of resource owners, users, or policymakers. Based on this analysis the economist can identify policy options and predict the probable consequences of each alternative.

The Wisconsin Farmland Preservation Law was adopted by the Wisconsin legislature in 1977. The law provides income tax credits to landowners whose county and town governments restrict their land to exclusive agricultural use through special zoning and planning programs. The FPL combines incentives for individuals, incentives for local officials, and regulations to guide agricultural land use. The resource and land use situation in which the FPL functions is typical of most urbanizing areas in the United States.

LAND USE, 1967–1977

In the 1960s and 1970s, Wisconsin experienced the same pressures on its agricultural land as many other states. Major changes in the U.S. economy followed World War II, and both population and economic activity shifted rapidly to urban areas. Throughout the 1960s and 1970s urban areas expanded very rapidly, both in terms of population and geographic area. In part this population growth was fueled by the baby boomers who became independent householders. Economic growth continued to favor cities (large and small) over rural areas, so city populations and the number of households grew rapidly. The geographic spread of urban areas resulted not only from the increased urban population but also from advances in highway design and automotive technology that enabled urban workers to reside far from their place of work and freed them from dependence on public transportation. Rising personal income increased the demand for the surburban or exurban lifestyle by lowering the proportion of family income that it would cost. The geographic spread of urban areas accelerated in the late 1960s and 1970s as more industry located on the urban fringe, but the urbanization (or suburbanization) occurred very unevenly in both time and space.

Urban growth presented a great economic opportunity for many farmers fortunate enough to own land in the vicinity of an expanding city. Land for development might sell from two to ten times as much as the prices farmers would be willing (or able) to pay for comparable land. Yet not all farmers were able to "cash in" on the opportunity, especially those with land further from the built-up areas. In addition, not all farmers were ready to sell when the development opportunity arose. Some wanted to continue to farm as a job/lifestyle. Others were too old to have much income-earning potential in an alternative occupation but also were too young to retire.

Many urbanites lamented the loss of open space on the urban fringe. Others objected to property taxes that they believed were inflated by the expense of providing public services to new residents living in widely scattered developments. Urban leaders indicted urban sprawl as one of the causes of the decline of downtown business districts. The rise of the environmental movement in the 1970s added concerns over the finite nature of agricultural land resources on "spaceship earth" and led many to advocate the preservation of good agricultural land for future generations and to preserve a rural community as an alternative lifestyle to the rapidly spreading suburbs and scattered exurban developments.

These general national trends were reflected in Wisconsin. In the ten years prior to the enactment of the FPL, the number of Wisconsin farms declined by 16.4 percent while the average farm size increased by 9.2 percent to 194.8 acres.[1] Dairying accounted for 60 percent of all farm receipts in 1977, compared to 54.8 percent in 1967. Between 1967 and 1977 about 1.9 million acres of farmland were taken out of production, which constituted 9.1 percent of the state's 1967 farmland base. The rate of decline accelerated in the latter part of the period to 1.53 percent per year. These declines occurred in spite of unusually favorable commodity prices and federal government policies designed to increase production and exports.

The rate of conversion of agricultural land to nonfarm use is not known; no state or federal agency regularly collects data at the substate level. However, population changes parallel changes in land use and provide some indication of changes in the 1967–1977 period. The Wisconsin population increased 17.1 percent over the period. The population of rural areas increased 23.3 percent even though the farm population was declining by 28.6 percent at the same time. In general, urban areas were expanding but much of the growth was taking place in rural townships near the central cities. In addition, many smaller cities and villages were growing, and a considerable amount of population growth was being accommodated in rural areas. Agricultural land values increased 328 percent over the period, compared to an overall property value increase of 181 percent. The greatest increases in land values were in counties experiencing rapid population growth. Property taxes increased in proportion to land values.

ANALYZING THE PROBLEM

The essence of agricultural land use problems in Wisconsin in 1977 and across the nation today is that of a natural resource that has two very different uses—agriculture, on the one hand, and urban housing or commercial development, on the other. The uses are almost perfectly incompatible; use of the land for development precludes agriculture and use of the land for agriculture precludes development. Those wishing to develop the land have one set of objectives; those seeking to keep the land in agricultural use have a very different set of objectives. The most basic question is: Whose interests will count in agricultural land policy? The answer involves fundamental questions of equity that the economist is not well equipped to answer. Yet the economist can still provide a great service by making clear the trade-offs between one use of land and another, and the trade-offs between the interests of one group and another.

The economist analyzing a natural resource policy issue begins by applying some of the principles of economic theory to the specific case. One convenient way to group some of the principles is to consider resource characteristics and resource institutions. These characteristics and institutions define the incentives under which different groups seek to use the resource. Individual and group behavior can thus be analyzed systematically.

Resource Characteristics

Agricultural land is a unique resource. Each parcel not only has a distinctive set of soil and topographical characteristics but occupies a particular position in space. It is the parcel's unique location that is the source of the conflict between its agriculture and development use. The public policy debates in Wisconsin, at both the state and at the local level, centered not on whether there should be any new development but *where* that new development should be located. Thus, the issue of converting agricultural land to development use is a location-specific problem.

One of the fundamental assumptions of the perfectly competitive model—a homogeneous product—is violated when considering agricultural land near an expanding urban area. Location is perhaps the single most important characteristic of property on the urban fringe, and location is unique to each parcel. Obviously, if a city is large enough then the amount of agricultural land near the edge of the city is also quite large and many parcels may have approximately the same location relative to, say, the central business district. But even in this case some parcels will be located closer to a major highway, or in the path of the main sewer interceptor, or have some other unique locational attributes.

A second important resource characteristic is the complete incompatibility between agricultural and development uses. Land used for one is completely unavailable for use by the other. Not only is the land occupied by the structure unavailable for agricultural use, but the development will severely interfere with agriculture in the immediate vicinity. For example, farm machinery may be difficult to move from place to place if development creates more traffic and changes road patterns. Or, land may be difficult to rent and impossible to buy, so that the nearby farmer may be unable to expand to take advantage of economies of scale and compete with others further from the city boundary.

The agricultural and development uses are also incompatible over time. The decision to convert agricultural land to development use is, for all practical purposes, irreversible. Once the land is developed in an urbanizing area, other nearby parcels are also likely to be developed, streets will be laid out, sewer and water systems constructed, and the entire land area will be split into smaller and smaller parcels. The cost of removing the structures on one parcel and restoring the land would be extremely high. The cost of doing this to enough parcels to assemble a working-sized farm would be totally prohibitive. Thus, once converted to development use, an agricultural land parcel has very little probability of ever being reconverted to agricultural use.

Agricultural land also has attributes of a joint-impact good. One of the most important "products" of agricultural land near a city is the open space amenity provided urban residents, although this open space is not usually available for public recreational use. Rather, the open landscape provides a visual amenity to urbanites accustomed to the built-up physical environment of the city.

Although U.S. citizens seem reluctant to base their land policy arguments on the amenity value of open space, some countries have very specific laws to maintain amenity values. For example, in order to protect the visual appearance of the English countryside, landowners are sometimes required to receive local government permission to cut down a deciduous tree growing in a pasture. One might expect homeowners on the edge of the city to favor open space preservation because it may increase the value of their house. But many more urban residents favor open space policies simply because they value open space.

It is impossible to exclude anyone from enjoying the amenity value of open space, unless the view is totally blocked by surrounding subdivisions. Further, one person's consumption of open space views does not reduce the amount of open space amenity available to others, provided that road congestion does not detract from the amenity or visual experience. These characteristics make it highly unlikely that the private market will provide a sufficient quantity of open space. Because exclusion is impossible, no urbanite has any incentive to pay for an open space product and no farmer has any means of collecting from those who consume the visual amenity. The free rider problem is present in classic form—if any open space is provided at all, everyone is able to share in its consumption. Finally, the number of urbanites who enjoy open space is so large that any privately organized provision of open space is unlikely—the transaction costs of organizing the group action are prohibitively high. Government and collective action through the political system is the only practical alternative for providing open space on a regional scale.

Institutions

The agricultural land use policy debate concerns the extent to which agricultural land should be allocated to different uses through market transactions versus administrative (governmental) transactions. The theoretical constructs of property rights and the boundary question are useful in analyzing the problem as it is debated in the public arena.

Property Rights. A property right in land is best considered as a "bundle" of potentially separable rights such as the right to use the air over the land, the right to the minerals under it, the right to mine the minerals, the right to use the land in particular ways, the right to water that falls on the land or runs through it, the right to sell or lease the land to others, the right to change the contours or drainage patterns of the land, the right to convert the use of open land to development or other uses.

The crux of the agricultural land use issue is, Who holds the right to develop the land? Is the development right exclusively held by the landowner? Or, is the development right shared by the owner and the public (government)?

Constitutional arguments are moot; there is no question that the public can restrict the right to develop land, within very broad bounds. Rather, the policy debate concerns who *should* hold the development rights. Specifically, the debate concerns whether the public should have the power to veto some specific subset of development plans of the landowner. For example, should the owner have the ability to develop houses on his or her land? Or should that right be limited to the development of only one house per two acres? One per twenty acres? No houses at all without government permission? In most states the debate over agricultural land policy was, and is, a debate over who should hold what property rights in agricultural land.

Boundary Issues. The boundary issue arises when the effects of agricultural land conversion occur outside the governmental jurisdictions that have the authority to control or regulate it. Many urban residents and leaders feel that agricultural land conversion affects their property tax for local public services, business activity in the downtown area, the future shape of the city, and the quality of the visual environment near the city. Yet the decisions to allow development, and the restrictions on development, if any, are usually the province of county governments that may be controlled by nonurban groups. In some states in the Midwest and New England, control over development may be exercised by township government, or control may be shared by township and county government. These smaller units of government are even less likely to be sensitive to the impact of development decisions on the nearby urban center. Political jurisdictions and land market areas seldom coincide. Thus, an important part of the policy debate is often which *level* of government should have the land use control authority.

In most states the boundary issue dominates the discussion of agricultural land policy. Urban groups who own no agricultural land nevertheless feel a keen interest in the land use conversion actions of agricultural landowners. Urban government has little or no control over the land use decisions of county or township government, yet the city and its residents are clearly affected by the decisions of rural landowners and governments. The debate over agricultural land policy is partly a debate about the relevant boundaries for public decisionmaking on agricultural land conversion.

Behavior

The mix of resource characteristics and institutions in a land-use issue gives rise to a wide range of behavioral responses from various groups. The responses are fairly predictable and are based on economic, political, or environmental incentives inherent in the resource under question and the institutions that govern its use. For example, some of the groups that behave in very different ways are farmers who want to develop, farmers who do not want to develop, urbanites/environmentalists, developers, and local elected officials. The behavior of each group can be analyzed and described as if everyone in the group were identical but of course this is not the case. Also, the groups themselves are not necessarily mutually exclusive. For example, the behavior of local elected officials partly depends on whether the official is also a developer, a farmer who wants to develop, or an environmentalist.

Given these cautions, the economist can paint a very general picture of the behavior of different groups, given the resource characteristics, institutions, and the incentives they produce for individuals. By thinking of behavior as a response to incentives that are created by resource characteristics and institutions, the economist can analyze the effect of different policy options by analyzing the changes in incentives for various groups.

Farmer/Developer. Farmers who want to develop their land respond to the basic economic incentive of the capital gains from land conversion. Some are able to capture the pure economic rent inherent in the unique locational advantage of their land as the city grows. If the local government does not jointly share the development decision, the landowner can ignore the boundary issue, the impact of the development on the city dweller, and even the impact on the neighboring farmer.

Farmers seeking to develop their land are sometimes victims of a classic social trap. A farmer who is able to subdivide his entire property can gleefully take the purchase price and leave the farm. More frequently, the farmer may only wish, or is only able, to sell a few lots along the frontage road. When many farmers in an area behave similarly, each reaps some benefits from land sale for conversion. However, the combined effect of the development in the area might restrict farm operations to the point returns from farming are reduced. Thus the overall effect might be negative, even though each farmer pursues his or her own individual best interest in developing as much land as possible.

This social trap is exacerbated by the nature of the market transactions for agricultural land near an urban area. The price of agricultural land, when sold for development, is typically many times higher than the price any farmer can afford to pay for land to farm. But this price is a *marginal* price, based on transactions that occur at a point in time. Only a small fraction of the farmland is offered on the market at any given time. The supply of agricultural land for development is largely a function of the farmer's life cycle. Land comes on the market at retirement or during the probate/estate process at death, but usually not at other times. Development occurs in a spotty fashion partly because developers are forced onto the parcels that happen to come on the market in any given year.

Demand and supply set price for those additions to the housing stock and for the relatively few acres developed in any year. Yet landowner *expectations* are considerably higher. Each owner may reckon that his or her land will sell for the going market price for development land. Yet in reality the city population will not grow enough, even over several decades, for development to occupy all the agricultural land in the area. Much more land is affected by the expectation of development than will ever conceivably be developed. Yet each landowner expects to be a winner in this game of real estate roulette. These high expectations of capital gains influence farmer behavior in the political arena. Each may strongly oppose any government interference with the right to develop, based on the unrealistically high estimate of the probability of being able to subdivide his or her land.

Long-Term Farmer. Some agricultural land owners have little interest in developing their land, at least in the forseeable future. Some may simply be committed to the idea and lifestyle of farming and do not want to move. Others may be attached to land and a farm that has been in the family for many generations. Others may simply be making a good living and would prefer to remain in agriculture. For many, the decision to remain in agriculture may be the result of considering their income earning potential in agriculture versus other occupations. Their earning potential in other occupations might be much lower than in agriculture, especially for those in the 50 to 60 age group who may be "too old to learn new tricks but too young to retire."

For whatever reason, many farmers near urban areas prefer to farm, at least for another decade or more. These farmers have little incentive to become active in the political process. If their farm operation is directly threatened by a neighbor's development plans, they might become very active in the local government decisionmaking process on that single issue. But the probability of a direct and substantial threat is not high. By far the greatest threat comes through the lot-by-lot decisions of a great many farmers in the area, but none of these decisions has a large enough impact to transform the long-term farmer into a political activist. Further, many might agree with the philosophical argument that land use should be determined exclusively by the landowner (those who might want to eventually develop their land would have a strong economic interest in maintaining this position). The result is that very few long-term farmers have a strong enough economic interest to oppose development in their area.

Urbanites/Environmentalists. The behavior of the "typical" urban resident or environmentalist is to favor a greater public role in the agricultural land development decision, particularly if that larger public role would give the urban resident some control over decisions taken in neighboring government jurisdictions. Urbanites might not oppose all development but might seek to control the location or pace of development. The urban resident may respond to the joint-impact nature of the amenity "products" of agricultural land, and may be particularly sensitive to the boundary issues. In general the urban/environmental interests would want the property rights in development shared by the landowner and the public sector, and would want the level at which public decisions are made to include representation of the urban interest.

Developers. In general the developer reacts to the same economic incentives as the farmer/developer. The more land allocation is determined by market transactions, and the less the allocation is dependent on administrative transactions, the more likely the developer will be able to respond to the market signals for housing demand. Of course not all developers oppose all government action in the land allocation process. The value of the development product may be enhanced by a land use plan that provides for open space near the developer's housing. The developer's marketing and construction plans may be enhanced by knowledge of what types of development will be permitted in the future. But, other things being equal, the developer generally prefers less government action to more in the agricultural land conversion process.

Local Officials. The behavior of the local official is the most difficult to describe because the local official may also be a farmer/developer, a long-term farmer, an urbanite, an environmentalist, or a developer. The private interest may outweigh any consideration of the broader interest in the official's mind, and the official's behavior depends on which government jurisdiction is discussed.

The typical elected official in a *rural* government near an expanding urban area is faced with several incentives. First, development brings some benefits to the rural government in the form of additional tax base and population. Second, the owner of the developable land is a rural voter who would gain from converting land, and many of the owner's relatives might also live (and vote) in the area. Opposing the new development might cause the official to lose a great deal of local support. On the other hand, the benefits of controlling the new development would accrue partly to local residents and partly to residents of the wider metropolitan area. The local official might well wish to control the location or pace of development but may have little or no political incentive to do so. As a result, in many rural government jurisdictions in urbanizing areas few development regulations are enacted until the suburban population increases sufficiently so that the newcomers can outvote the original rural residents. At that point the original elected officials are voted from office, new officials representing the land use preferences of the new residents are voted in, and a prodigious struggle ensues between the newcomers who want to preserve open space and guide development and the remaining farmer/developers and developers who want the development process to continue with as few administrative transactions as possible.

Outcomes

The results of the behavior can be described in terms of technical externalities, pecuniary externalities, political externalities, and the equity issue of the distribution of benefits and costs of agricultural land development.

The major technical externality is the loss of the amenity value of open space on the urban fringe. The decisions of agricultural land owners and developers, usually unhindered by any local policy to guide development, result in a loss of amenity values to the urban population. If rural governments and developers considered the loss of the open space as a cost of development, perhaps less development and more open space would be provided.

Several other externalities may also occur in the conversion process. Political externalities occur when the relevant costs and benefits of government decisions are not internal to the decisionmaking body. When many rural governments in an urban area make independent decisions on development, usually with little development control, a geographic pattern of development may result that is highly inefficient in the delivery of public services. Public service costs may increase for urban residents, a pecuniary externality caused by the underlying technical externality, which in turn is caused by the political externality. A related externality may exist as the new exurban residents place demands on city services such as roads or libraries, without sharing in the costs of the services.

Farmers may also face pecuniary externalities as agricultural land is developed in the rural government jurisdiction. As some agricultural land is developed, the market value (on the margin) of all land is increased. In Wisconsin, tax assessments follow market values, so the assessment increases as well. At the same time, the local government must increase its spending to provide public services to the new development. In fact, spending may increase more rapidly than the tax base because the new development may require higher levels of service than the farms; the new residents may demand new and different types of services as well. The tax rate may increase at the same time the farm assessment is increased. The result is a large increase in the farm property tax. New development may bring increased property taxes, and part of the increase will be paid by agricultural landowners who do not develop their land.

The political externalities are perhaps the most critical for public policy. The decisions of rural elected officials do not take into account the costs imposed on urban residents or the future costs to the metropolitan area of current development decisions. The effects of the rural government decision spill over the boundaries of the neighboring rural and urban jurisdictions.

The basic policy issues involve questions of equity. One key question is who should have which rights in agricultural land on the urban fringe. The answer to this question determines in part the timing and distribution of gains from land development. A related question is who should bear the cost of provision of open space on the urban fringe, and how much should be provided. Is it fair that the farmer must provide open space for urban residents without receiving compensation? Is it fair that the farmer is able to deny open space to residents of the city by ignoring the value of the open space when making land use decisions? Is it fair for the farmer to reap the economic gains of land development that result from growth of the city population and public investment in roads and sewers, rather than any action of the landowner? The general question is, How should the benefits and costs of agricultural land conversion be distributed? The institutions governing resource use will establish the rights of the various parties in deciding the use of agricultural land on the urban fringe. The conflict over natural resource use is translated into a set of questions about who has the right to do what with the resource. This is the policy issue that confronts the economist.

POLICY CHOICES

After first describing the natural resource use patterns and applying economic theory to analyze the resource characteristics, institutions governing resource use, the incentives these create for various groups, and the resulting outcomes, the economist is now ready to propose some policy options.

Identifying and Analyzing Polar Opposites

The economist might begin by identifying the basic types of policy options, rather than plunge immediately into an analysis of complex and extremely detailed alternatives. One type of policy might be financial incentives to the landowner to change land use behavior. In effect, this strategy would define all development rights to be in the exclusive control of the landowner. Public policy would seek to provide enough financial incentive to prevent the conversion of land that would impose significant costs on the community, or delay the conversion until the evolving pattern of land use change would minimize these costs.

A second type of policy might define the entire development as a right of the public domain so that development is solely a public decision. Regulation of land use would be the only policy tool, and the only question might be which level of government would exercise the control.

The economist has two ways to analyze these "polar opposite" policy options. The first approach is empirical: Look for policies actually adopted by state or local governments that are representative of the two polar types and examine the outcome of these policies. Use this analysis as the basis for predicting outcomes of the different policy options.

The second approach is more theoretical: Return to the analysis of the behavior of various groups under the current incentives, carefully analyze how each of the opposing policies would change these incentives, and predict group response to the new incentives that would be created by the two different types of policies.

In fact, the economist is well advised to adopt both approaches. The theory is useful in applying an analytical framework to the empirical reality. The empirical observation provides some grounding for the theory and ensures that the economist confronts the complexity of human behavior as it occurs in reality.

Let us assume that the economist pursues both an empirical and a theoretical approach to the analysis of the policy options. With minimal research, two representative types of policies appear. The use value assessment laws adopted by many states are representative of the incentive/voluntary policy, and strict zoning is representative of the regulatory approach.

The economist would quickly discover that use value assessment has been very ineffective in influencing land use change on the urban fringe.[2] Use value assessment laws provide that agricultural land is assessed at its value in agricultural use for property taxation purposes. As a city expands and land prices increase, use value assessment prevents any increase in the assessment of the farmland (except an increase caused by higher value in farm use). Studies of use value assessment laws in many states have produced very consistent results. First, such laws reduce farm property taxes, particularly on the urban fringe. Second, such laws do not result in any detectable change in land use patterns or conversion. Third, many of the benefits of the reduced taxes flow to nonfarm landowners, especially those on the urban fringe.

A more theoretical analysis produces the same conclusions. The farmer/developer will not be greatly influenced by a small reduction in property tax from use value assessment, compared to the gains from land development. As a simple illustration, the typical property tax rate is less than 2 percent of the value of the land. Even if the policy completely exempted the land from taxation, the benefit to the landowner would be less than 2 percent of the value per year. The gains from land development may be double or triple the agricultural value of the land, that is, 50 to 100 times as great as the annual tax reduction benefit. The farmer/developer is still subject to the social trap created by overly optimistic expectations of development and the fact that the aggregate of many development decisions, each positive for the individual landowner, has a net negative effect when the development strategy is pursued by all members of the group. Use value assessment does not change any of the key incentives for the long-term farmer. This individual still prefers to remain in agriculture (with or without the tax break) and still has little incentive to oppose development in his or her area. Use value assessment changes the incentives for the developer, by making it cheaper to hold land while waiting for the best time to develop. Instead of slowing or guiding growth, the tax policy accelerates the process of transferring land from farmers to developers without regard to the resulting land use patterns. The behavior of the local official is not greatly influenced by the use value assessment and still has little political incentive to try to control the development process.

The main advantage of use value assessment is that it is politically acceptable. The gains are high for the farmland owner, whether farmer or developer. The costs of the tax reduction are spread over many nonfarm taxpayers so the cost to each is small and the incentive to organize to oppose the use value law is weak. The effect on development patterns is minimal.

The other approach to policy—regulation—is typified by strict zoning.[3] Few zoning ordinances are strictly written and strictly enforced, but in general, zoning has proven ineffective when used as the only growth control on the urban fringe. Empirical studies are rare, but those that do exist indicate that zoning is often not very strictly enforced. Even more often, zoning is not even adopted by rural governments on the fringe. The theoretical analysis of group behavior in the previous section provides some insights for these results. The overly optimistic farmer/developer may perceive a large loss if strong zoning is adopted and enforced. These farmers have a very strong economic incentive to organize political opposition to the zoning. Developers also may perceive a very strong economic incentive to oppose the zoning. In this case the costs of the zoning are concentrated and a few individuals have a very strong incentive to overturn the policy or frustrate its implementation. At the same time the long-term farmer and the urban/environmental groups benefit from the zoning, but the level of benefit for

any single member is small compared to the level of cost for the farmer/
developer. The former have little economic incentive to favor the zoning or
insist on its strict enforcement.[4]

The local government official has little political incentive to support the
zoning and considerable incentive to oppose it. A specific example will
illustrate the point. In Wisconsin the land use regulatory power is essentially
shared by township and county government. A county may adopt a zoning
ordinance for unincorporated areas of the county, but the ordinance takes
effect in a township only with the approval of the township government.
Once a township adopts the county ordinance any rezonings require both
county and township approval, unless the township chooses not to vote on
the proposal. Any change to the county ordinance requires approval of a
majority of participating townships before the change can take effect. Under
these conditions, there is little chance that strict zoning will be adopted at
the county level. The township official will be subject to the political pressure
brought by farmer/developers and developers to oppose the zoning. Few
long-term farmers will have a large enough incentive to actively promote
the zoning. Some of those who benefit live in the urban area outside the
township, do not vote locally, and may have very little voice in local
decisions. The unit of government that *does* give a voice to the broader
geographic interests in land use decisions is the county. Yet the county
could not adopt strict agricultural zoning without the approval of a majority
of the townships. And within the townships the support for the zoning is
weak relative to the opposition. Thus, the zoning "rules of the game"
prevents any representation of the wider geographic interest in local zoning
policy decisions.

The economist who has completed the analysis of these polar opposites
might conclude that neither type of policy offers much potential for addressing
land use conflicts found on the urban fringe. Yet the 1977 Wisconsin
Farmland Preservation Law uses both zoning and tax relief, together with
some very subtle but important changes in the zoning process.

A Legislative Response

In 1977 the Wisconsin legislature was faced with precisely the type of land
use conflict described in this chapter. The legislature adopted the Farmland
Preservation Law, which can be analyzed in terms of how the law changed
the incentives faced by the various groups in the urban fringe.

Under the FPL agricultural landowners are eligible for income tax credits
if their land is covered by a local land use program designed to maintain
the land in agricultural use.[5] In effect, the FPL is a response to farmers
concerned about high property taxes that accompanied the development
process and escalating agricultural land values in the 1970s. At the same
time, the law responds to the urban concern about the process of conversion
of agricultural land and the problems the process causes for the urban
resident. The law also addresses an equity issue. In effect, farmers are
compensated with tax credits for an increased sharing of the development

property right with government. A more detailed description of the law will be useful in understanding the lessons for natural resource policy.

Land Policy Provisions. The FPL has different provisions for urban counties (population density over 100 people per square mile) and rural counties (density less than 100). This distinction is a response to the unique nature of the agricultural land resource and recognizes the importance of location in determining the degree of resource conflict.

In an *urban* county, land is eligible for tax credits *only if* it is included in an exclusive agricultural zone in a local zoning ordinance that meets state standards and is certified by a special state board. In a *rural* county, land qualifies for tax credits if it is in an exclusive agricultural zone *or* if the county government adopts an agricultural preservation plan that meets state standards *and* the landowner signs a 10- to 25-year contract with the state, agreeing not to develop the land. A preservation plan is a nonbinding land use plan focused on agriculture and must be certified by the state board as meeting the standards in the law. A contract is binding and requires the agreement of the owner, county, and state before it can be relinquished prior to its expiration date.

The details of the zoning provisions in the state law are extremely important, because it is in these details that the boundary issue is addressed and the incentives for local officials are shifted drastically.

The state law sets standards that a local zoning ordinance must meet in order for the landowners to qualify for tax credits. These standards are quite strict: Nonfarm housing is prohibited in the zone; any changes require full public hearings and must be based on certain findings of fact; the enforcement provisions of the ordinance are subject to state approval; and the land included in the exclusive agricultural zone on the zoning maps must be consistent with a coherent local plan to protect agriculture and guide urban development. This is one way the boundary issue is addressed. Through the state government the urban groups that ultimately pay for the tax credits are able to ensure that the local zoning takes into account more than the rural interest or the economic interests of a few rural landowners.

The process of adoption of exclusive agricultural zoning also shifts the incentives for local elected officials. With a few exceptions, the exclusive agricultural zoning must be adopted by county government. (The exceptions are a few counties in which the zoning power has been historically held only by township government.) County government represents urban as well as rural interests, so the urbanite's interest is represented and the boundary issue is again addressed.

The most important change is a provision that a change in the county zoning ordinance to allow exclusive agricultural zoning does *not* need the approval of a majority of townships in order to take effect. Instead, the exclusive agricultural zoning provisions are adopted as an amendment to the county ordinance and go into effect in a township unless the township board of supervisors vetoes the provisions for that town. If the township board vetoes the zoning, it can later reverse its vote and accept it. If the township board does not veto the zoning it automatically takes effect in the township. By doing nothing the town board can allow the zoning to take effect but blame can be shifted to the county government. Also, the strong tradition of local control is maintained. In the past, opponents of a county zoning change could argue that the township should vote against the change so as not to force other towns into an ordinance that is not acceptable to them. The new rules for exclusive agricultural zoning allow each township to approve or reject the new provisions only for itself. County board supervisors who favor exclusive agricultural zoning can adopt the zoning changes in the county ordinance and defend their position with the argument that no township is forced to adopt any of the new exclusive agricultural zoning provisions unless the township supervisors 'approve of the change. Further, one can argue that anyone who opposes the change at the county level is *against* local control because opposing the change prevents each township board from having the opportunity to approve or reject the amendment for its township.

Tax Provisions. The tax credit is based on the landowner's household income and property tax. The credit is refundable, it increases with increases in property tax (income constant), and it decreases with increases in income (property tax constant). Table 2.1 shows the credit for various levels of income and property tax.

The percentage of credit the landowner receives depends on the agricultural land policy adopted by the county and township government. The credit is 70 percent of the amount calculated under the formula if the land is in a rural county and is eligible through a county preservation plan and long-term contract. In both a rural and urban county, if the land is simply covered by exclusive agricultural zoning, the owner is eligible for 70 percent of the formula amount. If the land is covered by exclusive agricultural zoning and the county has also adopted an agricultural preservation plan, the owner is eligible for credits at the 100 percent level. Thus, the stronger the local land use policies the higher the level of tax credits.

Behavioral Response

By the end of 1985, 68 of the state's 71 counties had adopted agricultural preservation plans, placing virtually all of the state's farmland into a preservation district under a certified plan.[6] In 39 counties exclusive agricultural zoning was in effect in some or all of the townships in the county. By the end of 1985, 5.4 million acres of agricultural land were in an exclusive agricultural zone and an additional 1.1 million acres were covered by a contract. About 76 percent of all farms in urban counties were covered by exclusive agricultural zoning, and about 27 percent of all potentially eligible farms in rural counties were covered by either zoning or contracts. Figure 2.1 shows the approximate percentage of farmland covered by exclusive agricultural zoning and contracts in each county. It is clear from the figure that most of the land covered by exclusive agricultural zoning and contracts is concentrated in the southern and eastern parts of the state. This part of

TABLE 2.1: Schedule of Current Law Farmland Preservation Tax Credits Effective for Property Taxes Levied in 1983-1985[a] (in dollars)

Household Income[b]	Property Taxes					
	1,000	2,000	3,000	4,000	5,000	6,000 & over
0 and below	900	1,800	2,500	3,200	3,700	4,200
5,000	900	1,800	2,500	3,200	3,700	4,200
10,000	585	1,485	2,255	2,955	3,525	4,025
15,000	180	1,080	1,940	2,640	3,300	3,800
20,000	100	585	1,485	2,255	2,955	3,525
25,000	100	200	720	1,620	2,360	3,060
30,000	100	200	300	405	1,305	2,115
35,000	100	200	300	400	500	600
40,000 and above[c]	100	200	300	400	500	600

a Participants whose land is subject to exclusive agricultural zoning under a county, city, or village ordinance in a county which has adopted an agricultural preservation plan receive 100 percent of the amounts shown in the table. Participants whose land is subject to a town exclusive agricultural zoning ordinance and a county agricultural preservation plan receive 90 percent of the amounts shown in the table (effective 1985 tax year; prior to 1985 town zoning credit level was 70 percent). Participants with a farmland preservation agreement receive 70 percent of the amounts shown in the table. Participants whose land is subject to an exclusive agricultural zoning ordinance receive a minimum credit of 10 percent of property taxes, not to exceed $600.

b Household income indicates income of the farm operator, spouse, and dependents plus nonfarm business losses, plus nonfarm depreciation in excess of $25,000.

c Participants through zoning with incomes greater than $40,000 receive a credit equal to 10 percent of property taxes, up to a maximum $600 credit. Credit amounts below the line in each column reflect the 10 percent minimum credit.

Source: Calculated from formulas in the Wisconsin Statute 71:09(11).

FIGURE 2.1 Percentage of Farm Acres Protected by Exclusive Agricultural Zoning and Preservation Agreements on December 31, 1985

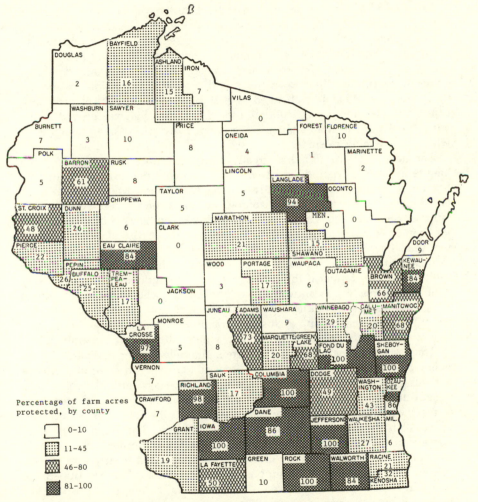

Note: Number in county is percent of total farm acres protected.

Source: Compiled from information of Department of Agriculture, Trade and Consumer Protection, local governments, and the 1978 and 1982 Federal Census.

the state has the best agricultural soils and accounts for most of the state's agricultural receipts. This same area is also the most subject to agricultural land conversion from suburban and exurban development.

Why the widespread adoption of exclusive agricultural zoning? We can ascertain the reasons by examining the problem from each group's perspective.[7]

Farmers who wish to develop their land still have the same economic incentives to develop. However, the tax credit now provides a slight incentive *not* to develop. This incentive is slight because the credit is quite small compared to the capital gains from land development, just the same as with use value assessment. These farmers are still highly motivated to apply political pressure to their township boards to gain permission to develop their property. What has changed is that now there is a local ordinance restricting the land to agricultural use. Changing this has proved to be much more difficult than changing the older, more permissive zoning, even when such zoning existed.

The advent of the FPL has greatly shifted the incentives faced by the long-term farmer. The individual who wants to continue in agriculture now has a very strong economic incentive to urge his or her township government to adopt exclusive agricultural zoning, and a strong incentive to see it enforced once adopted. The exclusive agricultural zoning establishes eligibility for the tax credit. The tax credit has averaged about $1,600 per household per year statewide since about 1979. This is a sizable addition to farm income, and the credit increases as farm income falls. The credit is available to the long-term farmer if the land is restricted to agricultural use, precisely what the farmer wants anyway. Thus, the farmer who wishes to continue in agriculture has very little to lose and much to gain, if the township and county government adopt exclusive agricultural zoning. In addition, this farmer will benefit from the protection zoning affords farm operation.

Thus, many farmers who did not enter the debate over agricultural land policy before 1978 have entered the discussion strongly in favor of exclusive agricultural zoning. In areas that adopt exclusive agricultural zoning it is usually farmers who lead the effort for adoption, and these are generally farmers who intend to farm for many years into the future or who intend to pass on their farm operation to their children. The large number of farmers in this category have outweighed the fewer farmers who want to develop their land or who are philosophically opposed to any government role in land policy. It is the support of these farmers that has tipped the scales in favor of adoption of exclusive agricultural zoning in township after township over the period since 1978.

Urban and environmental interests did not have any great change in incentives after the adoption of the FPL. Rather, these groups gained voice in setting agricultural land policy at both the state and the county levels. At the state level the law itself contained standards that ensured that the planning and zoning adopted by rural government would consider the interests of the broader urbanizing area. Plans had to consider future development paths and efficient provision of public services. Zoning had to be consistent with plans. Rezoning required public hearings and had to be approved by the county government in which urban people had at least some voice and sometimes had a majority. At the county government level, urban supervisors did not often propose the adoption of exclusive agricultural zoning but often supported the proposal when raised by rural supervisors. The urban interest in rural land development was clearly more represented after adoption of the FPL.

The developer's incentives were not greatly changed by the FPL. To the extent that development areas were more clearly identified, gaining development permission may have been made simpler and faster. On the other hand, many areas were restricted and the development opportunities were somewhat more limited. However, it is likely that the FPL had relatively little effect on housing prices because most villages and cities already had ample development land available within their boundaries. Ample rural land also was identified for development both around existing urban centers and in rural areas unsuited for agricultural use. Therefore, the developer had as much incentive to oppose the adoption of zoning after the FPL as before.

The local officials were given much incentive to adopt exclusive agricultural zoning by the FPL. First, county elected officials could adopt the zoning but argue that they were only giving the township governments a chance to have the zoning if local people really wanted it. Also, by opposing the zoning the elected official was denying tax credits to farmers. At the township level, the elected official could accept the county zoning change without action and blame the county. Much more often, however, township elected officials were willing to adopt the exclusive agricultural zoning because they began to receive pressure from the long-term farmers who wanted the tax credits. The political balance-of-power was greatly shifted at the local level because the majority of farmers now had a very clear economic incentive to support zoning, in addition to the less tangible benefit of the protection it gave their farm operation.

CONCLUSION

The lessons for natural resource policy are not complicated. A great deal of change in natural resource use can be brought about by some fairly small, subtle changes in institutions that set the rules-of-the-game and shape the incentives for individuals in both the political and economic systems. For the economist or policy analyst this presents a great challenge. Relatively slight changes in institutions and incentives can bring great changes in behavior vis-à-vis natural resources. Yet overlooking a relatively subtle relationship between an institution or a set of institutions and individual behavior can doom a policy initiative to failure or could even produce consequences that are opposite to those intended.

In analyzing or recommending natural resource policy options the economist or policy analyst must take into account the characteristics of the resource that lead to the resource conflict or problem. It is also critical to carefully analyze the institutions governing allocation of the resource, particularly the details of the institutional relationships, because these seemingly minute details may prove to be the critical links in determining human behavior.

The economist must pay close attention to the incentives that guide or influence individual behavior with respect to the resource. It is particularly useful to consider incentives in both the economic *and* the political spheres because natural resource is determined by a mix of market and administrative transactions. With a good understanding of the institutions governing resource use it is possible to identify incremental changes in institutions that can have significant effects on natural resource use.

NOTES

1. Data are taken from *Wisconsin Agricultural Statistics,* various years.

2. Some of these studies are summarized in the National Agricultural Lands Study, "Case Studies of State and Local Programs to Protect Farmland" (1981). Another source is Council on Environmental Quality, *Untaxing Open Space* (1976).

3. A review of some of the zoning literature and additional references can be found in David Ervin et al. (1977).

4. For an exception, see Richard Barrows and Carol Smith (1981) or Richard Barrows and John Redman (1981).

5. For a more detailed description of the law see Richard Barrows and Douglas Yanggen (1978).

6. Detailed data on the results of the program can be found in Richard Barrows and Kendra Bonderud (1986).

7. A discussion of some of the politics of local adoption of zoning ordinances can be found in Richard Barrows (1981).

REFERENCES

Barrows, Richard (1981). "Summary of Research on the Wisconsin Farmland Preservation Program." Staff Paper 198. Madison: Dept. of Agricultural Economics, University of Wisconsin.

Barrows, Richard, and Kendra Bonderud (1986). "Distribution of Tax Credits Under the Wisconsin Farmland Preservation Law." Staff Paper 261. Madison: Dept. of Agricultural Economics, University of Wisconsin.

Barrows, Richard, and John Redman (1981). "The Effects of Exclusive Agricultural Zoning in Columbia County, Wisconsin." Staff Paper 190. Madison: Dept. of Agricultural Economics, University of Wisconsin.

Barrows, Richard, and Carol Smith (1981). "The Effects of Exclusive Agricultural Zoning in Walworth County, Wisconsin." Staff Paper 195. Madison: Dept. of Agricultural Economics, University of Wisconsin.

Barrows, Richard, and Douglas Yanggen (1978). "The Wisconsin Farmland Preservation Program." *Journal of Soil and Water Conservation* 33:209–216.

Council on Environmental Quality (1976). *Untaxing Open Space.* Washington, D.C.: Government Printing Office.

Ervin, David, J. B. Fitch, R. K. Goodwin, W. B. Shepard, and H. H. Stoevener (1977). *Land Use Control.* Cambridge, Mass.: Ballinger Publishing Co.

National Agricultural Lands Study (1981). "Case Studies of State and Local Programs to Protect Farmland." Washington, D.C.: U.S. Department of Agriculture and Council on Environmental Policy, Government Printing Office.

Wisconsin Department of Agriculture (various years). *Wisconsin Agricultural Statistics.* Madison: Wisconsin Dept. of Agriculture, Trade and Consumer Protection.

SUGGESTED READINGS

Barlowe, Raleigh (1984). *Land Resource Economics,* 3d ed. Englewood Cliffs, N.J.: Prentice-Hall.

This book is a standard text in land economics, accessible to any undergraduate. The author reviews the institutions related to land, the basic economics of land use, and the physical and biological setting in which land use occurs. The discussion of rent is particularly useful.

Ervin, David, James B. Fitch, R. Kenneth Godwin, W. Bruce Shepard, and Herbert H. Stoevener. (1977). *Land Use Control.* Cambridge, Mass.: Ballinger Publishing.

The authors review the economics and politics of land use controls and provide a useful conceptual analysis of several land use control techniques. The theoretical framework varies by chapter but includes economics, sociology, and political science. The book is useful for undergraduates in any major field.

Hagman, Donald, and Dean Misczynski. (1978). *Windfalls for Wipeouts.* Washington, D.C.: Planners Press.

The authors review methods for redistributing the benefits and costs of land development to both compensate those who bear the costs and reduce the incentives for individuals who thwart the land use control process. The perspective is legal and economic and the book is useful for upper-level undergraduates or graduate students.

Hite, James C. (1979). *Room and Situation: The Political Economy of Land-Use Policy.* Chicago: Nelson-Hall.

The author provides a very broad analysis of the institutions relevant to land use decisions, the incentives that are created for individuals, and the policy choices facing government. The book is accessible to students of economics and other upper-level undergraduates.

STUDY QUESTIONS

1. Evaluate the argument that preservation of agricultural land in the immediate vicinity of urban areas imposes considerable costs on society.

2. Barrows suggests that from a farmer's perspective the increase in land value resulting from proximity to a growing urban area is a pure economic rent—that is a payment to a factor of production that need not be made. Alternatively, one might argue that the price of land is a measure of opportunity cost indicating forgone benefits if its use is not changed. Reconcile these two perspectives.

3. Using the framework of analysis developed in Chapter 1, describe changes in outcomes that could result from resolving the boundary issue for agricultural land by (1) vesting authority over land use in county government, or (2) vesting authority in the state government.

4. Identify and categorize by type and by group impact the kinds of externalities created by conversion of a parcel of agricultural land into a shopping mall.

Chapter Three

State Water Management Policy
The Florida Experience

Roy R. Carriker

Decline in groundwater quantity and contamination of aquifers are serious problems in many regions of the United States. Ground and surface water management issues, often interdependent, are the focus of this analysis of the Florida Water Resources Act. Issues include interference between wells, overdraft, contamination, and the interaction between surface and groundwater. Changes in water law from reasonable use to administrative law are described as are water sources and problems. Three cases are examined: (1) Technical externalities are discussed in a case dealing with frost protection for strawberry fields; (2) common property aspects of groundwater are considered in a case of water-to-air heat pumps; and (3) boundary issues are addressed in "water wars." This chapter demonstrates the important link between law and economics for analysis of natural resource and environmental policy issues.

Water management has a special meaning in Florida. It refers to the highly sophisticated exercise of regulatory authority by specially designated agencies over the development and use of freshwater within the state. Florida's concept of water management has evolved over the decades as a result of rapid growth in population, agricultural production, and industrial activity. But its essential nature was crystallized by the sweeping reforms in water law that were embodied in the Florida Water Resources Act of 1972. Florida's example illustrates many of the economic and institutional issues confronting state water policy.

From an economic perspective, water management may be broadly conceptualized as the process by which need for water is translated into effective demand for water, physical availability of water is translated into effective supply of water, and demand for water is reconciled with the supply of water. Water management, in reconciling demand with supply, must implicitly or explicitly recognize time, place, and the forms of water demand and supply. Hence, water management may include construction of storage reservoirs to make water available over time, interregional transfers to make water available at the desired place, desalinization or water treatment to make water available in the desired form, or other measures to enhance the supply of water. On the other hand, water management may include conservation, rationing, pricing schemes, or other measures intended to reduce or manipulate the demand for water. Various flood control measures are often called for to avert the undesirable effects of having more than a desired amount of water present at a particular place and time. These measures may involve structural devices or nonstructural measures such as flood plain zoning to prevent or modify construction in flood-prone areas. In addition, the relationship of water to natural ecosystems is critically important. Water management increasingly requires that environmental considerations weigh heavily in decisions affecting diversion, drainage, and consumptive use of water.

Water, like most natural resources, is scarce at certain times and certain places. Scarcity, in this context, occurs whenever quantity demanded exceeds quantity supplied under existing terms of human interaction. The condition of scarcity gives rise to the necessity of choice, which in turn suggests the need for a decision framework by which the scarce resource is allocated among competing uses and users over time and space. Basic to this selection process is the functional role of the institutional arrangements for resource allocation. The role of water policy then is to assess the adequacy of existing institutional arrangements, and where these are found deficient, the design of alternative institutional arrangements.

The law embodies much of the institutional framework within which water management decisions are made. Adequacy of the institutional framework for water management in Florida, as anywhere else, can be measured in part by the extent to which unresolved issues of water management generate persistent pressures for institutional change through the political process. Externalities in the pattern of interdependence on water resources are a persistent source of political controversy over water management. Other issues are commonly expressed in terms of efficiency and equity problems.

Many of the political issues confronting Florida's water management institutions stem from the peculiar nature of the resource. Water has been referred to as a "fugacious" resource (Levine, 1984), and institutional arrangements must account for the externalities that arise from its fugitive nature. This case study examines resource characteristics, institutions, and human behavior as they affect the outcome of water management decisions in Florida.

BACKGROUND

Water Sources

The state of Florida relies heavily on groundwater for municipal, industrial, and agricultural uses (Baldwin and Carriker, 1985). Florida has several prolific

FIGURE 3.1 Major Aquifers in Florida

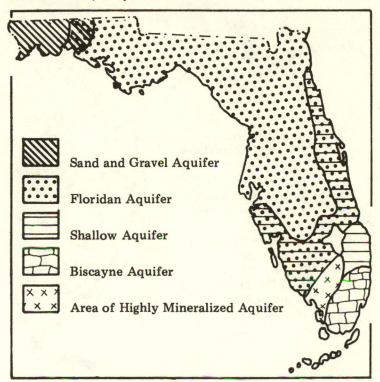

Source: Luther W. Hyde, *Principal Aquifers in Florida*, Map Series No. 16 (Tallahassee: U.S. Dept. of the Interior, Geological Survey, and Florida Dept. of Natural Resources, Bureau of Geology, 1975).

aquifers that yield large quantities of water to wells, streams, and lakes as well as some of the world's largest springs (Figure 3.1). The principal source of groundwater for most of Florida is the Floridan aquifer. It is the source of municipal water supply for such cities as Tallahassee, Jacksonville, Gainesville, Orlando, Daytona Beach, Tampa, and St. Petersburg (Klein, 1975). It also yields water to thousands of domestic, industrial, and irrigation wells throughout the state. The thick layers of porous limestone that comprise the Floridan aquifer underlie all of the state, although in the southern portion the water it contains is too highly mineralized for domestic, industrial, or agriculture use (Hyde, 1975).

The Biscayne aquifer underlies an area of about 3,000 square miles in Dade, Broward, and Palm Beach counties on Florida's lower east coast (Hyde, 1975). This aquifer is recharged directly from local rainfall and, during dry periods, from canals ultimately linked to Lake Okeechobee (a large, shallow, natural lake situated about 30 miles inland of Florida's lower east coast).

FIGURE 3.2 Major Rivers and Canals in Florida

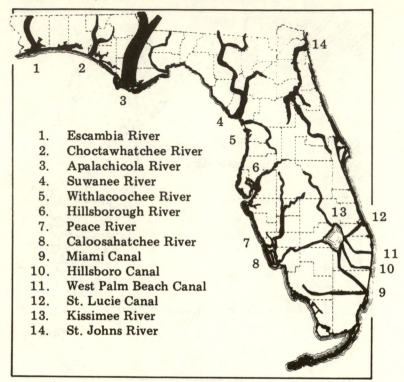

1. Escambia River
2. Choctawhatchee River
3. Apalachicola River
4. Suwanee River
5. Withlacoochee River
6. Hillsborough River
7. Peace River
8. Caloosahatchee River
9. Miami Canal
10. Hillsboro Canal
11. West Palm Beach Canal
12. St. Lucie Canal
13. Kissimee River
14. St. Johns River

Source: W. E. Kenner, E. R. Hampton, and C. S. Conover, *Average Flow of Major Streams in Florida,* Map Series No. 34, updated (Tallahassee: U.S. Dept. of the Interior, Geological Survey, and Florida Dept. of Natural Resources, Bureau of Geology, 1975).

The Biscayne is a major source of water supply for the lower east coast cities, including Miami.

The major source of groundwater in the extreme western part of the Florida panhandle is a sand-and-gravel aquifer (Hyde, 1975). Water in this aquifer is derived chiefly from local rainfall and furnishes most of the groundwater supplies used in Escambia County (Pensacola), Santa Rosa County, and part of Okaloosa County.

Shallow aquifers are present over much of the state, but in most areas these are not major sources of groundwater because a better supply is available from the deeper aquifers (Hyde, 1975). However, where water requirements are small, shallow aquifers are often tapped by small-diameter wells.

Surface water in Florida is visible in the form of numerous lakes and several major rivers (Figure 3.2). Of Florida's five largest rivers, four are in the drainage basins of northern Florida with headwaters in Alabama or

Georgia (Kenner, Hampton, and Conover, 1975). The fifth largest, the St. Johns River, involves an extensive system of wetlands and lakes lying along the eastern part of the peninsula from Indian River County (Vero Beach) to Jacksonville, where it turns to flow into the ocean. Southern Florida is dominated by the Kissimmee-Okeechobee-Everglades basin, which extends from the Orlando area to the southern tip of the state. This system currently involves hundreds of miles of canals and levees for surface water management and uses Lake Okeechobee as a reservoir. Many streams in the southern part of the state have been altered by a system of canals that relieve high-water conditions and deliver water to agriculture and growing population centers on the lower east coast. Some portions of the original Everglades function as shallow water conservation areas. The remaining Everglades at the southern tip of the peninsula comprise the Everglades National Park, which receives water from this managed system (Baldwin and Carriker, 1985).

With the exception of portions of the state bordering Alabama and Georgia, Florida is a hydrologic island relying on local rainfall to replenish its freshwater supply (Baldwin and Carriker, 1985). Florida receives an average of 55 inches a year according to U.S. Geological Survey (U.S.G.S.) records (Geraghty, et al., 1973). This compares to an average of 30 inches for the nation as a whole, and only 9 inches per year in Nevada, the driest state.

Water Use

According to estimates compiled by the U.S.G.S., withdrawals of freshwater for all uses in Florida averaged 7.3 billion gallons per day in 1980, about double the withdrawals estimated for 1960 (Leach, 1982). Irrigation accounted for the largest share of consumptive use of water. Of the 3 billion gallons per day withdrawn for irrigation, about half was considered to be consumptive use, according to U.S.G.S. calculations. Most of the water withdrawn for irrigation was accounted for by counties in the lower two-thirds of peninsular Florida. Surface water was the major source of irrigation water in Palm Beach and neighboring counties on the lower east coast. Groundwater was the principal source of water for irrigation in the northern two-thirds of peninsular Florida. The amount of water used to irrigate crops in any given year bears a close inverse relationship to the amount of rainfall received during the growing season.

In 1980, 532 utility systems supplied water to 7.8 million people (Leach, 1982). The seven most populous counties—Broward, Dade, Duval, Hillsborough, Orange, Palm Beach and Pinellas—accounted for 68 percent of the total freshwater used for public supplies. Except for Orange County, all seven countries are located on Florida's coastline.

Of the 839 million gallons per day withdrawn for industrial use, most went for pulp and paper processing, chemical products, and phosphate mining (Leach, 1982). Total water withdrawn by industries has decreased in recent years as a result of water conservation and recycling by industrial plants.

Water Control–Water Management

Historically, Florida's water law was based in common law, which, through case law and long established practices, provided a basis for water use rights (Kiker, 1977). In essence, owners of land adjoining lakes and streams could withdraw water for "reasonable" use provided they did not impair reasonable use by other riparian owners. Similarly, land could be drained by routing water to lower areas through an improved drainage system provided the owner of the lower land was not unreasonably damaged by the altered drainage. Groundwater rights were tied to land ownership, but again, withdrawals were subject to the reasonable use doctrine and the rights of adjacent owners to groundwater.

Under common law doctrines, disagreements over water use rights were resolved in court usually after damages were alleged as a result of some modification of water flow or quality. The pressures of rapid growth brought about comprehensive water resource management legislation in the 1970s, but portions of south Florida had been under some degree of water control for nearly a century (Baldwin and Carriker, 1985). During the late 1800s and the first half of the 1900s private and public projects sought to control the surface waters that could inundate most of the central-southern and lower east coast regions of the peninsula during extremely wet years. There were relatively few well-defined streams but a large portion of the area was "wetland." Water control required canals, levees, pump stations, dams, and other structures that involved substantial costs for planning, construction, and operation. It was not until an extensive flood control project was implemented, during the 1950s and 1960s, that water in south Florida could be viewed more as a resource than as a recurring threat to agricultural and urban areas.

State law provided for the formation of "drainage districts" (Chapter 298, Florida Statutes, 1913), with taxation and other powers to construct and operate water control systems over specified areas, usually not more than a few thousand acres. Special acts created larger districts, such as the Everglades Drainage District as early as 1907, the Central and Southern Florida Flood Control District in 1949, and the Southwest Florida Water Management District in 1961 (Baldwin and Carriker, 1985). The more recently formed districts usually provided water storage and conservation and not just drainage and flood control. Still, the power to regulate private water management and use was limited to controlling the connections of private water systems to district-owned facilities.

By the late 1960s considerable experience had been gained in the control of water in small districts and on a regional basis (Baldwin and Carriker, 1985). The intricacies of funding, structural design, and hydraulics could be managed. Where water conveyance and storage facilities were publicly owned and controlled, such as by the districts, some measure of resource management was available. Over a great portion of the state, however, natural streams and lakes constitute the surface water system and owners of lands adjoining these waterways (riparian landowners) could drain to or withdraw water from these waterways within the poorly defined constraints of existing water law. All landowners could tap groundwater supplies within these same constraints.

Administrative Structure

Florida's path toward a comprehensive system of administrative water law was marked by successive legislative efforts to respond to the exigencies of periodic droughts and catastrophic floods related to tropical storms. Legal scholars and other experts concluded that water regulatory districts defined on hydrologic boundaries should be established on a statewide basis. Starting with this concept, a group of water law authorities at the University of Florida Law School developed "A Model Water Code," designed to provide a vehicle for comprehensive state regulation of Florida's water resources, taking into account basic hydrologic principles (Maloney et al., 1980). In 1972, during a period of severe drought, members of a legislative committee used the code to draft new water resources legislation for Florida. Its essential chapters, with minor modifications, were enacted by the Florida legislature as the Water Resources Act of 1972.

The Water Resources Act of 1972 provided for a system of administrative regulation within the framework of the riparian water law system (Baldwin and Carriker, 1985). It created five water management districts, encompassing the entire state and established along hydrologic boundaries. A nine-member governing board makes policy for each district subject to provisions of the statute, a statewide water policy, and oversight by the Florida Department of Environmental Regulation. The districts are required to implement programs to regulate consumptive use of all waters of the state as well as diversions or other alterations in natural flow patterns of water. The basic standards for evaluating applications for consumptive use permits are provided by the statute. A proposed water use must be "reasonable" with respect to uses of other riparians, or, in the case of groundwater, to adjacent landowners. The proposed water use must be "beneficial" and must involve only the quantity of water necessary for an economically efficient operation in a use that is consistent with the "public interest." Established minimum stream, lake, and groundwater levels are included in the consideration of reasonable beneficial uses and in the granting of permits.

To cope with water allocation problems during periods of water shortage, districts are required to develop plans, classifying water by priority of use (Maloney et al., 1980). Reduction of water use during periods of shortage emergency are to follow preestablished priorities.

In all, the Florida Water Resources Act provided for development of a state water resources plan; regulation by permits of consumptive water use, management and storage of surface waters, and regulation of wells; and project financing and taxation (the districts were granted ad valorem taxing power by special referendum).

The Florida Department of Environmental Regulation also administers a water pollution control program under broad authority granted by the Florida Air and Water Pollution Control Act, as amended, which is now part of Chapter 403, Florida Statutes.

THE PROBLEM

Many water management issues in Florida arise because of the peculiar nature of the resource and its propensity for generating unexpected and unintended outcomes in response to efforts to develop, use, or otherwise manipulate it. Policy analysis must address the adequacy of the legal and institutional arrangements for averting or resolving these issues.

Hydrology: Understanding the Resource

Scientists have demonstrated that water moves in what is known as the hydrologic cycle. That is, water moves from atmospheric water vapor into liquid and solid form as precipitation, gathering then into lakes and streams as surface water, and evaporating from the earth's surface to once again become atmospheric water vapor.

Some of the water that falls as precipitation moves into yet another phase of the hydrologic cycle, the groundwater phase. In fact, groundwater is a subclass of a larger subsurface water classification. Subsurface water occurs in two primary zones. Water that seeps down to be available to the roots of plants is found in the rooting zone or zone of aeration (Tinsley and Fransion, 1979). Water not retained in the rooting zone percolates down to the zone of saturation, in which voids in the subterranean geologic formations are completely filled with water. It is the water in this zone that is available to supply springs and wells. The water-bearing formations are known as aquifers. Water in these aquifers is referred to as groundwater.

The water level can rise and fall in the shallow or surface aquifers, depending upon local rainfall conditions. When the shallow groundwater aquifer is underlain by a stratum of low permeability called an aquiclude, water can move laterally through the aquifer and emerge into a surface stream or lake (Tinsley and Fransion, 1979). On the other hand, when groundwater levels are low, water may flow in the opposite direction—from surface streams and lakes in to the shallow aquifer.

Sometimes freshwater exists deep underground in confined aquifers, so-called because the water-bearing aquifer is confined below a stratum of low permeability. Such a confined aquifer can sometimes hold water under sufficient pressure that the water will rise above the confining layer when a tightly cased well penetrates the aquiclude. These are known as artesian aquifers. When tapped, they sometimes produce free-flowing artesian wells. Naturally occurring springs also result from this same phenomenon. Water may enter the aquifer through recharge areas—those areas where the water-bearing stratum emerges at the surface or where the confining layer is broken up by faults or natural sinkholes, which allow the downward infiltration of water. Recharge areas may be some distance away from the spring or well that is fed by the aquifer.

Florida is almost entirely underlain by porous and permeable limestones that serve as aquifers for much of Florida's groundwater supplies. The Floridan aquifer underlies most of the state and is under artesian pressure throughout much of its extent. The Biscayne aquifer is a surficial (water table or unconfined) aquifer as are the smaller aquifer systems in the northwestern counties of the state.

Problems Due to Hydrologic Interrelationship

Some basic problems of water management fall under four general headings: (1) interference between wells, (2) overdraft of the aquifer, (3) contamination due to pollution and saltwater intrusion, and (4) interaction between surface water and groundwater. These problems are separable for analytical purposes, but they are interrelated in terms of cause and effect.

Interference Between Wells. If a well is pumped or allowed to flow (in the case of artesian wells), the water level (or the pressure surface, called the potentiometric surface in the case of artesian wells) in the area around the well is lowered as a result of the withdrawal of the water (Maloney and Plager, 1967). The water table surface (or the potentiometric surface) forms a depression in the shape of an inverted cone. The shape of the cone of depression or influence is governed by the size of the openings in the rocks forming the aquifer. The cone is flat if the openings are large, and steep if the openings are small. The cone of depression may extend a few feet from the well to a few miles. The amount of drawdown in the well depends on the rate of flow or pumping and the rate of release of the water from storage in the aquifer. Interference occurs between wells when the cones of depression overlap. The interference may occur if wells are spaced too close together, given rates of pumping and the yield potential of the aquifer. Alternatively, pumping rates may be excessive given the proximity of wells. In addition, what appears as interference between wells may actually be caused by the lowering of the water table or pressure surface as a result of inadequate recharge of the aquifer during periods of drought. In order to eliminate interference between wells, some adjustment must be made in well spacing, well depth, or rates of withdrawal.

Overdraft of the Aquifer. Overdraft of an aquifer occurs whenever the rate of withdrawal from an aquifer exceeds the rate at which that portion of the aquifer is recharged (Maloney and Plager, 1967). The water level is lowered and larger pumps may have to be installed to withdraw the water from the greater depth. Artesian wells may cease flowing and pumping may become necessary. Overdraft of an aquifer can lead to serious problems. Lower water levels may increase costs of obtaining water, since larger pumps, deeper wells, and additional wells may be necessary to obtain the same yield. The most serious problems occur in Florida in areas where the aquifer connects with the ocean, overlapping salty water. In those areas, excessive withdrawals of the freshwater may draw the salty water into the freshwater aquifer, thus contaminating the water supply.

Contamination. Contamination includes pollution of the water supplies by industrial, agricultural, municipal, or private domestic wastes and runoff (Maloney and Plager, 1967). It also includes saltwater encroachment into the aquifer. Pollutants released into the environment can be flushed by rainfall and runoff into streams and lakes. They can also be carried downward through the soil profile into groundwater supplies, especially in the deep sandy soils common throughout Florida. Aquifer recharge areas are susceptible to contamination of confined aquifers as well. Saltwater intrusion from the ocean, the Gulf of Mexico, or from underlying saline aquifers (called connate aquifers and left over from earlier geologic eras) is a major contamination problem with respect to groundwater in many parts of Florida. Saltwalter is more dense than freshwater and exerts a constant pressure to permeate the porous aquifers. As long as freshwater levels in the aquifers are above sea level, the freshwater pressure keeps saltwater from moving inland and upward in the aquifers. In some places, overpumping a well can increase the saltwater intrusion. As water is pumpted at a rate faster than the aquifer is replenished, the pressure of freshwater over saltwater in the land mass is decreased. This may cause the level at which the saltwater and freshwater meet to rise in the aquifer, degrading the water quality. This phenomenon is referred to as up-coning of the saltwater in response to reduced pressure from the overlying freshwater lens.

Surface Water–Groundwater Interaction. The hydrologic interrelationship between groundwater and surface water leads to interaction between the two. Problems arise when pumping from wells causes streams and ponds to dry up and springs to cease flowing. Problems also arise when ditching, diking, and draining of surface water systems cause wells to dry up through loss of normal recharge.

Institutional Factors

Historically, legal resolution of disputes arising over the use of water was achieved through litigation in the common law process (Brion, 1979; Carriker, 1985). Judicial adherence to precedent through the evolutionary process of custom and case law led to a loose body of doctrines addressing the more common types of disputes that arose over water resource management and use.

Several shortcomings plagued the common law dispute–settlement process, however, especially as Florida entered the era of rapid and sustained growth. First, separate common law doctrines evolved for water in watercourses (rivers and streams), groundwater, and diffused surface water (water from precipitation that has not yet reached a watercourse nor infiltrated into the ground). Early decisions were made in apparent ignorance of the interrelationship of water in separate stages of the hydrologic cycle.

Common law doctrines were heavily dependent on the concept of "reasonable use" as a condition of water use rights for both surface and groundwater. Reasonableness of each use was defined in part on the needs of other riparian owners, including the unforeseen exercise of a previously unused right as new water uses emerged. Additional uncertainty resulted from the need for litigation in order to establish the extent of a landowner's entitlement to reasonable use.

Critics of the common law doctrines argued that such uncertainty has costly economic consequences; for example, some industries might refuse to locate in an area for fear that the legal right to water may be diminished in some unforeseen manner (Maloney and Ausness, 1971). Moreover, critics argued that the courts were not capable of uniformity in the application of the law because they lack expertise and because they must address issues on a case-by-case basis, rather than on a comprehensive and generalized basis. Problems of maintaining streamflow and groundwater levels become increasingly important as growth in population, industry, and agriculture increases water demand. Common law doctrines are viewed by some legal scholars as inadequate to address these problems.

Research into the evolution of water politics and water law in Florida suggests that the issues were rarely defined explicitly as economic problems. Typically, issues were defined and discussed in terms of geology, hydrology, engineering, and law. This is not to imply that the economic implications of water policy decisions went unrecognized. Rather, they were treated implicitly, as an underlying motive for reforming legal institutions in a search for solutions to the vexing problems posed by the fugitive nature of water as a resource.

The conventional literature in natural resource economics has approached issues in natural resource management from the perspective of market economics. It has identified particular characteristics of natural resources and environmental amenities that inhibit the formation of markets for the efficient allocation of those resources and amenities, or which attenuate the effectiveness of such markets as do exist. These characteristics and the consequent failure of markets have been blamed for pollution problems and conflict over natural resource use and availability.

The same characteristics that inhibit the development of markets also pose challenges for other institutional forms. Water resources possess several of these characteristics, and the Florida experience with water resource management illustrates some of the consequences. To some extent, water resources are *nonexclusive* (Randall, 1987; Schmid, 1978). That is, water in the environment tends to be more or less equally available to all individuals, regardless of nominal ownership. Groundwater exists in geologic formations that lie beneath lands owned by many different individuals. Owners of one parcel of land have little, if any, ability to exclude neighboring landowners from access to underlying groundwater. The inability to exclude access to the resource precludes meaningful ownership of it. It also precludes pricing of the water as a device for efficient allocation. It mitigates against individual efforts to prevent overexploitation of the resource.

Groundwater has characteristics of *nonrivalry* (Randall, 1987), also referred to as *joint impact* (Schmid, 1978) in consumption. That is, water in an aquifer is more or less equally available to anyone able to sink a well into it. Consumption by one individual does not reduce the amount remaining for other water users. This is especially true for prolific aquifers that are subject to periodic and rapid recharge. Eventually, however, the addition of more wells and more users reduces the amount or quality of water available to all users. At this point, the resource is said to be *congested*, and in this sense, groundwater is more accurately referred to as a *congestible resource* (Randall, 1987). The resulting conflicts among well owners are very difficult to resolve through individual negotiations among affected parties, especially given the nonexclusive nature of groundwater. Although two, three, or a few well owners may strike an accord to limit withdrawals consistent with the sustained yield of the aquifer, they lack the ability to deny access to the aquifer to those well owners who refuse to join in the voluntary accord.

Persistent *negative externalities* are basically the result of nonexclusion and/or nonrivalry in consumption (Randall, 1987). A negative externality is an activity by one party that imposes costs on another party for which the latter is not compensated. The characteristics of groundwater have given rise to persistent negative externalities, and several specific examples are available from the Florida experience.

Nonexclusion and congestibility can lead to a state of affairs referred to as a *social trap* (Schmid, 1978). Social traps occur when the incremental, optimal decisions of individuals add up to an aggregate effect that is counter to the preferences of any individual. They refer to circumstances under which like-minded people fail to act in concert to obtain shared objectives. In the case of well owners and a congested aquifer, all recognize the collective need to limit withdrawals for the good of each and every well owner. But no single well owner can achieve the mutually preferred objective by any unilateral act.

There is a set of property rights issues that can best be understood as *boundary issues.* These issues concern how a given person as a consumer or voter is grouped with other people (Schmid, 1978). One's ability to have the government act in accordance with one's tastes depends on the tastes of one's fellow citizens. Who one's fellow citizens are is affected by where one lives and how political boundaries are drawn. The drawing of such boundaries can make a person a member of a majority or minority group by the mix of other people in one's decisionmaking unit. Individuals who find themselves in a decision group where their preferences are always losing out have several alternatives. Each person can try to change the preferences of the dominant group, use vote and voice more effectively, try to change the boundary, or move. The property rights involved in boundary definition determine which of these are real opportunities. Boundary issues are implicit in some of the more acerbic debates among Floridians over the matter of interjurisdictional transfers of water. Arrangements to move water from well fields in rural counties to densely populated urban counties have highlighted some boundary issues.

The difficulties among people that result from nonexclusion, congestion, social traps, and boundary issues will inevitably challenge the institutional framework within which such issues must be addressed. In Florida, that framework consists of administrative water law. The Florida Water Resources Act of 1972 supplanted the common law approach to water rights and created the system of comprehensive administrative water law envisioned by A Model Water Code and currently in force within the state. The Model Water Code was intended to be a comprehensive and fully integrated system designed for the management of water resources in an eastern state (Maloney, Ausness, and Morris, 1972). The authors of the code intended for it to take into account the close interrelationships of surface and groundwater as well as the relationship between water quality and consumptive use patterns. The code provides for overall planning for water use, considering all waters of the state through time. The heart of the system is the permit program and the administrative agency that implements it.

OUTCOMES: THREE EXAMPLES

The Florida experience offers several examples of resource management issues that illustrate fundamental concepts of natural resource economics. Three cases are presented in this chapter. The first case illustrates the concepts of negative externality and nonexclusion. The second illustrates a negative externality with the added complexity of a social trap involving a congestible resource. The third subsumes issues identified in the first two, focusing on the boundary issue.

Freeze Protection for Strawberry Fields

The Setting. Farmers have been growing strawberries in the Dover–Plant City area for at least a hundred years (Hinton, 1987).[1] This strawberry-growing area is located in eastern Hillsborough County, about 20 miles east of the city of Tampa. Given the semitropical climate of central peninsular Florida, early producers of strawberries in the area were able to bring their produce to market earlier than producers in colder climates and were therefore able to claim a higher price. Once the packing, shipping, and distribution infrastructure had been established for the Dover producing area, further expansion of strawberry production was possible. In addition, the soil in this area drains well, and there is abundant groundwater of good quality for irrigation. As the nearby Tampa Bay urban center has expanded into rural Hillsborough County, and as nonagricultural development has followed the Interstate 4 corridor through eastern Hillsborough County, competition for land has intensified. Because strawberry production generates a high valued yield per acre, it has been able to compete more successfully than some other agricultural enterprises with nonagricultural uses for acreage in the area. There are about 4,500 acres of strawberries in the Dover–Plant City area as of 1987, and about 150 producers.

Strawberry production depends on irrigation. The production season begins in October each year. The new transplants require overhead sprinkler irrigation as their bare roots are not yet able to draw moisture from the soil, making it necessary to spray moisture over the plant and roots until the new plants are established (Hinton, 1987). Once plants have their roots well established, it is possible to irrigate them with the newer type of low-volume, drip irrigation systems. Such systems have the advantage of reducing the consumptive use of water per acre of irrigated strawberries. They also offer advantages for fertilizer application and disease control.

The normal season for strawberry production in the area is October to May (Hinton, 1987). During the winter months temperatures occasionally drop briefly into the freezing range. Because freezing temperatures cause severe damage to strawberry plants, growers must arrange for protection from the cold temperatures or else suffer significant losses in yields and income. So far, the only feasible means of freeze protection available to the strawberry farmers is the constant application of water to the crop via overhead sprinklers. The spray forms ice on the strawberry leaves and maintains temperatures on the plants at a level just above the damaging freezing levels. Once ambient air temperatures rise above the danger level, the irrigation pumps can be switched off.

The Problem. Although the technology for strawberry production, including that for freeze protection, had been well established for many years, signs of trouble began to crop up during the mid to late 1970s (Hinton, 1987; Weber, 1987[2]). There had been an increase in acreage devoted to strawberries in this area over the preceding decade or two. The number of residential developments in this part of eastern Hillsborough County had also increased. Generally speaking, most of these homes were not on central water supply systems. Sometimes there would be several residences on one well, but typically each residence had its own well. On those occasions when low temperatures, and thus the need for freeze protection, persisted for more than a few hours, homeowners in the vicinity would experience loss of water from their water supply wells. Aside from the discomfort and inconvenience of losing their domestic water supply, some of these homeowners discovered that their well pumps had burned up because the pumps had continued to run even after there was no more water available to them. They were consequently damaged or ruined and had to be repaired or replaced.

Complaints were intermittent but were always associated with a freeze event. Once the temperatures rose (which they always do within a matter of days if not hours), the aquifer recovered and the controversy would quiet down. Some years there would be no freeze of sufficient duration to create problems for the domestic wells. However, in 1980 there were two freezes within ten days, causing enough complaints from homeowners that the governing board of the Southwest Florida Water Management District ordered a formal investigation (Weber, 1987).

District staff studied the geology, hydrology, and pumpage in the affected area. The district found that there was a low-yield shallow aquifer that most of the domestic wells were in (Weber, 1987). This shallow aquifer was not prolific enough to satisfy the pumping requirements of the strawberry growers, but a deeper aquifer, separated from the shallow aquifer by a confining layer, served their purposes quite well. Therefore, their irrigation wells had always been drilled deeper—through the confining layer at about 110 to 150 feet, to a depth of perhaps 500–600 feet. Although construction of large-diameter wells must now meet rigorous standards imposed by the district's regulatory program, district staff felt that some of the irrigation wells installed before regulations were in place were not cased all the way through the confining layer between the surficial aquifer and the deeper aquifer. The district staff suspected that the existence of such wells allowed interaction between the two aquifers. Thus, during brief periods of intense, heavy pumping by the growers, water levels were drawn down in the shallow aquifer as well as in the deeper aquifer. The study also indicated that most complaints were filed by homeowners having shallow wells or wells with pumps set shallow.

The case illustrates the concept of negative externality. The decision by growers to protect their crops from freezing temperatures did not anticipate the impacts on shallower domestic wells in the vicinity. Property rights to the resource were, at best, unclear. Essentially, the consumptive use permits that had been issued by the Southwest Florida Water Management District to the strawberry growers were the nearest thing to a property right in water held by any party to the issue. However, the permit, as an entitlement to use the resource under prescribed conditions, is strictly limited and is transferable only in the sense that the regulatory agency (the district, in this case) could conceivably reallocate the entitlement from growers to some competing user category on the expiration of the permit, provided the district could demonstrate that the growers' use of the water was harmful to the resource or was no longer a reasonable or beneficial use in the public interest. Such a finding was unlikely on the face of it and would be politically controversial. On the other hand, the domestic homeowner wells were typically small enough as to be exempt, by statute, from the regulatory authority of the water management district. What would be their recourse if their wells were periodically affected by the activities of the growers? For the most part the growers were there first. The relatively large number of homeowners, on the one hand, and growers on the other, mitigated against private transactions to resolve the problem. In any event, no party to the issue was in a position to exclude anyone else from access to the resource.

The Search for Solutions. In the recollection of participants, early efforts to define the problem and arrive at solutions were frought with discord and political strife (Hinton, 1987; Weber, 1987). The issue continued to be intense, however, as a number of sinkholes opened up in the Dover area after a particularly severe bout of freezing temperatures at Christmastime in 1983. Although sinkholes are a natural phenomenon in many parts of Florida, the fresh sinkhole activity was generally attributed to the quick drawdown of groundwater levels that resulted from withdrawals for freeze protection. Another cold spell in January of 1985 also produced adverse effects on homeowner wells in the area, although there was not a repeat of the sinkhole activity.

Eventually, communication among growers, homeowners, and the water management district improved to the point where serious efforts to find solutions to the problem could be sustained. For its part, the district launched a public information program designed to teach home builders and home-owners the importance of installing wells and pumps sufficiently deep so as to minimize the chances of their being affected by the hydrologic reaction to freeze protection activities (Weber, 1987). The district requires strict adherence to well construction standards to ensure that no additional interconnection between the two aquifers is created. There was no attempt to require strawberry growers to retroactively case wells that had been installed before standards became mandatory. The district did not institute new regulations nor did it alter the conditions on growers' consumptive use permits. The district has funded research through the University of Florida's Institute of Food and Agricultural Sciences to seek alternative methods of achieving freeze protection. Apparently, it was generally conceded that strawberry growers had no alternative means of freeze protection and that freeze protection was necessary in order to avert a genuine disaster for the local economy.

The strawberry growers made a concerted effort to minimize the negative effects of misinformation and misunderstanding that can result from poor communication among growers, homeowners, and water management authorities. For example, after the 1985 freeze the Florida Strawberry Growers Association, in cooperation with the Southwest Florida Water Management District, began issuing press releases resembling weather bulletins to alert homeowners and others of the likelihood that impending weather conditions could precipitate intense pumping for freeze protection (Hinton, 1987). Homeowners who, based on past experience, have reason to fear that such pumping will temporarily affect their wells are advised to store water and arrange to switch their pumps off to prevent damage to them in the event the water level in the aquifer declines temporarily. Pumps can be fitted with an inexpensive switch that will automatically turn the pump off if water pressure in the well declines.

The strawberry growers have also supported research for alternative ways to achieve freeze protection, including one new method involving a special cover for the crop (Hinton, 1987). However, the growers are reluctant to adopt any method of freeze protection that is not economically competitive with the use of overhead irrigation. The growers have begun to adopt drip irrigation as a cost-effective alternative to overhead delivery for established plants. However, drip irrigation will not provide adequate freeze protection nor is it suitable for new plant establishment. Growers have begun to incorporate tailwater recovery into the designs for irrigation systems, spe-cifically on land being brought into strawberry production for the first time. By recovering irrigation water that runs off the field and reapplying it, the growers are able to reduce the amount of water pumped from the aquifer, at least temporarily.

No one claims the problem has been solved. When the next protracted freeze hits, the growers will run their pumps. If no complaints arise from the owners of domestic wells, it will be because they have all deepened their wells and reset their pumps or have otherwise taken measures to mitigate the effects on the water supplies of temporary hydrologic responses to freeze protection. In any event, the problem involving negative externalities was addressed with technical solutions—solutions that involve well depths, well casings, tailwater recovery, pump switches, the search for alternatives for freeze protection, and user education for all parties. The problem was not treated as an institutional problem. No change was made in the institutional framework for water management. Solutions were sought within the existing institutional framework.

Water-to-Air Heat Pumps

The Setting. During the 1950s homeowners in Brevard County, Florida, discovered a way to use water to conserve energy and reduce their home heating and cooling costs. They discovered reverse-cycle, water-to-air heat pumps, which could be furnished with water from the underlying Floridan aquifer. Over the next two decades thousands of Brevard County homeowners took advantage of this discovery, with the result that the local groundwater resource was seriously threatened to everyone's detriment. The Brevard County experience illustrates the challenge for water management when a congestible resource is exploited by a large number of individuals. The resulting negative externalities were of sufficient magnitude to elicit collective action via public agencies to resolve the problem.

Water-to-air heat pumps offered a unique advantage for many Brevard County homeowners due to the accommodating nature of the groundwater aquifer beneath their community. In this particular coastal extent of the Floridan aquifer, artesian pressure was about 30 feet above sea level (Frazee, 1987).[3] This means that a well tapping the pressurized aquifer would deliver water to a point 30 feet above sea level without having to be pumped. Because much of Brevard County is no more than 10 feet above sea level, homeowners could have groundwater for their heat pumps without having to incur pumping costs. All they had to do was sink a 2-inch well roughly 250 to 300 feet into the limestone of the Floridan aquifer and water would immediately rise out of the depths and flow without cost or interruption. Groundwater, which maintains a constant year-round temperature of about 76 degrees Fahrenheit, could be routed through the heat pump to provide cool air during the hot summer months and to provide a source of home heat during cold days. The artesian pressure was such that a 2-inch well would deliver 5 to 15 gallons of clean fresh water per minute. At least for the time being.

During the 1950s, 1960s, and 1970s, as many as 16,000 wells were installed for the primary purpose of supplying water-to-air heat pumps for home comfort (Frazee, 1987). Virtually all of these wells were small 2-inch wells. Installation costs were very low, and pumping costs were nil. When the thermostat setting required a cooler room temperature (or a warmer room temperature), the heat pump would circulate the water through its coils and room temperatures were thus maintained at the desired comfort level. When the heat pump was not needed, the water from the free-flowing artesian well was automatically diverted through a garden hose to a circular irrigation sprinkler head to irrigate the homeowner's lawn—continuously, day in, day out, year-round. Some homeowners diverted the flow to the nearby Indian River estuary or to the Atlantic Ocean in the case of oceanfront homes. At first, salt spray in the coastal environment caused corrosion problems for the outdoor heat pump units, but this problem was easily solved by installing the units indoors.

Water-to-air heat pumps were used in other parts of the country, to be sure. In some instances, water could be pumped from underlying aquifers for the desired heating or cooling effect. Whether the water-to-air technology was preferred to other conventional heating and cooling systems was a matter of comparative installation and operating cost analysis (Frazee, 1987). Usually the hydrogeology of an area ruled which type of system would be used. In this particular part of Brevard County, the deeper Floridan aquifer with its clean water and artesian pressure dominated the microeconomics of technology selection. So thousands upon thousands of 2-inch wells tapped the aquifer and delivered its water to the surface in an unending flow.

The Problem. Eventually several difficulties began to emerge. With so many wells flowing constantly, the artesian pressure in the Floridan aquifer beneath Brevard County began to decline (Frazee, 1987). The potentiometric surface in the area began to decline an average of 6 inches per year. In those parts of the county where the pressure surface had been barely above surface level to begin with, homeownevers had to fit their wells with pumps—at substantial costs for installation and operation—in order to bring the groundwater once again to their heat pumps.

Hydrologists monitoring the interface between saltwater and freshwater in the aquifer beneath this coastal community noticed movement of the interface upward and inland (Frazee, 1987). In many areas, the quality of water being delivered by the wells deteriorated as the saltwater interface moved into what had previously been a freshwater zone. As the chloride content of the water increased, corrosion problems made it unsuitable for use in heat pumps.

The problem was compounded by a secondary, surficial aquifer positioned above the Floridan in this region (Frazee, 1987). The lower portion of this surficial aquifer is referred to as the shallow rock zone by hydrologists, a water-bearing stratum known to geologists as Tamiami limestone. Water in this shallow rock zone is inherently high in chlorides and consequently is unsuitable for heat pump applications. Therefore, homeowners developing wells for their heat pump installations would always push their wells through the Tamiami limestone to reach the freshwater of the deeper Floridan. This may not have posed a problem had the well installers used a tight casing through the full depth of the well. Instead, the common (cheaper) practice of "short-casing" was usually employed. That is, the well casings were typically seated on the Tamiami limestone instead of being continued on through the intervening geologic formations and into the Floridan aquifer. The uncased portion of the wells had the effect of connecting the freshwater of the deeper Floridan aquifer with the high-chloride water of the overlying surficial aquifer. Freshwater emerging from the Floridan aquifer would be mixed with the more saline water in the uncased portion of the well through the shallow rock zone of the surficial aquifer. Not only was high-chloride water hard on heat pump equipment, it was also hard on foliage and other salt-sensitive life-forms receiving the irrigation overflow from the wells.

Three interrelated negative externalities resulted from the circumstances that had developed in Brevard County. First, newcomers imposed externalities on existing homeowners in the form of a reduced pressure surface, which made it necessary for some homeowners to install pumps not required before. Second, to the extent that wells were short-cased, they created externalities in terms of reduced water quality due to aquifer mixing. Third, reductions in the pressure surface caused saltwater encroachment as the saltwater/freshwater interface moved upward and inland. The pressurized freshwater in the Floridan beneath Brevard County was, originally, a joint-impact, or nonrival resource. Thousands of new users were able to tap it to their immediate benefit with no cost or loss of utility to any other user in the area. Clearly, at some point, the further addition of wells in the area began to overcome the ability of the aquifer to maintain artesian pressure from its distant recharge areas, with the consequence that some wells had to be fitted with pumps and others had to be abandoned because the decline in pressure had permitted saltwater encroachment.

A social trap existed. From an individual homeowner's perspective, a water-to-air heat pump was the most economical method of maintaining home comfort, and there was no compelling reason to refrain from tapping the Floridan aquifer just because the cumulative impact of many new wells was adversely affecting neighbors with wells located closer to the saltwater interface. Existing well owners whose water was adversely affected had no means of excluding newcomers from access to the aquifer. Those who developed new wells in unaffected areas were creating problems for other homeowners but did not have to bear any of the costs associated with those problems. And the sheer numbers of households involved precluded private, individual negotiations to discourage further exploitation of the aquifer for heat pump applications.

The Search for Solutions. As the magnitude of the problem became apparent to homeowners and public officials alike, the search for explanations and solutions began. Scientists and engineers from the St. Johns River Water Management District became involved in the task of monitoring changes in water quality and pressure from the aquifer (Frazee, 1987). The St. Johns River Water Management District intervened on the strength of a nondeterioration policy stipulated by Chapter 373, Florida Statutes, from which the district derives its regulatory authority. According to its statutory mandate, the district can intervene with regulatory measures to prevent deterioration of any groundwater aquifer in its jurisdiction.

To prevent groundwater deterioration, the district had two regulatory measures at its disposal. First, it had authority to regulate well construction according to preestablished standards (Frazee, 1987). Second, it had authority to regulate withdrawals for consumptive use from wells that exceeded 6-inches in diameter or that withdrew more than 100,000 gallons per day. The district immediately imposed restrictions on new well construction, abolishing the practice of short-casing and requiring tight casings full length for any additional wells drilled through the Tamiami into the Floridan to prevent mixing of the lower quality Tamiami water with the fresh Floridan water.

The district faced a discouraging problem as it attempted to restrict further use of Floridan water for heat pumps. The rules adopted by the district for consumptive use regulation had explicitly excluded wells smaller than 6 inches in order to avoid unnecessary regulation of low-yield, backyard wells, which, because of their low volume, would not likely cause problems associated with the nonexclusive, congestible nature of groundwater. The district lacked regulatory authority to release Brevard County homeowners from the social trap in which they found themselves.

An institutional innovation to address this unique problem evolved in the form of a cooperative management arrangement between the Brevard County government and the district, offering a good example of cooperation between a local unit of government and a multicounty regulatory agency (Frazee, 1987). Drawing upon scientific, engineering, and legal expertise from the district staff, as well as from the county government, representatives from both government units developed a water management ordinance for Brevard County. Fortunately, the geographic extent of the problem and its impacts were well contained within Brevard County boundaries.

The ordinance adopted by the county requires all existing water-to-air heat pumps be fitted with demand control valves, ensuring that flow from the well ceases except when the heat pump is in operation (Frazee, 1987). Studies had shown that heat pumps would run from four to 20 hours per day during those seasons of the year when heating or cooling was needed; they would not run at all for several months of each year when coastal temperatures were comfortably moderated by the influence of the ocean. The artesian wells had been allowed to flow constantly, all year, 24 hours a day. Imposition of the demand control valve requirement led to an 80 percent reduction in flow from the aquifer almost immediately.

In addition, the ordinance required that all new wells into the aquifer incorporate a two-well design (Frazee, 1987). Water could be withdrawn from the aquifer through one well, but must be returned to the same aquifer through the second well once the water had cycled through the heat pump. In this manner, consumptive use from the aquifer could be capped.

Further, the ordinance stipulated that when existing heat pumps require replacement, or when they require repairs or renovation that equals half the cost of the original installation, they must be equipped with a second, return well (Frazee, 1987). The cost of such a well was estimated at $1,000 to $2,000 per homeowner.

The cost to homeowners of complying with the ordinance may have eliminated most of the economic advantage of water-to-air heat pumps over other types of heating and cooling systems. On the other hand, preexisting practices had not taken into account the social costs of this method of heating and cooling.

In any event, the search for solutions in the heat pump case included, first, some institutional changes and, second, some technical changes in residential water management practices. The former was necessary before the latter could be imposed.

The Water Wars

The Setting. Growth in demand for potable water has roughly kept pace with the rate of population growth in Florida. Most of Florida's drinking water comes from groundwater aquifers. These aquifers are extensive and prolific. However, they are vulnerable to saltwater encroachment in coastal areas. Ironically, much of Florida's population growth is occurring in coastal communities where such saltwater intrusion is most likely to be a problem. As water supply authorities explore options for solving the water supply problems facing coastal communities, they encounter difficult issues.

For example, South Brevard Water Authority is responsible for supplying water to 120,000 people within its jurisdiction (Koenig, 1986). The authority serves the city of Melbourne on Florida's Atlantic coast. The city's primary water source, Lake Washington, is merely a wide spot in the upper reaches of the St. Johns River. Water supply officials consider the lake to be unreliable—too shallow to afford comfortable reserves during the periodic droughts that are normal for Florida, and susceptible to contamination by organic pollutants flushed from the upper St. Johns watershed. The authority made plans to develop a well field at Holopaw, 20 miles inland from Lake Washington, as the Floridan aquifer there contains plenty of freshwater, remote from the coastal threat of saltwater encroachment.

On the opposite side of the Florida peninsula, historical precedents were set in Pinellas County, which has become completely urbanized as the site of the cities of St. Petersburg, Clearwater, and their suburbs, and which is situated on the finger of land between the Gulf of Mexico and Tampa Bay. Wells located in Pinellas County turned salty during the 1930s, and water supply companies arranged to pipe water from neighboring northwest Hillsborough County (Koenig, 1986). They also acquired well field sites in rural Pasco County to the north. As the entire Tampa Bay area has grown, the investment in freshwater supply facilities has increased and the search for additional developable supplies has intensified.

The Problem. As coastal communities look inland for freshwater supplies, they encounter resistance and sometimes open hostility from the inland residents. The problem with South Brevard's new well field site near Holopaw is that it is located, not in Brevard County, but in neighboring Osceola County. Elected officials in Osceola County fear that their country's prospects for growth and prosperity will be diminished if access to the freshwater beneath it is preempted by agencies serving the interests and citizens of another jurisdiction. Osceola County went to court in an attempt to block the planned diversion of water across county boundaries (which, in this case, also happened to be across water management district boundaries) (Koenig, 1986).

In the Tampa Bay area, Pasco County was the reluctant party in plans to develop water supplies in the rural community for distribution to the coastal cities (Koenig, 1986). In that instance, pressure from the state legislature induced Pasco to sign on with Pinellas and Hillsborough counties, along with the cities of Tampa and St. Petersburg to form the interjurisdictional supply network called the West Coast Regional Water Supply Authority. The authority operates a sophisticated network of reservoirs, well fields, treatment plants, and transmission lines to provide for the growing water supply needs of the communities it serves.

Local newspapers and periodicals often carry stories reflecting the resentment felt by many rural residents over the manner in which urban officials approach the problem of ensuring adequate water supplies. Pasco County residents contend well fields operated by the West Coast Regional Water Supply Authority are draining local water supplies and in some cases have affected the surface water sources in the county as well (Koenig, 1986). This contention is disputed by officials at the Southwest Florida Water Management District. The Pasco County Commission has threatened to sue the regional water organization, claiming it is sacrificing water Pasco will need in the future to support Pinellas County.

A frequent lament of the rural interests in these disputes is that the coastal residents are profligate users of water, inclined to waste it because it is made available to them at low rates that do not reflect the lost opportunities suffered by the rural communities. Whether those communities have truly lost opportunities is difficult to prove. That people use less water if they are required to pay more for it has been documented.

The controversy surrounding interjurisdictional transfers of water in Florida illustrates the boundary issue. Governmental entities—water supply authorities, water management districts, the courts, the legislature—have made binding decisions affecting water resource development and allocation that have implications for the wellbeing of people residing in political jurisdictions not really enfranchised with respect to the relevant decision process. The boundary issue is summed up in the words of those involved. A former water management official said, "Water is like freedom of speech. You start messing with somebody's water—whether or not he has an inalienable right to that water, he thinks he has" (Koenig, 1986). A rural legislator concedes,

"Water is 99 percent political. It's between those that have it and those that don't. Unfortunately, in Florida today, the most political clout is with those that don't" (Koenig, 1986). And his urban counterpart argues, "Water knows no political boundaries. If the legislature saw fit to realign political entities along watershed lines, we'd all have plenty of water" (Koenig, 1986).

The Search for Solutions. It is not clear that the objections of rural water interests will ever be sustained with sufficient political influence to produce concessions and a willingness to negotiate on the part of their urban neighbors. At a minimum, alternatives to interjurisdictional transfers will have to be suggested, as the growth in coastal populations compels the attention of water supply officials. Several options of a technical nature have been studied and, to some extent, adopted.

The most widely publicized option is reverse osmosis, a process for removing minerals and other unwanted substances from salty water (Koenig, 1986). Desalinization was once very expensive, but advances in membrane technology have cut the cost of desalinization to the point that it has been adopted as the primary means of preparing water for human consumption in several Florida cities, including Venice and Sarasota. There are some problems with reverse osmosis. It is energy intensive, a fact that could make it more expensive should energy prices soar again. Also, reverse osmosis plants usually use brackish water that is considerably less saline than seawater. Heavy withdrawals of brackish water from coastal pools lead to the same problem as heavy withdrawals from freshwater aquifers: saltwater intrusion. The saltier the source, the more expensive it is to purify it.

Another promising innovation is aquifer storage, sometimes referred to as recharge-recovery. During rainy reasons, excess water is collected and injected underground (Koenig, 1986). Then, in dry seasons, it is recovered for use. Utilities that have tried this technique in Florida have found aquifer storage costs one-third as much as building a surface reservoir, and surface reservoirs lose 35 percent or more to evaporation.

Reuse of treated wastewater offers potential. St. Petersburg installed a dual system that includes one conduit for treated effluent for lawn irrigation and similar, nonhousehold uses and a separate conduit for potable water for drinking, cooking, and bathing. A disadvantage is the cost of building the separate distribution system required for this approach.

Maybe the most cost-effective option for Florida is also the simplest: water conservation devices in every home (Koenig, 1986). Orlando installed flow restrictors in faucets and water reduction devices in toilet tanks throughout the city. The result was an 18 percent decline in water consumption. Ironically, the conservation program was motivated by a critical shortage of sewage treatment capacity, not by concern for water supplies.

The attractiveness of these alternatives to interjurisdictional transfers of water depends in large part on how costly they are relative to the cost of developing water supplies from remote locations and piping them to population centers. Unless customers see a price advantage in the alternative technologies, they will be reluctant to adopt them. The state legislator representing Pasco County has a bill before the legislature that, if adopted, would require urban jurisdictions to demonstrate that alternative means of water supply are not feasible before they are allowed to develop water supplies in remote jurisdictions. One press account referred to this bill as more or less a futile last stand by parochial water interests (Koenig, 1986).

COMMENTARY:
PERSISTENT WATER MANAGEMENT ISSUES

The case studies reported in this chapter illustrate the type and complexity of issues that the institutional framework for water management must somehow address. Has water law reform in Florida been a success? Are there further changes to be made that will improve the performance of Florida's water management institutions? Are there lessons to be learned from the Florida experience that will benefit policymakers in other states?

Generally speaking, administrative water law seems to be well established in Florida. The fundamental legal precepts have apparently survived initial legal and political challenges. Water management issues persist, but, for the most part, solutions to those issues are being sought within the context of the existing framework and not in terms of fundamental institutional reform.

The administrative structure seems to have demonstrated some of the hoped-for advantages over the common law dispute–settlement process that had been intended by drafters of the Model Water Code. In the case of freeze protection and again in the case of the heat pumps, the water management districts were able to take an active role in helping to protect the resource and resolve the disputes, and were not relegated to the passive and reactive role available to the courts had the issues been the subject of litigation. Moreover, the districts were able to marshall technical expertise and research capabilities not directly available to the courts, a fact that no doubt aided in the process of resolving the resource management issues. The administrative structure allows water management to account for the fugacious nature of the resource and to explicitly account for interaction between surface water and groundwater. In a limited geopolitical setting, such as those represented by the freeze protection and the heat pump examples, the administrative structure averted the boundary issue. In a broader context involving interjurisdictional transfers of water, for example, the boundary issue persists.

It may well be that Florida's system of water management has not yet faced a serious test. Certainly, as the population continues to grow, each successive period of drought will bring greater challenges to the ability of water management districts to protect water resources and somehow accommodate or otherwise manage the competing demands for water. A criticism of the Model Water Code and, by extension, of Florida's system of water law, focuses on its provisions for allocating water when competing demands exceed the available supply (Trelease, 1974). The plan for shortages includes classification of permits according to source, method, and use; and the governing board may order a temporary reduction in total water use, impose restrictions on certain uses, change conditions of a permit, or suspend a permit. The code's solution to the legal uncertainties of riparian rights, say the critics, is the substitution of these administrative uncertainties.

Another criticism focuses on the question of the length of time a permit is to be effective and the related question of how permits for limited supplies can be shifted to new uses (Trelease, 1974). Flexibility in allocating water is relinquished for the term of a permit. If the term of the permit is too short, it may be impossible to amortize the investment in water-using technology. Moreover, a permit holder may, on the expiration of a permit, lose a going concern of considerable value if the permit renewal is denied in favor of a new one.

One view holds that a model water code and similar administrative structures would be strengthened by issuing a water right of indefinite duration, held in fee simple, which is transferable (Trelease, 1974). By substituting the transferable water right for the permit, provision is made for the reallocation of water supplies through time while strengthening the position of water rights holders.

These and other institutional issues will be revisited as Florida's policy-makers struggle with the water management problems that growth and change will generate. The economic nature of problems confronting common law doctrines and modern regulatory systems is compelling. Externalities, the boundary issue, and many other aspects of resource allocation and service flows will be a central focus of the issues and the analysis leading to their resolution.

NOTES

1. Dr. Charles Hinton is the Executive Director, Florida Strawberry Growers Association, Plant City, Florida.

2. Ken Weber is the Senior Hydrologist, Resource Regulation Department, Southwest Florida Water Management District, Brooksville, Florida.

3. James Frazee is the Chief Hydrologist, Water Well Construction, of the Department of Resource Management, St. Johns River Water Management District, Palatka, Florida.

REFERENCES

Baldwin, L. B., and R. R. Carriker (1985). *Water Resource Management in Florida.* Bulletin 206. Gainesville: Florida Cooperative Extension Service, Institute of Food and Agricultural Sciences, University of Florida.

Brion, Denis J. (1979). *Compendium of Water Allocation Law in the Eastern United States.* Lexington, Va.: Washington and Lee University, School of Law.

Carriker, Roy R. (1985). *Water Law and Water Rights in the South.* SRDC Synthesis— Bibliography Series No. 16. Mississippi State, Miss.: Southern Rural Development Center.

Frazee, James (October 28, 1987). Private communication.

Geraghty, James J., David W. Miller, Frits Van Der Leeden, Fred L. Troise (1973). *Water Atlas of the United States.* Port Washington, N.Y.: Water Information Center, Inc.

Hinton, Charles F. (October 28, 1987). Private communication.

Hyde, Luther W. (1975). *Principle Aquifers in Florida.* Map Series No. 16. Tallahassee: U.S. Dept. of the Interior, Geological Survey, and Florida Dept. of Natural Resources, Bureau of Geology.

Kenner, W. E. (1969). *Runoff in Florida.* Map Series No. 22. Tallahassee: U.S. Dept. of the Interior, Geological Survey, and Florida Board of Conservation, Division of Geology.

Kenner, W. E., E. R. Hampton, and C. S. Conover (1975). *Average Flow of Major Streams in Florida.* Map Series No. 34, updated. Tallahassee: U.S. Dept. of the Interior, Geological Survey and Florida Dept. of Natural Resources, Bureau of Geology.

Kiker, C. F. (1977). *Water Rights and Allocation.* Florida Food and Resource Economics Leaflet No. 17. Gainesville: Florida Cooperative Extension Service, Food and Resource Economics Dept., Institute of Food and Agricultural Sciences, University of Florida.

Klein, Howard (1975). *Depth to Base of Potable Water in the Floridan Aquifer.* Map Series No. 42, Revised. Tallahassee: U.S. Dept. of the Interior, Geological Survey, and Florida Dept. of Natural Resources, Bureau of Geology.

Koenig, John (1986). "Fighting Gets Fierce as Water Wars Spill into the Courts." *Florida Trend* 29 (October):101–110.

Leach, S. D. (1982). *Estimated Water Use in Florida 1980.* Map Series No. 103. Tallahassee: U.S. Dept. of Interior, Geological Survey.

Levine, Steven J. (1984). "Groundwater: Louisiana's Quasi-Fictional and Truly Fugacious Mineral." *Louisiana Law Review* 44:1123–1148.

Maloney, Frank E., and Richard C. Ausness (1971). "A Modern Proposal for State Regulation of Consumptive Uses of Water." *The Hastings Law Journal* 22 (February):523–560.

Maloney, Frank E., Richard C. Ausness, and J. Scott Morris (1972). *A Model Water Code (with Commentary).* Gainesville: University of Florida Press.

Maloney, Frank E., and Sheldon J. Plager (1967). "Florida's Ground Water: Legal Problems in Managing a Precious Resource." *University of Miami Law Review* 21:751–776.

Maloney, Frank E., Sheldon J. Plager, Richard C. Ausness, and Brian D. E. Canter (1980). *Florida Water Law, 1980.* Publication No. 50. Gainesville: Water Resources Research Center, University of Florida.

Randall, Alan (1987). *Resource Economics: An Economic Approach to Natural Resource and Environmental Policy.* 2d ed. New York: John Wiley & Son.

Schmid, A. Allan (1978). *Property, Power, and Public Choice: An Inquiry into Law and Economics.* New York: Praeger Publishers.

Tinsley, Ray K., and Joseph B. Fransion (1979). *Water Resource Engineering.* 3d ed. New York: McGraw-Hill Book Co.

Trelease, Frank J. (1974). "The Model Water Code, the Wise Administrator and the Goddam Bureaucrat." *Natural Resources Journal* 13 (April):207–229.

Weber, Ken (October 28, 1987). Private communication.

SUGGESTED READINGS

Baldwin, L. B. and R. R. Carriker (1985). *Water Resource Management in Florida.* Bulletin 206. Gainesville: Florida Cooperative Extension Service, Institute of Food and Agricultural Sciences, University of Florida.

This 15-page bulletin provides an introductory overview of Florida's water resource, patterns of water use, and the evolution and implementation of administrative water law in Florida. The bulletin was written for general audiences and represents a useful background piece for anyone interested in understanding the context for state water management policy in Florida.

Carriker, Roy R. (1985). *Water Law and Water Rights in the South.* SRDC Synthesis-Bibliography Series No. 16. Mississippi State, Miss.: Southern Rural Development Center.

This work is organized into two parts. The first includes an essay providing background about major areas of water law, a discussion of water law reform, and summaries of water law for each state in the southern region. The second part consists of an annotated bibliography for 193 sources applicable to regional water issues, primarily in the southern United States. This synthesis and bibliography is intended to save time for individuals who, without training in law, have need of information about law as it pertains to state and regional water policy issues.

Maloney, Frank E., Sheldon J. Plager, Richard C. Ausness, and Bram D.E. Canter (1980). *Florida Water Law 1980,* Publication No. 50. Gainesville: Water Resources Research Center.

This study, written by legal scholars at the University of Florida College of Law, represents a comprehensive overview of Florida water law, including both consumptive uses of water and land use activities that affect the aquatic environment. It supplements the synthesis on water law and water rights by Carriker (1985), focusing exclusively on Florida water law.

Randall, Alan (1987). *Resource Economics: An Economic Approach to Natural Resources and Environmental Policy.* 2d ed. New York: John Wiley & Son.

This is a textbook in natural resource economics presented at the intermediate level, appropriate for upper division and undergraduates and beginning graduate students in economics. It provides a good policy-oriented treatment of economics in the context of natural resource and environmental issues, providing an excellent synthesis and critique of the "conventional" literature, and integrating the natural science, legal, political, and administrative concerns that round out the milieu within which natural resource policy decisions are made.

Schmid, A. Allan (1978). *Property, Power, and Public Choice: An Inquiry into Law and Economics.* New York: Praeger Publishers.

This book makes a good text for students who have already completed a standard course in natural resource economics. Schmid tries to wean his readers from the implicit presumption in favor of markets that tends to pervade the conventional literature in natural resource economics. He reintroduces many of the standard concepts of natural resource economics in what he calls a "nonpresumptive" inquiry into the relationship between human agreements on property rights, formalized institutions, and the performance of the economy.

Trelease, Frank J. (1974). "The Model Water Code, the Wise Administrator, and the Goddam Bureaucrat." *Natural Resources Journal* 13 (April):207–229.

This journal article provides a useful critique of "A Model Water Code" upon which Florida's water management statute is based. The article makes a case for including market-like arrangements for dealing with water allocation decisions, injecting the perspective of a legal scholar who favors incorporating some aspects of western prior-appropriations doctrine into proposals for eastern water law reform.

STUDY QUESTIONS

1. From your reading of this chapter would you consider groundwater in Florida to be a renewable or nonrenewable resource? How can the order in which users have access of water alter the effective supply?

2. Distinguish how riparian water law differs from the scheme implemented under the Florida Water Resources Act.

3. Evaluate the merits of the argument that those having used water from an aquifer for the longest period of time should have the right to maintain that use.

4. How would implementation of the proposal in Florida to substitute transferable water rights for permits likely affect "outcomes," as described in Chapter 1?

Chapter Four

Land Use Policies, Water Quality, and the Chesapeake Bay

Philip Favero
David G. Pitt
Dean F. Tuthill

Nonpoint sources of pollution such as runoff from agricultural and urban activities are major factors in declining water quality. This chapter describes the interaction between land use decisions and water quality in the Chesapeake Bay. The authors examine the creation of new land use regulations designed to protect the Bay. Economic concepts applied and refined in this case include externalities, common property, transactions costs, irreversibilities, and free rider situations. Other concepts related to the issue include the role of symbols and myths, especially as used by interest groups, and preservation versus management values. Economic and political factors are used to explain how interest groups effect and are affected by a natural resource policy process.

THE CHESAPEAKE BAY: BACKGROUND

The Chesapeake Bay is the largest estuary in the United States. This drowned valley of the Susquehanna River is approximately 200 hundred miles long and its width varies from 4 to 30 miles. Although the Bay's surface area of 4,400 square miles is extensive, its depth averages only 28 feet. Two-thirds of the Bay has a depth of 10 feet or less. The salinity of the Bay's water ranges from zero at the northern freshwater inflows during the spring, to 30 parts per million (the definition of ocean water) at the Bay's mouth in the autumn. This range of salinity enables the Bay environment to provide habitat for freshwater, marine, and anadromous species. The diversity and abundance of plant and animal species populating the Chesapeake Bay make it an immense "protein factory."

The Chesapeake Bay drainage basin (Figure 4.1) includes 64,000 miles of land that extends over six states (Maryland, Virginia, Delaware, West Virginia, Pennsylvania, and New York) and the District of Columbia and

FIGURE 4.1 The Chesapeake Bay

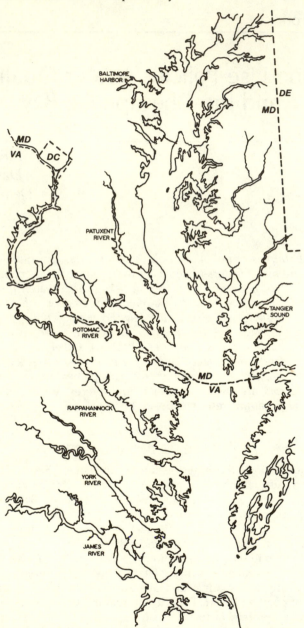

Source: Environmental Protection Agency Field Office, Annapolis, Maryland.

spans four physiographic provinces (the Atlantic Coastal Plain, the Piedmont, the Ridge and Valley, and the Allegheny Plateau). Approximately 12.7 million people currently reside in the tri-state Maryland, Virginia, Pennsylvania portion of the drainage area, and the U.S. Environmental Protection Agency (EPA) expects an additional 1.9 million by the year 2000 (U.S. EPA, 1983). Over three-fourths of this population resides in one of five large metropolitan areas immediately adjacent to the Bay or its major tributaries (U.S. Army Corps of Engineers, 1984).

Bounteous Resources

As a large natural system that lies in a heavily populated region, the Chesapeake Bay constitutes a natural resource having multiple and sometimes conflicting uses. In spite of the Bay's overall shallowness, the deep channel of the drowned Susquehanna river valley has enabled Baltimore, Maryland, and Hampton, Virginia, to become two of the nation's five most important North Atlantic ports. The commercial fishing industry in the Bay is over 350 years old and generates an annual dockside value in excess of $75 million. More than 120,000 pleasure craft are registered in Maryland alone, and during 1979, more than 4 million recreational activity days were recorded on the Bay. The Bay sport fishing industry directly and indirectly generates $770 million of income per annum (U.S. EPA, 1983). The Bay is an important part of the Atlantic migratory bird flyway, serves as an overwintering ground for several waterfowl species, and provides opportunities for wildlife observation. The Chesapeake also serves as a receptacle for the discharge of treated and untreated waste effluent from domestic, municipal, and industrial sources. Finally, 7 of the 16 Maryland counties immediately adjacent to the Bay or its tributaries experienced at least a 20 percent increase in population between 1970 and 1980, well above the 7 percent state average. These additional Bay country residents have become consumers of the ambience associated with the Bay's resources.

Decline of Resources

The Chesapeake Bay is beginning to show signs of distress under the influence of so many people trying to use a finite system in so many ways. Enrichment of nitrogen and phosphorus in Bay water, especially in the northern and middle Bay, has been dramatic. This increase in nutrients has caused a 15-fold decrease in oxygen levels in the waters of the Bay.

Heavy metals and organic compounds have contaminated Bay water and sediments. Partly because of changes in these physical parameters of water quality, oyster harvests and freshwater-spawning fish have declined. Aquatic vegetation, an important habitat for many Bay species, has all but disappeared. The diversity and abundance of benthic (bottom-dwelling) organisms important in nutrient recycling have diminished (U.S. EPA, 1983).

Bay Decline as a Function of Land Use

In its eight-year study of Chesapeake Bay pollution, the EPA concluded that the quality of the Bay doesn't solely depend on what is discharged from the end of pipes (1983). The contribution of these so-called point sources of pollution is often exceeded by the contribution of dispersed and disaggregated nonpoint sources. Surface runoff from agricultural fields or urban streets can carry contaminants by pushing them along the stream bed, by suspension, and by solution. When discharged into the Bay or its tributaries, these contaminants become major sources of pollution. In an average year, for example, nonpoint sources are responsible for 39 percent of the phosphorus entering the Bay and two-thirds of the nitrogen loading. In high rainfall years, nonpoint contributions of phosphorus can exceed 64 percent while nonpoint nitrogen loading can exceed 80 percent (U.S. EPA, 1983). Urban runoff and agricultural runoff are equally capable of delivering excessive loadings of nitrogen and phosphorus to the Bay and its tributaries (Northern Virginia Planning District Commission, 1979). Nonpoint sources also deliver toxic compounds and heavy metals to the Bay. For example, 28 percent of all lead and 15 percent of all cadmium found in the tidal freshwater Potomac River is attributable to urban runoff (U.S. EPA, 1983).

Development of Critical Area Criteria
to Protect Resources

Given the social and economic significance of the Chesapeake Bay to the people of Maryland and the decline of Bay resources as documented by the EPA study, Governor Harry Hughes announced in November 1983 a sweeping plan to restore the Bay to its 1950 condition. Known as the Chesapeake Bay Initiatives, the plan included ten pieces of proposed legislation and numerous administrative procedures to protect critical Bay resources and reduce both point and nonpoint sources of pollution. Point sources of pollution were addressed through programs to upgrade and expand industrial and municipal wastewater treatment facilities and enhanced enforcement capabilities. Nonpoint sources were addressed through an expanded program to manage nontidal wetlands; a program to facilitate farmer adoption of agricultural Best Management Practices (BMPs)[1] to control nonpoint pollution generated by agricultural operations; and the proposition of the Chesapeake Bay Critical Area legislation to protect the natural resources adjacent to the Bay's shoreline. The primary purpose of the critical area proposal was to foster more sensitivity among developers for the impact development had on land surrounding the Bay. The Governor requested the formation of the Chesapeake Bay Critical Area Commission charged with formulating critical area management criteria that would be implemented by local jurisdictions of the state (chiefly counties).

POLITICAL ECONOMICS OF THE BAY'S DECLINE

Externalities

Some costs of resource use are borne directly by the recipient of whatever benefits accrue from the resource. Industrialists, for instance, directly bear the costs of building and maintaining devices to dump wastes into the Chesapeake Bay. (Some industrialists, to be sure, may pass those costs on to consumers.) Other costs spill over to and are borne by individuals not able to enjoy the benefits accruing to the initial user. For example, oyster propagation is sensitive to the presence of industrial wastes, and oyster harvesters may suffer significant losses from industry's use of the Bay as a waste receptacle. Such spillover costs are external to the initial user's decisionmaking framework. The indusrial waste disposer is unlikely, of its own volition, to consider costs imposed on oyster harvesters.

Results of studies conducted by numerous public and private organizations reveal many external costs created by Chesapeake Bay users. Many individuals and groups use the Bay as an expedient to dissolve and transport nearly anything, nearly everywhere. Table 4.1 illustrates a set of major external costs for the Bay. Four major types of negative externalities are identified and criteria for their measure suggested. The externalities are attributed to certain "origin" activities and distinguished by their impacts on Bay users.

It was not by chance that Governor Hughes's proposal for critical area regulations followed closely the publication of the most comprehensive water quality study of the Bay, EPA's *Chesapeake Bay: A Framework For Action* (September 1983). As part of its Chesapeake Bay program, the EPA sponsored over fifty research projects. The subsequent reports and studies by other organizations provide credible evidence of the presence, magnitude, source, and impact of external costs. Scientific evidence reduced uncertainty about relationships among Bay users, reduced the ability of creators of negative externalities to disassociate themselves from or avoid bearing their external costs, and motivated members of the attentive public to join certain interest groups.

Common Property

Impacts of negative externalities are compounded by common ownership of Chesapeake Bay resources. When the physical characteristics of a natural resource are such that property rights cannot or have not been distributed among users, the resource can be described as common property. However, when many individuals simultaneously use a common property resource and their individual use subtracts from that available to others, dilemmas arise. Individual users seeking to maximize their self-interest are then motivated to obtain first use and resist policies designed to constrain individual use (Hardin, 1968).

TABLE 4.1: Negative Externalities in the Chesapeake Bay

Type	Criteria	Origin	Impacts
Water quality degradation	Declining dissolved oxygen Increasing collifom bacteria Sediment delivery Increasingly abnormal pH Nutrient transport Increasing temperatures Heavy metal movement	Municipal waste disposal Industrial waste discharge Oil spills Suspended material runoff Fertilizer and pesticide runoff Channel dredging and dumping	Aesthetics Food supply Industrial use Recreation services
Modification of fresh-water inflow	Abnormal salinity levels Riparian zone flooding Sediment delivery Nutrient delivery Heavy metal movement	Municipal and industrial withdrawals and diversions of fresh-water inflow Increased areas of impervious surfaces	Aesthetics Food supply Industrial use Recreation services
Wetland alteration -- dredging and filling	Diminished areas of marsh and wetlands	Dredging and filling	Food supply Hunting Wildlife observation
Shoreline utilization	Dimished shoreline areas for other future uses	Development by riparian landowners	Future sites for ports, industries, recreation, and residential development

An example of a common property resource dilemma is the management of an oyster bed in Maryland's portion of the Chesapeake Bay. The state of Maryland owns all surface water and underlying land resources of its part of the Bay. Oyster harvesters have historically resisted leasing of native oyster beds. As indicated by the comment of an Eastern Shore oyster harvester, most users prefer to leave the harvest to whomever can take it: "What's mine is mine, and what's someone else's is mine if I can get it" (Pitt, Bellows, and Sorter, 1975).

When unchecked, this philosophy can promote severe overuse and eventual depletion of a healthy resource. When negative externalities are already affecting a common property, the tendency to overuse the pool's threatened resources is encouraged and compounds the risk of depletion.

Transaction Costs of Resource Allocation

Resolution of problems associated with negative externalities and common property suggests transactions among resource users and between users and resource managers. For example, resolution of negative externalities involves determining the nature of damages incurred, identifying both the origin and impacts of these damages, and establishing a system of payments or charges to offset damages (Fisher, 1981). Resolution of common property dilemmas involves either establishing and enforcing rules of allocation among common property users or distribution of property rights among users (Hardin, 1968). Both situations require identifying the set of users involved and organizing and conducting collective action among users. Identifying users and organizing collective action implies pecuniary and nonpecuniary costs that must be borne either by users or society.

When the number of users involved is small, such transaction costs are relatively minor and their allocation is straightforward (as when legal fees in a tort are assigned by a judge to one of the involved parties) (Coase, 1960). However, when the number of users involved is large, transaction costs escalate, and their assignment among affected parties becomes complex (Dick, 1976). The escalating magnitude of transaction costs and complex damage assessment procedures inherent in the large-numbers case often preclude determination of a final settlement. As a result, problems of negative externalities and common property resource allocation involving large numbers of users tend to remain unresolved.

Many of the externalities and common property dilemmas associated with the decline of the Chesapeake Bay involve complex interactions among diverse and numerous Bay users (e.g., waterfront industrialists, shoreline property owners, recreational boaters, commercial and sport fishers). Consequently, the associated transaction costs provide deterrents for problem resolutions.

Irreversibility

In general, two values have been associated with the Chesapeake Bay (Sagoff, 1985): (1) its "management" value as a developable source of human food, recreation, and waste disposal; and (2) its "preservation" value, inherent in protecting the Bay as a healthy ecosystem.

Land use decisions in the watershed around the Bay, especially as they affect the ecological health of that estuary, fall into the category of "nontrivial irreversibilities" (Krutilla and Fisher, 1975). That is, land use decisions that affect the Bay's ecological health will endure virtually undiminished. For example, once filled and paved, a wetland, the heart of the Bay ecosystem in terms of primary productivity, is not easily restored to its natural state or function.

No study exists to compare the relative values of the Bay as a managed versus a preserved resource. It seems likely, however, that preservation values are increasing relative to management values. This conclusion rests on the following assumptions: Technical progress increasingly compensates for Bay management values, but the same option does not exist for the Bay as a healthy estuary. In other words, substitutes can be found for the Bay as a waste receptacle, source of food, or recreation resource, but no substitutes can be created for the Bay as a natural ecosystem.

Krutilla and Fisher (1975) have shown that if management values are decreasing relative to preservation values, then the following holds true for nontrivial irreversible investments: (1) the optimal scale of new investments to create management values decreases; and (2) the net present value to the environment will be maximized by stopping management value investments even though they are still profitable. The incentive for individuals to continue investing in management values exists until internal marginal costs equal internal marginal returns. However, when management values are declining relative to preservation values, each marginal increment of management value investment is associated with increasing marginal costs in forgone opportunities for preservation values.

Unfortunately, the calculus of preservation value estimation has yet to be developed. There is little agreement on how to balance preservation and management values; commonly, political debate exists. Profit maximizing firms have an incentive to continue management value investments. Those people and groups seeking to maximize preservation values have an incentive to curtail development. Public sector authorities have a responsibility for deciding between the conflicting interests of the opposing groups. Among Krutilla and Fisher's suggested policy options for establishing this public interest balance is one directly related to land use regulations in Bay critical areas—legislative zoning to preserve ecological value, with provision to make rezoning difficult.

Free Rider Situation

Almost by definition, public policies for natural resources are characterized by high-exclusion costs. That is, it is difficult for those individuals and groups who work to produce a public policy to exclude individuals from enjoying the benefits of that policy (Olson, 1965). The proposed critical area criteria exhibit the high-exclusion cost characteristic common to many natural resource policies. The costs arise in preventing others from enjoying the benefits. Land use controls surrounding the Chesapeake Bay would provide benefits that would be ubiquitously shared by all present and future users of the Bay whether they are wanted.

Because the benefits of the policy could not be packaged for sale, however, little incentive exists for individuals to invest in the formulation of the policy. Rather, the incentive is to ride free on the policy efforts of others. The free rider situation for the development of new policies can be overcome by interest groups in at least two ways: interest groups can sell membership services to obtain funds needed to engage in the policy process (Olson, 1965); or public agencies can be created that represent the interests of certain collections of individuals and groups and thereby use tax dollars to overcome the situation. Individuals not involved in interest groups or associated with public agencies are left to resolve the free rider problem independently. Their values will therefore not be well represented in the policy process.

Symbols and Myths

"Symbols and myths" affect the generation of natural resource policies (de Neufville, 1983). In this context, a symbol means the image of a desired condition, the benefits of which commonly appeal to certain individuals and groups with policy interests. A myth is defined as the belief (true or not) that the behavior prescribed by a particular public policy is connected with the desired symbol. Thus, symbols have the potential to motivate interest groups, public agencies, and organizations, and perhaps even the general public to action. They reduce transaction costs for policymaking by establishing common values. Myths possess the potential to gain the support of groups for certain policy options. Of course, opposing groups strive to create competitive symbols and myths so as to differentially influence the policy process.

One symbol of the Bay that faded as the result of scientific studies of Bay water quality was "the Bay as a multiple and full use resource." Attached to that image was the myth that policy norms should support the complete spectrum of investments to create management values. The studies revealed, however, the presence of numerous and large external costs among Bay users and, as a result, significant threats to preservation values and some management values. The new symbol created by the studies was "the Bay as a threatened ecosystem"—an "incredibly complex living organism" threatened by the pressure of human use. The related myth is that new policies are needed to "save the Bay."

Another symbol of the Bay still in vogue but undergoing scrutiny is "the Bay as a treasure chest." The related myth contains the notion that government expenditures to preserve and enhance Bay water quality can support increasing numbers of private and public, individual and group consumers of the Bay's treasures. In fiscal year 1985 Maryland state government expenditures for Bay-related activities ran about $70 million, or more than 1 percent of the total state budget. Moreover, expenditures are increasing. For example, Bay-related expenditures by Maryland's Department of Agriculture increased threefold over the fiscal year 1985–1986 period to total approximately $9 million in 1986.

The symbol of "the Bay as a treasure chest" has a dynamic and potentially expansive character. To the extent that public expenditures to maintain the Bay as a treasure chest are successful, increasing numbers of Bay consumers are attracted to its use. Thus public expenditures to maintain the Bay as a treasure chest are absolutely required, but only at increasing real marginal costs to accommodate increased use. This dynamic character has the quality of a social trap (Platt, 1973). The alternative symbol is, again, "the Bay as a threatened ecosystem," with the related myth that uses of the Bay as an intermediate or final product must be modified to avoid increasing public expenditures.

Several other Bay symbols and myths exist and played prominently in the development of critical areas policymaking.

1. "The Bay as it was in 1950." The related myth is that Maryland legislators could help restore the Bay to that of recent memory by supporting the creation of the Critical Area Commission.

2. "The noble ploughman." This symbol portrays the farmer as a wise and trustworthy steward who cannot afford to and in any case would never squander land resources for personal gain. Farmers used this symbol to gain support for the related myth that voluntary actions by farmers will suffice to achieve agricultural conservation of land resources in a critical area.

3. "Private property." The Fifth Amendment to the United States Constitution specifically prohibits the taking of private property for public use without just compensation. The property rights sumbol portrays any government limitation on the exercise of property rights as an uncompensated taking. The associated myth is "that government governs best which governs least." Realtors and developers used the property rights symbol to promote the myth in Maryland that government should not intrude in the management decisions of landowners.

4. "There's no life west of the Bay." This sentiment, commonly seen on Eastern Shore bumper stickers, symbolizes the regional attitude of Shore dwellers to the rest of Maryland. Its related myth is that Eastern Shore natural resources should be managed differently than resources in the rest of the state.

The critical area experience suggests that symbols are important in providing opportunities to galvanize support around related myths. Symbols and myths create common images and policy implications for interest group transactions. These images rally interest groups and probably alter their definitions of self interest.

Institutions

Institutions, defined here as the formal and informal rules and procedures that govern behavior, are important determinants of public policies because these rules are the standards for conducting transactions to establish those policies (Schmid, 1978). Institutions also establish parameters for the realm of acceptable behavior by setting limits or creating incentives for prescribed patterns of resource use. State and local governments exercise their inherent police and taxation powers, for example, in establishing administrative regulations or setting standards and charging fines for exceeding the limits of acceptable waste discharge into the Chesapeake Bay. Institutions such as these provide incentives or disincentives for achieving a prescribed pattern of behavior by Bay users.

Finally, institutions may themselves become objects of attention as interest groups strive either to redefine the rules of the policy process or reestablish bounds of acceptable resource use behavior. To the extent that interest groups are able to impact existing legislative or administrative doctrine, the norms produced become institutions in their own right.

OUTCOMES OF THE GOVERNOR'S PROPOSAL

Establishment and Activities of the Commission

A bill-drafting committee, established by Governor Hughes in anticipation of the 1984 session of the Maryland General Assembly, made specific the governor's proposal for critical area controls. The legislature then passed the governor's bill, with amendments, and established the Chesapeake Bay Critical Area Commission. The commission met during 1984 and 1985 to develop a set of criteria that local jurisdictions could use to create and administer land use controls in the critical area. Actions by the drafting committee, General Assembly, and commission all reveal attempts to balance institutions in the Maryland land use policy environment.

Balancing Institutions

Private Property vs. Public Trust. In an article on the workings of the bill-drafting committee, a member of that group described the concern given to both private property rights and public trust (Liebermann, 1985). The bill produced by the committee was weighted, however, on the public trust side of the balance as it stressed the preponderant public necessity to minimize water pollution from land use; conserve fish, wildlife, and plant habitat; and ensure scenic qualities of the Bay shoreline. The General Assembly, in adopting legislation, tilted the balance toward private rights by dropping the necessity to ensure scenic qualities and by requiring the commission to write criteria that would "accommodate economic growth." In establishing its administrative procedures, the Critical Area Commission strove to obtain information from all groups with interests in public trust, private property, or both (Liss, 1985).

County Jurisdiction vs. State Guidance. In Maryland, critics of local government control over land use contend that counties operate under a strong incentive that is little concerned with environmental quality. That incentive is to attract businesses that add to the local demand for labor and to the county property tax base. The incentive is said to create a "competition of laxity" with respect to environmental protection. To guard against such laxity, the bill as introduced and enacted provides a strong state role. County governments are required to obtain commission approval for critical area management plans and any subsequent amendments affecting critical areas. Moreover, an amendment to a zoning map may be granted by a local authority "only on proof of a mistake in the existing zoning." Thus relatively rigid zoning is mandated, and change is allowed only as part of a review conducted at least once every four years.

The drafting committee also gave preliminary consideration to the applications of land use controls across all Maryland county jurisdictions in the Bay watershed or, at least, across the counties that adjoin the Bay. Staunch local government resistance was anticipated, however, so the committee settled on a corridor approach. As enacted, the "initial planning area" for the critical area includes all land under the Bay, waters of the Bay, and uplands within 1,000 feet of state and private wetlands to the head of the tide. Certain exclusions or inclusions by local jurisdictions, with the Critical Area Commission's approval, can expand or contract this area, in accordance with law and regulations.

Legislators, for their part, amended the bill in a way that reflected their concern for local land use control. As proposed, the commission would have included 15 members. That number was increased to 25 by the General Assembly so as to require the governor to appoint a representative member from the local government in each of the affected 16 counties.

The commission, in establishing its working procedures, sought also to balance local control with state guidance. Thus the commission developed criteria that included a mix of state prescriptions requiring strict local compliance but allowed some local flexiblility.

Strong Executive vs. Jealous Legislature. In recent decades the political power of Maryland's governor has increased. That development is not, however, universally admired. The General Assembly jealously guards its power, diminished though it may be. In particular, legislators tend to criticize attempts by state agencies to increase their budgets. Thus, to avoid creating a large new state bureaucracy, the bill and subsequent legislation avoided making the commission a permitting agency. Rather, the commission was given oversight authority to intervene in local government procedures so as to ensure adherence by local programs to commission criteria. As a check against the authority of the commission, the General Assembly required the commission to report its activities to an oversight committee of members of the legislature. Moreover, the General Assembly also amended the draft bill to require legislative approval of commission criteria by joint resolution of both legislative houses during the 1986 session, with the provision that if unapproved, the criteria would take effect in 1987.

Summary of the Commission's Activities in 1984 and 1985

The Chesapeake Bay Critical Area Law required the Critical Area Commission to conduct two sets of public hearings in preparation of a set of criteria for creation of local government land use controls in the critical areas. The first round of seven regional hearings was conducted in late 1984 and a second round of nine hearings in mid-1985. The initial hearings provided a forum wherein private and public interest groups could express their concerns prior to the start of substantive commission activities; the latter round served as a sounding board for the commission's preliminary criteria released between the two rounds.

Analysis of transcripts from all 16 hearings reveals that approximately one dozen private interest groups presented testimony. Among the most active groups were environmentalists, farmers, and developers (chiefly home builders and real estate professionals). Among public groups, municipal and county government representatives also frequently testified.

Elements of state government were also active in various ways in establishing critical area criteria for land use. In addition to the governor, who was viewed as the source of the policy initiative, five executive departments participated in the draft writing, lobbied for legislation, and helped formulate criteria by serving on the Critical Area Commission. Two departments that viewed their roles, in part, as assisting private interest groups to articulate policy positions were Agriculture (for farmers) and Natural Resources (for various interest groups concerned with the environment and natural resources).

Commission Criteria

The commission criteria, as submitted to the General Assembly, addressed three major areas: (1) development activity, (2) resource-based activities, and (3) habitat protection.

Development Activity. Local jurisdictions are required to prohibit solid or hazardous waste collection or disposal activities and sanitary landfills in their critical areas unless no environmentally acceptable alternative exists outside the critical area. The critical area corridor is divided into three types of land use for development purposes:

1. Intensely Developed Areas (IDAs) comprising at least 20 contiguous acres where residential, commercial, or industrial uses predominate
2. Limited Development Areas (LDAs) where low or moderate intensity uses prevail
3. Resource Conservation Areas (RCAs) where agriculture, fisheries, forestry, wetlands, barren lands, surface water, and open space prevail; no water or sewer services exist; and/or density is less than one dwelling unit per five acres. New developments must not exceed one dwelling per 20 acres.

Local governments are required to establish land use policies for the three land types. For IDAs the policies must be designed to minimize the impacts of existing land use practices and control the impacts of future development. For LDAs the policies must allow, in addition, only that kind of development that does not change the designated character of the area and that meets certain criteria for habitat and water quality protection. Forest removal in LDAs, for instance, must be limited to 20 percent of existing tree cover and impervious surfaces to 15 percent of the total area. For RCAs the policies must conserve, protect, and enhance overall ecological values; habitats for wildlife; and the resource base for agriculture, forestry, and aquaculture. A requirement that new development be restricted to densities of one dwelling unit per 20 acres is imposed in RCAs.

Resource-based Activities. Forest and woodland protection is encouraged by requiring that local jurisdictions develop a forest preservation plan for wooded areas of one or more acres in the critical area, with regulations to prohibit cutting and clearing of most trees within a 100-foot buffer adjacent to the Bay. Each farmer in the critical area is required to initiate a program of Best Management Practices, which would restrict cultivation near the Bay or its tributary streams, add runoff controls, or alter tillage practices. Water dependent facilities are also regulated according to type. These regulations include a prohibition of new commercial marinas in RCAs and the establishment of limits on community piers. Shore erosion protection works are to be regulated by local policies that encourage protection of eroding shoreline.

Habitat Protection. Local governments are required to establish policies to maintain an area of transitional habitat for upland aquatic wildlife, maintain the natural environment of streams, and protect riparian plant and wildlife habitat for certain named species.

Legislative Passage

During its 1986 session, the Maryland General Assembly considered 32 bills related to the proposed criteria as submitted by the commission. A highly publicized attack was mounted against the commission's proposals, led by rural lawmakers from Maryland's Eastern Shore counties. The attack focused heavily on the one dwelling per 20 acre–density limitation for RCAs. In the end, however, only minor amendments were approved. A joint resolution to approve the commission's criteria passed and was signed by the governor.

Substantive Outcomes

Critical area land use controls were accomplished by a process of balancing institutions and associated symbols and myths. The final policy outcomes, moreover, involved a sharing of substantive gains and losses among several private interest groups. Policy change thus occured in an evolutionary manner with no absolute winners or losers among affected groups.

Environmental Groups. Although they compromised on specific issues, environmental groups were the largest overall gainers among affected parties.

Land use controls for critical areas represent a distinct change in Maryland land use policy, a change sought by environmental groups. For the first time in its history, the state now requires local governments to apply uniform criteria for specific land use controls, with a provision for state administration if local governments do not comply. The Critical Area Commission, which includes state and local members, developed and oversees the program. Local governments enforce land use controls in their respective portion of the critical area.

The relative success of environmental groups can be explained, in part, by the strong political push the governor, as head of a dominant administrative institution, gave in promoting critical area policies. Also, through the sale of membership services, environmental groups were able to raise money to increase their involvement and effectiveness in the policy process. They were vocal participants at all the hearings, and their staffs regularly attended meetings of the commission and its constituent committees. This direct involvement allowed environmentalists to remain abreast of rapidly evolving policies and to provide specific information at key points in the process. Environmentalists are also among the clientele groups of the Maryland Department of Natural Resources (DNR), a key public interest agency in the formation of policies for critical areas. This clientele relationship has an established history that is manifested by client representation on several DNR policy bodies. The combination of resources acquired through membership services and representation through the DNR provided environmental groups with improved knowledge of and access to key decisionmakers and allowed environmentalists to overcome free rider problems and transaction costs in influencing public policy for the critical areas.

Finally, the success of environmental groups can be attributed to skillful use of three symbols—"the Bay as a treasure chest," "the Bay as a threatened ecosystem," and "the Bay as it used to be." These symbols helped lodge the Bay and the critical area concept on the governor's policy agenda, galvanize a consensus among all interests that something had to be done with respect to the Bay cleanup, and establish the myth that land use management is a cornerstone of Bay enhancement.

Farmers. Farmers also did reasonably well. Although BMPs are required by the critical area criteria, such practices should not impose large costs or cause major disruptions in farming operations. Farmers, even more than environmentalists, have departmental representation in the state government through the Maryland Department of Agriculture, whose secretary was a commission member. Again, such representation reduces, at public expense, free rider problems for institutional changes having high-exclusion costs. The presence of the secretary also provided an opportunity for an effective and carefully orchestrated inflow of information to the commission from an agricultural community organized by the Maryland Farm Bureau.

Farmers benefited, finally, from the institution of voluntary adoption of conservation practices. The presence and strength of this institution makes the regulation of farm management far less palatable to decisionmakers, especially when coupled with the symbol of the farmer as the "noble ploughman."

Foresters. Foresters and the wood products industry were reasonably successful in influencing decisionmakers for reasons similar to the success of environmentalists and farmers. Like the environmental group, the industry is a clientele group of the Department of Natural Resources, and it possesses knowledge of and access to key DNR policymakers. Many DNR employees are educated and trained as professional foresters and therefore share the lore of multiple and full use of forest resources through scientific management (Dana and Fairfax, 1980). Historical connections to the DNR policy process coupled with this shared perspective on intensive resource management enabled the forest industry to overcome potential free rider problems and provide timely information during commission deliberations.

The success of environmentalists, farmers, and foresters can be attributed lastly to the specificity with which they presented their interests to the commission. All of these interest groups presented specific recommendations for what the commission should allow as acceptable behavior in critical areas. Environmentalist testimony during the 1984 hearings was laden with many of the specific development restriction and habitat protection measures that were later embodied in the preliminary draft criteria. Farmers and foresters proposed specific amendments in their testimony in 1985 that were incorporated into the final draft criteria. In contrast, developers and landowners, the most significant "losers" in the interest group struggle, presented globally oriented, nonspecific testimony at both sets of hearings. This testimony focused broadly on institutions and symbols and myths and failed to match the level of specificity proposed in 1984 by environmentalists and in 1985 by farmers, foresters, marine operators, and seafood processors.

Developers and Landowners. The losses sustained by both developers and landowners include density restrictions imposed in the RCA, development regulations in the LDA, and community and private pier restrictions. Neither group had representation equalling that of environmentalists, farmers, or foresters in the public sector groups making policies for critical areas. Although organizations such as the Maryland Association of Realtors, the Suburban Maryland Building Industry Association, the Maryland Institute of Homebuilders, and various chambers of commerce and boards of realtors could have enabled developers to overcome the free rider problems associated with exclusion costs, these groups did not have the strong institutional representation of environmentalists, farmers, and foresters. Development groups are not normal components of DNR's clientele, and there was not a dedicated representative for development serving in any of the public agencies involved in criteria development. The developers' focus on property rights as both a symbol and an institution was overpowered by the environmentalists' references to the Bay as a threatened ecosystem and the Bay as a treasure. Finally, the strength of the natural allies of developers and landowners—rural counties seeking additional economic growth—has been significantly reduced by post–World War II changes in Maryland's political culture.

CONFLICTS AS PRESERVATION vs. MANAGEMENT VALUES

Almost without exception, interest group conflicts over critical area policies involved a struggle between environmentalists and commodity-oriented user groups. The underlying difference in the struggle revolved around environmentalists seeking some form of preservation value (e.g., habitat protection or water quality enhancement) and resource users seeking some combination of management values (e.g., foresters harvesting board feet of timber, farmers reaping bushels per acre, and developers building dwelling units).

Conflicts between environmentalists seeking preservation values and commodity groups seeking management values extend back to the birth of systematic natural resource management in the United States. A late nineteenth-, early twentieth-century feud between conservationist Gifford Pinchot and archetypical preservationist John Muir (founder of the Sierra Club) set the stage for much of the management versus preservation conflicts that have characterized natural resource policy in the United States (Pitt and Zube, 1987).

Muir's transcendental views were spiritual and ecological, not economic. He did not believe the earth was created solely to serve humankind. Benefits would flow to anyone who acknowledged nature as a power greater than him or herself (Petulla, 1977). In this sense, the preservation values associated with habitat protection and development restriction have greater value than the dollar value associated with any combination of commodity production.

In contrast, Pinchot's utilitarian perspective viewed the natural environment as the bestower of objects and systems of practical value to society. These natural elements are conceived as natural resources to be used in accomplishing the societal goal of "the greatest good for the greatest number for the longest time" (Dana and Fairfax, 1980). Failure to realize maximum and fullest human use of the resource (as in setting aside habitat protection areas wherein maximum multiple use values cannot be realized or restricting development to a level below the land's capability) is viewed as precluding the achievement of society's goal.

The struggle between environmentalist and commodity-oriented advocates in the critical area issue represents a Maryland manifestation of the preservation-management value conflict that underlies natural resource policy issues. The success of the environmental advocates in shaping critical area policy partly reflects the growing emphasis in our society on preservation values.

CONCLUSION

Land use restrictions in the critical area surrounding the Bay will affect some but not all of the human reasons for the Bay's decline. Negative externalities in the form of nonpoint source pollution emanating from the critical area will be reduced. In effect, the burden for externalities will be shifted back to those land users who have previously created them or who can be expected to create externalities in the future. Some shifted externalities will be borne by existing property owners, such as landowners with restricted building rights; some by future property owners such as purchasers of new shoreline homes with higher prices brought about by the reduced supply of such homes; and some by taxpayers through public subsidies to farmer investments in conservation systems.

Critical area policies also attempted to avoid irreversible private investments in management values. The policies established a public choice for preservation values by using a variety of policy instruments, which will probably include rigid zoning, depending on how local governments choose to meet the commission's criteria.

Finally, the critical area policies took an important step in recognizing the Bay as a common property resource and in confronting the associated social trap of ever increasing public expenditures to preserve and enhance Bay water quality subject to growing population and economic development pressures. The critical area policies are based on the assumption that population growth must be restricted and economic activities limited in a corridor around the Bay. All shoreline will not be available for home construction, for instance, and certain business practices, including some agricultural and forestry practices, will be prohibited. In addition, existing and future consumers and firms will be required to adjust their behavior as a result of limitations on impervious surfaces in subdivisions and the requirement for the use of BMPs in agriculture.

Yet the step taken was a small one. Population growth restrictions and limitations on business practices apply to only a part of the critical area corridor that is itself only a portion, albeit an important portion, of the Bay's watershed. Moreover, only a part of the Bay watershed falls in Maryland.

Future attempts to preserve and enhance Bay water quality are likely to involve additional policies to (1) use technical means of waste export, recycling, and treatment; (2) selectively guide business development and population growth; and (3) coordinate state efforts through multistate agreements and federal intervention.

ACKNOWLEDGMENTS

We thank Dr. Sarah J. Taylor, Executive Director, Chesapeake Bay Critical Area Commission, for her suggestions and comments. The conclusions are our own.

Research reported in this chapter was supported by a grant from the University of Maryland Water Team and the Maryland Water Resources Research Center.

NOTES

1. William Magette (1987) defines Best Management Practices as "structural, nonstructural, and managerial techniques that are recognized to be the most effective

and practical means to control nonpoint pollutants yet are compatible with the productive use of the resource to which they are applied."

REFERENCES

Coase, R. H. (1960). "The Problem of Social Cost." *Journal of Law and Economics* 3:1–44.

Dana, S. T., and S. K. Fairfax (1980). *Forest and Range Policy*. New York: McGraw-Hill.

Dick, D. T. (1976). "The Voluntary Approach to Externality Problems: A Survey of the Critics." *Journal of Environmental Economics and Management* 2:185–195.

Fisher, A. C. (1981). *Resource and Environmental Economics*. Cambridge, England: Cambridge University Press.

Hardin, Garrett (1968). "The Tragedy of the Commons." *Science*, no. 162:1243–1248.

Krutilla, John V., and Anthony C. Fisher (1975). *The Economics of Natural Environments*. Baltimore, Md: Johns Hopkins University Press.

Liebermann, G. W. (1985). "The Chesapeake Bay Critical Area Act: The Evolution of a Statute." *The Daily Record*, April 20, 1985.

Liss, S. (1985). *Process and Structure: The Chesapeake Bay Critical Area Act and Commission*. Baltimore: Maryland Institute of Continuing Professional Education of Lawyers, Inc.

Magette, William L. (1987). *Citizens' Guide to Environmental Terminology*. Water Resources 18. College Park, Md.: Cooperative Extension Service, University of Maryland.

de Neufville, J. I. (1983). "Symbol and Myth in Land Policy" in William N. Dunn, ed. *Values, Ethics, and the Practice of Policy Analysis*. Lexington, Mass.: Lexington Books.

Northern Virginia Planning District Commission (1979). *Guidebook for Screening Urban Non-Point Pollution Management Strategies*. Washington, D.C.: Washington Metropolitan Council of Governments.

Olson, Mancur, Jr. (1965). *The Logic of Collective Action: Public Goods and the Theory of Groups*. New York: Schocken Books.

Petulla, J. M. (1977). *American Environmental History*. San Francisco: Boyd and Fraser Publishing Co.

Pitt, D. G., W. J. Bellows, and B. W. Sorter (1975). "Farmers and Fishermen: Interaction in the Coastal Zone" in *The Present and Future of Coasts: Proceeding of the First Annual Conference of the Coastal Society*. Bethesda, Md.: Coastal Society.

Pitt, D. G. and E. H. Zube (1987). "Management of Natural Environments" in D. Stokols and I. Altman, eds., *Handbook of Environmental Psychology*. New York: John Wiley and Sons.

Platt, John (1973). "Social Traps." *American Psychologist* (August):641–651.

Sagoff, M. (1985). "Fact and Value in Ecological Science." *Environmental Ethics* 7(1):99–116.

Schmid, A. A. (1978). *Property, Power, and Public Choice: An Inquiry into Law and Economics*. New York: Praeger Publishers.

U. S. Army Corps of Engineers (1984). *Chesapeake Bay Study Summary Report*. Baltimore, Md.

U. S. Environmental Protection Agency (1983). *Chesapeake Bay: A Framework for Action*. Annapolis, Md.

SUGGESTED READINGS

Krutilla, John V., and Anthony C. Fisher (1975). *The Economics of Natural Environments.* Baltimore, Md.: Johns Hopkins University Press.
The authors use irreversibility and other economic and institutional concepts to consider natural environment management theory and five case studies. Here students will find a seminal source on the theory of irreversibility.

de Neufville, Judith Innes (1983). "Symbol and Myth in Land Policy" in William N. Dunn, ed., *Values, Ethics and the Practice of Policy Analysis.* Lexington, Mass.: Lexington Books.
Myth making in public policy, particularly in natural resource policy, is defined and discussed by the author. The author provides students with aid and direction for incorporating the concepts of symbol and myth in resource policy analysis.

Olson, Mancur, Jr. (1965). *The Logic of Collective Action: Public Goods and the Theory of Groups.* New York: Schocken Books.
This book includes a theory of political organization behavior and its use in explaining the actions of a variety of interest groups. Economic theory is blended with political science in an insightful and provocative manner.

Schmid, A. Allan (1978). *Property, Power, and Public Choice: An Inquiry into Law and Economics.* New York: Praeger Publishers.
The author develops a paradigm of institutions and performance that provides a method to analyze public policymaking. This thoughtful book is essential reading for the student of law and economics.

U.S. Environmental Protection Agency (1983). *Chesapeake Bay: A Framework for Action.* Philadelphia.
This publication summarizes findings of the agency's research and suggests policy directions to protect the Bay. This publication is the place to begin to learn about the Bay's problems and some broad policy options.

Warner, William W. (1976). *Beautiful Swimmers: Watermen, Crabs and the Chesapeake Bay.* Harmondsworth, Middlesex, U.K.: Penguin Books, Ltd.
Both a natural history of the Atlantic blue crab and the story of the Bay watermen are provided in this Pulitzer Prize–winning book. It informs the reader in a delightful way about the Bay's history and ecology.

STUDY QUESTIONS

1. How do the issues addressed in this chapter correspond to the Wisconsin farmland development issues discussed by Barrows in Chapter 2?

2. Explain, using concepts from Chapter 1, why nonpoint pollution is more difficult to control than emissions from well-defined sites.

3. Pollution taxes are often advanced by economists as a means to control pollution. These taxes are rarely used in practice. Evaluate the positive and negative features of a tax on polluters of the Chesapeake Bay. Given the political economy of Maryland described in this chapter, how would a pollution tax proposal probably fare?

4. To what extent are increased urban growth and additional amenity uses of the Bay (even when these uses are nonpolluting) irreconcilable with maintaining the "quality" of the Bay. In what sense is the attractiveness of the Bay an example of a social trap?

Chapter Five

Nuclear Waste Disposal Policy
Socioeconomic Impact Management Issues

Ronald C. Faas

The disposal of highly radioactive wastes forces us to ask who will bear the risk of exposure. This chapter explores the nature of the low-probability, high-consequence risk factors of nuclear waste. The analysis is applied to the proposed Hanford, Washington, nuclear waste repository site. Drawing from statistical theory, the author discusses types of decision errors and statistical loss functions. Policies that affect the allocation of risk—performance bonding and insurance, for example—are analyzed in the context of the prolonged time horizon presented by high-level radioactive wastes. The chapter provides a framework for use in environmental impact policy analysis. Key elements of the framework are uncertainty, potential irreversibilities, and intergenerational effects. Institutional designs to account for these elements are analyzed for their effect on potential risk-bearing interest groups.

The generation and disposal of hazardous waste present many unresolved public policy issues. One set of those issues, the siting of a high-level nuclear waste (HLNW) repository, raises a basic policy question: What burdens should have to be borne by residents of an area, state, or region adversely impacted by a project or policy that generally benefits residents elsewhere?

A fundamental premise of the National Environmental Policy Act of 1969 (Public Law 91-190) has been that citizens and officials of impacted local communities should have available the necessary policy tools to mitigate externally imposed adverse impacts, should they choose to do so. *Impact mitigation* is the reduction or elimination of adverse impacts created by the specific development project or policy change at issue. However, local capacity problems (that is, part-time, elected officials, small staffs, scarce finances) often limit the identification and effective utilization of available impact management options, even when dealing with standard socioeconomic impacts. These difficulties are greatly compounded with the introduction of unique impacts of hazardous waste disposal, including environmental risk considerations associated with low-probability, high-consequence occurrences.

WHAT IS NUCLEAR WASTE
AND WHY IS ITS ISOLATION A PROBLEM?

Since the beginning of the atomic age in the 1940s, the national need for permanent high-level nuclear waste disposal sites has risen due to the increasing volume of high-level waste and decreasing availability of on-site storage space. More than 80 nuclear power plants operating in the United States today are producing nuclear wastes. The highly toxic radioactive wastes are currently in temporary storage at each power plant, awaiting permanent disposal. Many storage facilities at power plants will reach capacity before the end of the century.

Nuclear wastes are hazardous because they are radioactive and remain so for a long, long time. The radiations emitted can cause death or damage to cells and cell components. The nature and severity of the damage depend on what is struck, on the amount of radiation—the exposure—and on the sensitivity of the struck cell. There is no question that radiation can cause cancer or genetic mutation; what is questioned is the relationship between the dose—particularly below one rem—and the number of resulting cancers or mutations. For both types of damage, the latency period—the time between exposure and the effect—is long, 25 or so years for cancer, and a generation or more for genetic damage. In both cases, other possible causes—chemical carcinogens, for example—can confuse the issue. It is claimed that nuclear waste, properly handled, will add miniscule amounts of radiation to the environment. However, if accidents occur, the wastes can present a significant hazard for generations. Some experts propose that an isolation time of 300 to 500 years for HLNW is adequate, and others refer to the "million-year" waste disposal problem. One reason for the wide discrepancy in estimates is the vast difference in half-lives among the different radio-isotopes in wastes. Another reason is the wide latitude available in choosing a level of acceptable risk for a given benefit. Taking these uncertainties and difficulties into account, scientists have developed several models for predicting the effects of low-dose radiation. Therefore, risk estimates for low amounts of radiation are based on incomplete data and involve a large degree of uncertainty (League of Women Voters Education Fund (LWVEF), 1982).

Types of Nuclear Waste

Highly radioactive wastes differ from other types of radioactive or hazardous wastes. The following paragraphs describe the differences between spent fuel, liquid high-level waste, and waste produced in U.S. government activities (Washington Nuclear Waste Board, 1984).

Commercial "spent" fuel consists of nuclear power plant fuel assemblies that have exhausted their "useful" life. These assemblies contain most of the uranium as well as additional radioactive elements (fission products, such as strontium and cesium, and actinides, such as plutonium) produced during plant operation. Each year a typical nuclear reactor creates about 30 tons of commercial spent fuel. When the spent fuel is removed from the reactors, the 12-foot long assemblies are both extremely hot and highly radioactive. Electric utilities are temporarily storing commercial spent fuel in water-filled pools on plant sites until a more permanent disposal method is available. By the year 2000, commercial spent fuel will total about 50,000 metric tons.

High-level nuclear waste is, technically, the liquid residue resulting from reprocessing of spent fuel. Highly radioactive, this liquid waste requires conversion to glass or a similar solid form before disposal. About 600,000 gallons of *commercial* liquid high-level waste exists in storage today.

Spent wastes generated by U.S. government activities (nuclear research, weapons production) can be low-level or high-level waste. About 48 million gallons of high-level waste is in temporary storage at Hanford.

Spent fuel and high-level waste should not be confused with *low-level radioactive wastes,* which are disposed of in shallow land burial sites. Low-level wastes are produced by research, medical procedures, hospitals and industry, as well as nuclear power plants. There are larger volumes of low-level waste, compared to high-level waste, but they contain lower levels of radiation. Three commercial facilities for disposal of low-level waste exist in Washington State (Hanford), Nevada (Beatty), and South Carolina (Barnwell). In addition, hazardous chemical or toxic wastes that are by-products of other, nonnuclear industrial manufacturing are handled at treatment and disposal facilities elsewhere.

Isolation Alternatives

Many nuclear power plants are now facing a growing storage problem. Without permanent storage facilities, nuclear power plants could find it impossible to operate. This potential problem has stimulated the federal government to find a safe method of disposal. Nuclear scientists have considered a number of options for disposing high-level nuclear wastes, ranging from deep sea disposal to launching waste containers into space.

The U.S. Congress gave direction to the search for high-level waste disposal by passing the Nuclear Waste Policy Act of 1982 (Public Law 97-425). The act, to be implemented by the U.S. Department of Energy (USDOE) by the end of this century, defines a schedule for permanent disposal of spent fuel and highly radioactive wastes. As an interim step, USDOE is planning to send commercial spent fuel to a Monitored Retrievable Storage site (MRS) for packaging and, perhaps, temporary storage. Spent fuel would then be shipped from the MRS site to a repository for permanent disposal.

The federal act specifies that the preferred form of permanent waste isolation and disposal will be in two, deep, geologic repositories. The USDOE examined potential repository sites across the country in a variety of geologic media, including basalt, granite, salt, and tuff (hard volcanic ash). Of nine potential sites in six states considered for the first repository, three were selected in May 1986 by the president for a more detailed, federal evaluation called site characterization (Washington Nuclear Waste Board, 1985a).

The Hanford, Washington, Site

One of these sites is located on the federally controlled Hanford Reservation in southeastern Washington, which covers 570 square miles of the Pasco Basin within the Columbia River Basalt Plateau. The Columbia River flows through the northern part of the Hanford site and also forms part of the eastern boundary. The cities of Richland, Pasco, and Kennewick, with a combined population of about 90,000, are located on the Columbia River southeast of the Hanford site.

The USDOE began studies at the Hanford Reservation in 1976 to determine the suitability of basalt rock for geologic radioactive waste isolation. The Hanford basalt is a dark, dense, volcanic rock deposited in lava flows 9 to 17 million years ago. The repository would be located near the center of the reservation and occupy about three fourths of a square miles on the surface. A maze of tunnels and shafts covering nearly two square miles would be dug approximately 3,200 feet underground. The shafts would be up to 12 feet in diameter and would be used to transport waste and workers, provide air intake, and vent exhaust. The tunnels would be divided into storage areas, each holding approximately 1,900 tons of spent fuel. The proposed repository would employ an average of about 450 workers per year throughout the eight-year initial development phase, and could employ 1,100 workers at peak operation.

Once the repository is constructed, solidified high-level waste and spent fuel would arrive in shipping casks by truck, train, or both from around the country. Estimates place the total number of shipments at 17 trucks or 2 railcar loads per day. At the repository, the waste would be taken from the transportation casks. Fuel rods would be removed using remote-controlled devices and packed tightly in canisters of 3-inch thick steel. Each canister would be about 15 feet long, weigh approximately 30 tons, and be designed to contain waste for at least 300 years. Once filled, the canister would be welded shut, then taken in a large elevator to one of the storage tunnels beneath the earth's surface. Workers dressed in protective clothing and riding in radiation-shielded vehicles would transfer the casks to "placement" holes. Using remote control, workers would place the casks into bored holes in the basalt rock. The cask would then be covered with crushed basalt and bentonite clay.

This method of storage would continue for about 20 years. Once the repository was filled to its 47,500–metric ton capacity and stopped receiving wastes, it would be monitored by both the state and federal governments. Although secure, it would remain unsealed for a number of years. Should reprocessing become economical, spent fuel could then be retrieved and reprocessed. After 50 years, the repository would be sealed and would rely on natural barriers such as layers of basalt to contain the wastes (Washington Nuclear Waste Board, 1985b).

Expected Impacts

It is difficult to comprehend fully the ramifications of a project that is unique in human history. The USDOE identified two postclosure objectives related to the isolation of spent fuel and high-level waste from the accessible environment and prevention of adverse impacts to the health and safety of the public. These objectives are to minimize the adverse health effects attributable to the repository during the first 10,000 years after repository closure, and also during the period 10,000 to 100,000 years after closure. Such time spans for projected impacts and the number of people involved are indeed extraordinary: 500 to 5,000 human generations—the latter equal in time to the period of evolution since Neanderthal man—and, assuming a constant population, involving 28 billion future residents of the state of Washington (Impact Assessment, Inc., 1987).

Failure prior to repository closure may affect people and property downwind from the site of an accident during transportation of waste to the repository or at the repository itself. Postclosure failure could lead to contamination of natural resources and economic goods from groundwater migration to wells to the Columbia River. There are a wide variety of potential economic losses from airborne and waterborne releases. Beyond the health effects of mortality (loss of life) and morbidity (sickness and injury), there are potential short-run and long-run effects to agricultural, fishing, industrial, and other commercial activities. Short-run losses would include the value of crops destroyed, fish killed, and other commercial and industrial products damaged, as well as the costs of removal and disposal of contaminated crops, fish, and other goods. Long-run effects include decreases in property values of contaminated land, buildings, and equipment due to decreased productivity, and also the costs of displacement, retraining, and/or relocation of owners, managers, operators, and laborers in farming, fishing, or other commercial and industrial activities. Residential property effects include decreases in property values and the costs of permanently relocating people (if necessary). Beyond losses to tourism-related businesses, the recreational/environmental effects include nonmarket losses to recreational fishing, hunting, boating, and the aesthetic value of scenic vistas and sightseeing.

Local and state government fiscal effects include decreased tax revenues from devalued property, depressed sales, and declining gasoline tax receipts. Costs could include emergency public services for evacuation, temporary storage, and food for evacuees and clean up, along with abandonment and relocation of some public offices. In case community drinking water from the Columbia River were contaminated by a release of radionuclides, fiscal effects could include extra expenses for water treatment or shifting to an alternative, higher-cost source. Furthermore, perceptions that agricultural, fish, and other commercial or industrial products were contaminated by a HLNW repository failure would likely depress the market for these commodities. Such economic loss would be "real" even if there were no "objective" evidence of such contamination.

The state of Washington has identified several categories of socioeconomic impacts that the state, local governments, business enterprises, or citizens might incur as the basis for mitigation or compensation claims (Washington Department of Ecology, 1986). "Standard" impacts include the full range of economic, demographic, community service, and fiscal impacts as well as social, cultural, and psychological impacts. "Special" impacts unique to the nuclear nature of the repository include (1) economic and social consequences of accidents and failures (and of public concern regarding such), the extended time period over which such consequences may be experienced, and the potential of a repository to attract or engender ancillary industry; (2) the risk of transporting, storing, or disposing of nuclear wastes; (3) equity considerations in the distribution of these costs and benefits; and (4) unforeseen events, such as changes in the policy arena. Transportation impacts, given the alternative modes (truck, train, barge) and routes from generating sites to the repository, include risks and hazards associated with increased traffic and the radiological nature of the cargo.

CONCEPTS FOR ANALYZING HLNW IMPACT MANAGEMENT ISSUES

This section will summarize physical and socioeconomic characteristics of nuclear waste that create socioeconomic impacts. Next, institutions and transactions that govern behavior and outcomes in impact management decisions will be identified.

Physical Characteristics

The preceding overview emphasized that nuclear waste remains potentially hazardous for a very long time span. What is unknown, however, is the capacity of the repository and its surrounding natural environment (rock and water) to contain the radionuclides in a safe manner throughout this time span. As with other environmental risk problems (National Planning Association and Haldi Associates, 1978), the probability of occurrence (radiation exposure from repository failure) is claimed to be so low and the underlying mechanism so uncertain that even the most informed estimates of risk are highly subjective and vary widely. At the same time, however, the level of potential damages is catastrophic, overwhelming both the underwriting capability of the private insurance mechanisms and the prospects of reasonable public provision. Furthermore, such consequences of environmental risks, once incurred, cannot be reversed for long periods of time—for tens of thousands of years in the case of nuclear wastes.

Socioeconomic Characteristics

In terms of the framework introduced in Chapter 1, the risk of radiation exposure from repository failure is a nonoptional, joint-impact good (bad) that is costly to avoid. In the parlance of environmental risk problems, the risk is latent, thus may be borne unknowingly and involuntarily for long periods of time. Such risk situations would likely involve collective exposure of large segments of society. Furthermore, parties who bear such risk receive a disproportionately small share of benefits of the undertaking, thus the value of the good is positive to some parties while negative to others. When one person places positive value on the good and another places negative value, the problem of nonoptional joint-impact goods (and bads) becomes more complicated; those harmed want to veto production of the good (bad) or be compensated for its adverse impacts.

Institutions and Transactions

In part due to the resource characteristics outlined above, it is difficult to establish a legally defensible cause-and-effect relationship between the parties liable for the exposure and those who bear the losses. These difficulties are exacerbated, however, by institutions that grant unequal power in the administrative transactions involved in repository siting and other impact management decisions. (An obvious example is the recent action by the federal government declaring itself immune to being sued for damages due to radiation exposure from defense or other federal activities.) Elements of institutions significant to the nuclear waste issue can be discussed in terms of property rights, transaction costs, uncertainty, burden of proof, and boundary issues.

One precondition of an effective nuclear waste repository siting policy is that the state and local governments should have negotiating leverage, defined as the power of one party to grant or withhold something desired by another party, in this case the federal government. A basic source of leverage would be the property rights of respective parties defining who has to deal with whom. One of these property rights is the power regarding siting—that is, the federal power to preempt siting versus the state's power to veto siting.

Transaction costs condition the ability to effectively utilize such ownership rights, however (Schmid, 1978). Different parties face differing costs of acquiring information and differing costs of being wrong. In addition to information costs, there are contractual costs of organizing and reaching agreement with another party, as well as policing costs of maintaining such an agreement once reached.

The question of who has to bear the burden of proof is a key factor in determining what kinds of transaction costs must be borne and by whom. A mitigation and compensation process imposing high-transaction costs on the local community may indeed nullify the effective exercise of a nominal right held by the local community.

That some parties value the good positively and others negatively creates complex boundary issues. Those of a geographic nature involve not only the many regions generating nuclear waste and the few states that have candidate repository sites, but also locally those who may realize economic gain from repository activity and others more exposed to risk of repository failure. Boundary issues are also temporal between current and future generations. These boundary questions and related uncertainties pose difficulties in determining whose preferences count in repository siting and impact management decisions.

Continuing with the framework introduced in Chapter 1, the next section examines behavior and outcomes associated with decisions concerning repository siting and impact management.

ANALYZING IMPACT MITIGATION DECISIONS AND OUTCOMES INVOLVING RISK

The two components of risk commonly accepted are (1) the *probability* of a hazard and (2) the *consequences* of exposure to it. There is less agreement, however, on which measures are to be used to operationally define the probability and consequence components.

Selective Perceptions of Risk

There are two common ways to think about risk. Technical experts in the field of risk assessment often refer to risk as the product of scientific research, primarily public health statistics, experimental studies, epidemiological surveys, and probabilistic risk analyses. Emphasizing the *low probability* of an occurrence, this group calculates risk in nuclear waste management to be quite low when compared to more commonly confronted risks. In contrast, the general public tends to focus on the degree of magnitude, or *high consequence* of the risk, almost ignoring probability. From the perspective of the potential victim of contamination, low-statistical probability is of little comfort; it is the high magnitude that is of concern (Peters, 1983).

In developing a theory of risk averse behavior, Kenneth Arrow in 1974 observed that (1) individuals tend to display aversion to the taking of risks, and (2) that risk aversion in turn is an explanation for many observed phenomena in the economic world. These selective perceptions may be related to differential incentives of different parties, each exhibiting risk averse behavior in their own way. It is in the interests of the nuclear industry, allied scientists, and federal agency personnel responsible for obtaining a solution to the nuclear waste management problem to downplay the high consequences of an occurrence and advocate repository siting based on low probability of an occurrence. It is equally in the interests of responsible people in an affected region to question estimates of low probability of an occurrence and to argue against siting a repository in their region on the grounds of high consequences of an occurrence.

Decision Errors Involving Risk

In any particular case of uncertainty regarding whether a proposition is true or false, decisionmakers face two hypotheses. In the case of a HLNW repository failure, the tendency of the technical community to focus on the

TABLE 5.1:   Comparison of Alternative Risk Choices With
Alternative Failure Outcomes

| | Failure Outcomes | |
Risk Choices	Low Consequences	High Consequences
Accept risk of HLNW repository failure:	No catastrophic consequences will occur.	Type II error -- fail to predict catastrophic consequence by presuming safe situation.
Avoid risk of HLNW repository failure:	Type I error -- falsely predict catastrophic consequence when situation is safe.	Catastrophic consequence if repository fails (but avoided by avoiding risk of failure -- not siting repository in area).

low probability of failure and for the general public to focus on the catastrophic consequences of failure corresponds with the following mutually exclusive hypotheses: (1) Repository failure *will not* expose the region to catastrophic consequences; or alternatively, (2) Repository failure *will* expose the region to catastrophic consequences.

The choice between either hypothesis cannot be made with certainty. An important principle in statistical hypothesis testing is that the researcher's decision that the hypothesis is true or that it is false is never made with certainty; one always runs a risk of making an incorrect decision. Statistical hypothesis testing is essentially a means of controlling and assessing that risk (Glass and Stanley, 1970).

Types of Decision Errors. Actual testing of a statistical hypothesis requires empirical data. However, because observations concerning failures of HLNW repositories are not available, decisions about the potential consequences of a repository failure depend on a choice between two competing scientific hypotheses based on judgment rather than empirical data. Choice of either hypothesis involves the possibility of two types of decision errors, as shown in Table 5.1.

A decision to accept risk of failure if the low-consequence outcome were actually true would be a correct decision. No catastrophic consequences would occur because the situation turned out to be safe. Likewise, a decision to avoid risk of failure if the high-consequence outcome were true would also be a correct decision, if the catastrophic consequences that would occur with the repository failure could be avoided by actions, such as not siting the repository in the area.

On the other hand, a decision to avoid risk of failure if the low-consequence outcome were actually true would be an incorrect decision. Such a decision is called a Type I error, which in this case would be to falsely predict a catastrophic consequence when the situation is safe. Similarly, a decision to accept risk of failure if the high-consequence outcome were actually true would also be an incorrect decision. This error is called a Type II error, that is, in this case failing to predict a catastrophic consequence by presuming a safe situation.

Statistical Loss Function. Ideally, it is desirable to minimize the chance of both Type I and Type II errors and thus minimize the total error. In fact, however, it is impossible to simultaneously minimize both types of errors, because as the probability of one type is reduced, the probability of the other is increased. However, the concept of a loss function allows an evaluation of total expected loss by considering the cost of each type of error, the probability of each type of error, and the prior probability that each of the two competing hypotheses are true. Many researchers often are so prone to using the habitual and arbitrary levels of 5 percent and 1 percent for the probability of Type I error that they never consider either the costs or size of the probability of a Type II error. Yet, in the case of medical research, for example, if a Type II error means the loss of human life and a Type I error involves $10.00 wasted on useless drugs, who would approve of a procedure that ignores the probability and cost of a Type II error (Manderscheid, 1971)? Similarly, the probability and cost of the Type II error must be considered in choosing which risk of repository failure is acceptable.

Which Decision Is Acceptable to Whom?

Why might the two "correct" decisions be unacceptable as a basis for initial policy choice? The primary factor is uncertainty, based on the lack of confidence that either will be a "correct" decision and the belief that the impact outcome will be other than that on which the choice of risk is premised. To illustrate, given the need to resolve the long-term waste disposal problem, some would argue against avoiding risk of failure by not siting the repository anywhere on the basis that at least one decision to accept siting is needed. As there have been no catastrophic impacts from waste repositories (the fact that there have been no repositories of the type under consideration notwithstanding), there is no justification to not proceed with siting. Others would argue against accepting the risk of HLNW repository failure on the basis of the skepticism that has developed regarding the ability of scientists to develop nuclear waste management techniques that will both stand the test of time and protect the local interests (Brenner, 1979).

Under conditions of uncertainty, neither of the two choices about the risk of failure, that is, either to accept or to avoid the risk, can be made without facing the possibility of decision error. Given "there is no risk-free environment," the issue then becomes, Which type of decision error is acceptable, at what cost, and to whom? Advocates of a decision to accept the risk of failure under uncertainty of the consequences of failure are apparently willing to accept the Type II error—the failure to predict catastrophic consequences by presuming a safe situation. Alternatively, advocates of a decision to reject the risk of failure are apparently willing to accept the Type I error—the false prediction of a catastrophic outcome from a relatively safe or harmless situation.

Some Hard Questions

An important function of national policy is to allocate exposure to risk, either explicitly or implicitly. The two basic repository siting choices and their associated risk impacts involve the following questions:

- Should national policy allow areas, states, and regions anywhere the right to "veto" siting and, in so doing, choose to accept the Type I error, thus rejecting siting everywhere?
- Alternatively, should national policy proceed with siting somewhere and, in so doing, impose exposure to the Type II error upon that impacted area, state, and region?

The latter policy choice, to proceed with siting somewhere, presents two mitigation issues generally ignored in the technical discussion of siting decisions. First, under what conditions should an area, state, or region accept exposure to the risk of a Type II error, that is, possible failure to predict a catastrophic impact outcome? An alternative formulation of this issue is under what conditions should an area, state, and region be forced to accept such exposure?[1] The USDOE claims that cumulative releases of radionuclides to the accessible environment would be so low as to be insignificant in comparison with both the EPA standard and natural background radiation (USDOE, 1986). Under conditions of uncertainty, this choice implicitly accepts (and imposes upon the impacted area) the Type II decision error, apparently without consideration of its costs.

The second mitigation issue is, Could alternative institutional designs link exposure to consequences of a low-probability, high-consequence occurrence more effectively with reduced probability of such an occurrence? In other words, if those who could affect the probability of an occurrence were to individually and collectively bear the consequences of such an occurrence, would they have sufficient incentive to drive the probability of a high-consequence occurrence to zero? In contrast, some aspects of current institutional design tend to insulate consequences of a high-consequence occurrence from those who could affect its probability. This assertion is examined in the next section, which examines several dimensions of building an effective impact management policy, including the mitigation of standard impacts, problems in compensating for exposure to environmental risk, and approaches to minimize the probability of a high-consequence occurrence.

BUILDING AN EFFECTIVE MITIGATION
AND COMPENSATION POLICY

The term "mitigation" is used both broadly and narrowly in the impact literature. Broadly, mitigation strategies include measures to maximize positive impacts and to avoid, minimize, or compensate for negative impacts. Narrowly, mitigation means the lessening of negative impacts that cannot be avoided entirely. A comprehensive impact management strategy includes four components: (1) impact enhancement measures to maximize the positive effects of impacts such as economic benefits and local business participation; (2) impact avoidance measures by which negative or undesirable impacts might be avoided in advance to prevent demands on local systems from reaching unmanageable levels; (3) impact mitigation measures by which negative impacts that cannot be avoided directly might be mitigated or lessened; and (4) impact compensation measures to compensate fully and equitably all persons or communities exposed to the potential for unavoidable or unmitigable impacts now and in the future. Such measures may include incentives for acceptance of risks.

Mitigating Standard Impacts

Considerable infrastructure investments such as housing, schools, roads, and other public facilities are often required to minimize the standard adverse economic, fiscal, and social effects of development. The early and candid presentation of impacts leaves time for mitigation efforts to be designed and implemented. Yet, the local community may face considerable costs in acquiring such information or critiquing the information provided. For example, the ability of a state to participate in the Nuclear Regulatory Commission and USDOE waste management programs depends upon the technical capabilities within or available to the state. While most states handle administrative, procedural, and broad-based environmental concerns in siting other major industrial facilities, states (and local governments) face constraints in participating in the technical portions of complex federal waste management programs.

This raises the question of how to offset the advantage of concentrated interests in generating information favorable to their interests. One approach is to strengthen the capacity of the local community as a diffuse interest to extract the information needed to effectively protect its interest. An example of this approach is the federal funding under the Nuclear Waste Policy Act of 1982 (Public Law 97-425) for affected states, local governments, and Indian tribes to participate more fully in the federal waste management program. This allows each state nominated for a site to perform a technical review of the USDOE plans for such a facility from the point at which USDOE announces the commencement of planning for a specific facility.

Another approach is to create an incentive for the concentrated interest and a competitor to generate the information needed by the local community. Competition between two or more applicants for a fixed size of the pie leads to a more rigorous project review, with more informed decisions resulting in better site design and planning. Would the impacted community be better informed about possible impacts if two federal agencies, such as the Departments of Energy and Defense, had to compete for a prospective waste repository site? This concept could be combined with O'Hare's (1977) compensation proposal to be discussed below. Each bidder for the site might supplement its bid with a critique of the competitor's ability (or lack thereof) to manage a repository effectively and with the impacts likely to result from such management.

Uncertainty regarding whether an announced project will be built leads to sluggishness of public and private sector responses to provide for impending development. Unless public officials and private developers receive assurances that they will not be left "holding the bag" in the case of a federal pullout, adequate preparation for newcomers will not occur. Such contractual costs on the part of the local community could be reduced by requiring an "earnest money" type of deposit with the local government to guarantee needed construction of infrastructure. This action would follow the precedent of a series of deposits required of the energy developer by Washington's Energy Facility Site Evaluation Council (EFSEC) at successive stages in the site certification process to partially cover costs of analytical work.

One party's contractual cost is another's right to the status quo. Contractual costs are affected by the assignment of the burden of proof and can be shifted from one party to another by reassigning the burden of proof. For example, site certification agreements drafted by the Washington EFSEC are required to include conditions to protect state or local government or community interests affected by the construction or operation of the proposed energy facility (State of Washington, 1978). Two such conditions in previous site certification agreements have provided for the applicant to (1) monitor primary and secondary socioeconomic impacts during construction, and (2) pay for adverse impacts of the project. However, as this latter condition has generally been written, the burden of establishing the validity of any such claim shall be upon the claimant (Washington EFSEC, 1976). Such an assignment of the burden of proof imposes high-transaction costs on the impacted community to prove its claim. What if, on the other hand, contractual costs were to be borne by the developer by radically shifting the burden of proof such that the applicant was required to establish to the community's satisfaction that no adverse impacts would result from the proposed activity or the applicant would agree to be liable for those that do occur?

Problems in Compensating for Exposure to Risk

Because accepting high-level wastes is for the local jurisdiction nearly a no-win proposition, involving unknown risks and little conceivable gain, Abrams and Primack (1980) concluded that the federal government will have the choice of either negotiating incentives to encourage a region to accept siting of a nuclear waste repository or of forcing it to do so by a raw exercise of power. Although western states apparently oppose "special incentives," all states have agreed that the federal government should pay what they call "compensation for the direct and indirect costs of repository siting." Abrams and Primack noted, however, that when the USDOE finally points the finger, "indirect costs" may very well be indistinguishable from "special incentives."

O'Hare claims that an important failing of current practice in siting an ugly or dangerous facility is the strategic problem that results from failure to pay compensation to neighbors who suffer costs (losses in property values or less measurable amenity costs) not found to be a taking under law (1977). He notes that unless such compensation is paid, a socially beneficial project can be stalled or blocked permanently on each possible site. If local sufferers are compensated, O'Hare suggests that choosing the right amount to pay is more important than accurately estimating (uncompensated) costs for purposes of benefit-cost analysis. He concludes that auctioning the facility to the community demanding the least compensation effects correct compensation and overcomes important strategic, efficiency, and equity problems in the siting process. His approach, however, oversimplifies the boundary issue by ignoring the preferences outside the defined community, such as in other states along the transportation routes to the repository.[2]

The foregoing has addressed compensation as part of the siting process prior to construction. There is also the alternative of compensation after the fact to redress the impacts of a high-consequence occurrence. However, those asking redress from environmental risk problems generally face insurmountable information costs in establishing a legally defensible cause-and-effect relationship between the loss incurred and the parties liable for the event that may have occurred years earlier. At issue is a shift in the burden of proof to affect what constitutes cause-and-effect suits in the case of hazardous waste repository impacts, and who will have standing to sue whom.

One approach would be to shift the impact of contractual costs. Allowing class action suits with lawyer's fees paid out of the court settlement gives an incentive to the lawyer to organize the suit and does not require explicit cooperation by all of the affected parties (Schmid, 1981).

Minimizing Probability of High-Consequence Outcome

The emphasis in the previous two sections was on compensation for impacts, including both standard impacts and high-consequence occurrences. The discussion will now turn to the question of incentives to minimize the probability of a high-consequence occurrence so that a decision to proceed with siting might more likely result in a safe outcome.

The key issue under discussion is whether institutions can be designed to link rather than separate the probability and consequences of an occurrence. The premise is that people in a position to affect the probability of a high-consequence occurrence would be more likely to take appropriate actions to minimize the probability of such an occurrence if directly exposed to its consequences, while those more divorced from the consequences would appear to be less concerned with the level of probability. It will be illustrated below that some risk-sharing concepts, such as assurance and insurance, already have been applied in a manner that leads toward an outcome pervasively counter to the objective of minimizing probability of a high-consequence occurrence.

Performance Bonding. In the case of a contractor constructing streets for a new subdivision, new home buyers want assurance that the construction will not be defective. One approach is to rely on the contractor's verbal "trust me" assurances that there is a low probability that the work will have defects. In the event of faulty work, such as a deep hole in the asphalt and base, or manholes protruding six inches above the street surface, new residents are stuck with the options of living with the damages, or filing individual suits, or bearing the contractual cost of organizing a collective suit against the contractor.

Performance bonding is an alternative institutional design that restructures the incentives for the contractor to minimize the probability of faulty work. A local ordinance requiring the contractor to post a performance bond of sufficient value to allow the local jurisdiction to bring the street up to standard shifts the burden of proof and related contractual costs from the new residents to the contractor. The consequence of faulty performance is borne by the contractor in the forfeiture of the performance bond, an incentive that effectively minimizes the probability of shoddy work. Applied to the nuclear waste repository issue, the USDOE's "trust me" claim of low probability of a high-consequence occurrence might have considerably more credibility if backed up by an offer to post an appropriate performance bond or comparable form of assurance.

Insurance. Another way to compensate for the specific occurrence of unpredictable events is to buy insurance; a small certain annual payment is accepted to avoid an uncertain large loss. Whether insurance against the probability of a high-consequence occurrence from a waste repository should be provided, the questions who should provide it and who should pay for it are matters of public choice. However, it must be emphasized that the current rules concerning insurance for nuclear accidents run counter to the objective stated above to link the consequences of an occurrence with those who can affect the probability of an occurrence.

As things stand now, a catastrophic accident involving nuclear wastes could result in financial ruin for local residents and fiscal ruin for local government jurisdictions where evacuated homes were located. In the event an accident occurs involving commercial nuclear wastes, any damages that might accrue to third parties would be subject to liability claims. However, total liability for any single nuclear accident is currently limited to $560 million by the Price-Anderson Act of 1957. Some critics maintain that any limitation of liability improperly relieves companies in the nuclear business from being fully responsible for their actions (Hebert et al., 1978). As the Price-Anderson Act requires the nuclear industry to purchase all available insurance coverage, individual homeowners cannot buy any nuclear insurance to supplement the $560 million maximum provided by the 1957 act, even though study after study has shown that potential damage would be well up in the billions of dollars. The system appears to be designed more to protect the industry than the homeowner.

The requirement that the nuclear industry purchase all the available insurance coverage effectively prohibits homeowners and business operators from buying supplemental insurance. Rather than linking probability with consequences, these rules tend to insure and cushion those who could affect the probability from bearing the consequences and thus leaves those who have no influence on the probability entirely exposed without insurance coverage.

CONCLUSION AND POLICY IMPLICATIONS

The introduction posed a basic impact mitigation policy question: What burdens should have to be borne by residents of a jurisdiction adversely impacted by a project or policy that generally benefits residents elsewhere or society in general? The argument here is based on the premise that citizens and officials of impacted communities should have available the necessary tools to mitigate adverse impacts, should they choose to do so.

Recognizing that local capacity problems often limit the identification and effective utilization of available impact mitigation options even when dealing with standard environmental impacts, the impact management challenge is greatly compounded with the introduction of the unique impacts of high-level nuclear waste disposal. Two special features of nuclear waste, uncertainty/irreversibility and intergenerational effects, lead to environmental risk problems associated with low-probability, high-consequence occurrences.

Although two components of risk, the probability of a hazard and the consequences of exposure to it, are widely accepted, there is wide disagreement on which objective and subjective measures are to be used to operationally define the probability and consequence components. The selective tendencies of technical experts to emphasize the low probability of failure and of the general public to focus on catastrophic consequences of failure can lead to two kinds of decision errors. The first type is to falsely predict a catastrophic outcome from a relatively safe or harmless situation, and the second type is to falsely predict a safe outcome from a catastrophic situation.

Given "there is no risk-free environment," an important function of public policy is to allocate exposure to risk, either explicitly or implicitly. Two basic repository choices and their associated risk impacts are to (1) accept the first decision error and reject siting everywhere; or (2) proceed with siting somewhere and impose exposure to the second type of decision error upon the impacted area, state, and region.

The choice to proceed with siting somewhere presents two key mitigation issues analyzed in this chapter. First, under what conditions should the area, state, or region accept exposure to the risk of the second type of decision error, that is, possible failure to predict a catastrophic impact outcome? The analysis examined how assignment of the burden of proof, a public policy choice, can effectively shift transaction costs from one party to another, not only affecting the mitigation of standard impacts, but also the operational effectiveness of measures to compensate for exposure to environmental risk.

The second mitigation issue examined was, Could alternative institutional designs more effectively tie exposure to consequences of a low-probability, high-consequence occurrence with reduced probability of such an occurrence? Evaluations of performance bonding and insurance showed that these two examples of institutional designs currently tend to insulate, rather than link, consequences of a high-consequence occurrence from those who could affect its probability. In the recent congressional debate on raising the Price-Anderson Act insurance limits, for example, industry representatives and financial experts calmly argued that the risk would be so high for industry to bear that without the current protection the nuclear industry would come to a halt. Yet pleas by community interests for measures to limit community exposure to those same risks are labeled as emotional, uninformed, or worse. Similarly, while the cost of an effective performance bond or comparable assurance is considered unrealistically expensive for the USDOE or the generators of nuclear waste to bear, current public policy effectively shifts that exposure to an impacted public unable to bear the high-transaction cost of obtaining relief from catastrophic consequences should such occur.

This analysis of nuclear waste disposal policy has addressed reasons why "scientific" claims of low probability by those insulated from catastrophic impacts are increasingly perceived as lacking credibility by those most likely to be exposed to potential high consequences of repository failure. This mitigation issue is one of many socioeconomic impact management issues raised in the selection of the first underground site for permanent, deep geologic storage. Although Hanford, one of the three potential first-round sites under consideration, has been featured to illustrate the policy issues, the economic concepts of this analysis apply not only to the selection of a first site, but also to the choice of a second underground site or an aboveground, monitored, retrievable storage facility for disposal of the nation's high-level nuclear waste.

ACKNOWLEDGMENTS

Research for this chapter was supportd by the Washington State Institute for Public Policy project "Risk of Economic Loss due to Failure or Perceived Failure of a High-Level Nuclear Waste Repository" and the Western Rural Development Center project "Socio-Economic Analysis of Repository Siting" contracted through the U.S. Department of Agriculture (USDA) with the USDOE.

NOTES

1. Those who find this alternative formulation of the mitigation issue unduly harsh should note that this formulation is indeed the effect of a policy allowing federal preemption of siting combined with a presumption of no catastrophic impacts.

2. For a critique of O'Hare's "siting by auction" scheme, see Brenner (1979). For a more thorough examination of the compensation, see Cole and Smith (1979).

REFERENCES

Abrams, Nancy E., and Joel R. Primack (1980). "Helping the Public Decide—The Case of Radioactive Waste Management." *Environment* 22(5):14–20 and 39–40.

Arrow, Kenneth J. (1974). *Essays in the Theory of Risk Bearing.* Amsterdam: North-Holland.

Brenner, Robert D. (1979). "The Social, Economic, and Political Impacts of Nuclear Waste Terminal Storage Repositories." Princeton: Center of International Studies, Princeton University. Report prepared under Contract E512-01200 with Battelle Memorial Institute, Project Management Division, under Contract EY-76-C-0601830 with the Department of Energy Office of Nuclear Waste Isolation.

Cole, Roland J., and Tracy A. Smith (1979). "Compensation for the Adverse Impacts of Nuclear Waste Management Facilities: Application of an Analytical Framework to Consideration of Eleven Potential Impacts." Report prepared as part of Social Science Support for the Office of Nuclear Waste Isolation, by Battelle Human Affairs Research Centers, Seattle. Report No. B-HARC-311-022.

Glass, Gene V., and Julian C. Stanley (1970). *Statistical Methods in Education and Psychology.* Englewood Cliffs, N.J.: Prentice-Hall, Inc.

Hebert, J. A., W. L. Rankin, P. G. Brown, C. R. Schuller, R. F. Smith, J. A. Goodnight, and H. E. Lippek (1978). "Nontechnical Issues in Waste Management: Ethical, Institutional, and Political Concerns." Seattle: Battelle Human Affairs Research Centers.

Impact Assessment, Inc. (1987). "A Proposal-Report on the Socio-Economic Impacts of a Potential High-Level Nuclear Waste Repository at the Hanford Site, Washington." La Jolla, Calif.: Proposal submitted to the Socioeconomic Committee, Office of High-Level Nuclear Waste Management, Department of Ecology, State of Washington. Revised version. January 29, 1987.

League of Women Voters Education Fund (1982). *A Nuclear Waste Primer*, rev. ed. Washington, D.C.: League of Women Voters.

Manderscheid, Lester V. (1971). "An Introduction to Statistical Hypothesis Testing." East Lansing: Dept. of Agricultural Economics, Michigan State University. Mimeograph.

National Planning Association and Haldi Associates, Inc. (1978). *Social Decision Making of High Consequence, Low Probability Occurrences.* Report prepared for Corvallis Environmental Research Lab, Ore., Report No. EPA-600/5-78-121.

O'Hare, Michael (1977). "'Not on My Block You Don't': Facility Siting and the Strategic Importance of Compensation," *Public Policy* 25 (4):407–458.

Peters, Ted E. (1983). "Ethical Considerations Surrounding Nuclear Waste Repository Siting and Mitigation," in Steve H. Murdock, F. Larry Leistritz, and Rita R. Hamm, eds., *Nuclear Waste: Socioeconomic Dimensions of Long-Term Storage.* Boulder, Colo.: Westview Press.

Schmid, A. Allan (1978). *Property, Power, and Public Choice: An Inquiry into Law and Economics.* New York: Praeger Publishers.

——— (1981). "Predicting the Performance of Alternative Institutions" in Warren J. Samuels and A. Allan Schmid, eds., *Law and Economics—An Institutional Perspective.* Boston: Martinus Nijhoff Publishing.

Washington, State of. (1978). *Revised Code of Washington*, Chapter 80.50, *Laws Relating to Siting Energy Facilities.* Olympia: Energy Facility Site Evaluation Council.

Washington Department of Ecology (1986). "Request for Proposals for a Report on Social and Economic Impacts of a Potential High-Level Nuclear Waste Repository at the Hanford Site, Washington." Olympia: Office of Nuclear Waste Management.

Washington Energy Facility Site Evaluation Council (EFSEC) (1976). *Site Certification Agreement Between the State of Washington and the Washington Public Power Supply System*, WPPSS Nos. 3 and 5. Olympia. October 27.

Washington Nuclear Waste Board (1984). "Newsletter '84," vol. 1, no. 1. Olympia.

———(1985a). "Newsletter '84," vol. 1, no. 4. Olympia.

———(1985b). "Overview: High-Level Nuclear Waste Management in Washington." Fact Sheet Number 1. Olympia. January.

U.S. Department of Energy (1986). *Recommendation by the Secretary of Energy of Candidate Sites for Site Characterization for the First Radioactive-Waste Repository.* Report no. DOE/S-0048. Washington, D.C.: Office of Civilian Radioactive Waste Management

SUGGESTED READINGS

Covello, Vincent T., Joshua Menkes, and Jeryl Mumpower, eds. (1986). *Risk Evaluation and Management.* New York: Plenum Press, Society for Risk Analysis, "Contemporary Issues in Risk Analysis" series, vol. 1.
Leading experts in the field of risk analysis cover a wide range of topics, including perceptions of risk, risk evaluation methods, and risk management in government, in this compendium of current research sponsored by the National Science Foundation's Division of Policy Research Analysis.

League of Women Voters Education Fund (1982). *A Nuclear Waste Primer*, rev. ed. Washington, D.C.: League of Women Voters.
Aiming to offer the nonexpert a brief, balanced introduction to nuclear waste, this publication outlines the dimensions of the problem, discussing the types and quantities of waste; then defines the sources, types, and hazards of radiation and sketches the history and current status of waste management; and finally reviews the choices for managing radioactive wastes over the short- and long-term.

Murdock, Steve H., F. Larry Leistritz, and Rita R. Hamm, eds. (1983). *Nuclear Waste: Socioeconomic Dimensions of Long-Term Storage.* Boulder, Colo.: Westview Press.
This 15-chapter book by 19 authors (primarily from rural sociology) examines the strategies and options of nuclear waste disposal facility siting, and is organized into four major sections: dimensions of the nuclear waste problem; impacts of storage and facility siting; mitigation of such impacts; and local community response.

U.S. Department of Energy (1987). *OCRWM Backgrounder.* Washington, D.C.: Office of Civilian Radioactive Waste Management. DOE/RW-0137, DOE/RW-0140, April. Published by the Office of Policy and Outreach to provide current background information on program facts, issues, and initiatives.

STUDY QUESTIONS

1. Faas discusses issues associated with a point-source potential environmental problem. How do these issues compare to those raised in Chapter 4 regarding the environmental condition and management of the Chesapeake Bay?

2. What are the important public policy features that distinguish high-consequence/ low-probability events from high-probability/lesser-consequence events such as cigarette smoking?

3. Design alternative legislation to substitute for the Price-Anderson Act of 1957. How would your design likely affect "behavior" and "outcomes" as defined in Chapter 1?

4. Given the existence of significant volumes of high-level nuclear waste, the question is not whether we wish to find a disposal/storage site but where that site will be. Given the overwhelming "not-in-my-backyard" reaction of residents of potential locations, how would you determine a location, and how should residents of that location be compensated?

Part Two

Economic Efficiency
in Policy Analysis

Most economists use efficiency as a criterion to judge the desirability of various natural resource and environmental policies. A more efficient solution increases the total quantity of output available to consumers. Economists agree, however, that efficiency is a *limited* criterion for three reasons: (1) different initial distributions of property rights yield different potential efficient solutions that are noncomparable; (2) ideal competitive markets yield efficient outcomes, but actual markets are never ideal and thus fail to achieve efficiency; and (3) an efficient solution is not necessarily an equitable solution. If a society produces more or if it uses less of an input (other factors remaining constant), a desirable outcome results. From an efficiency standpoint, then, if the wealthy have become richer, providing no poor are worse off, the solution is just as desirable (efficient) as making the poor wealthier and not impoverishing the rich.

Despite these limitations as a criterion to judge policy outcomes, efficiency is useful in pointing to possible gains for consumers. The authors in Part 2 use efficiency as well as standard market concepts in the examination of their case analyses. The standard concepts include supply, demand, production, and cost functions as well as marginal analysis. The case studies offer opportunities to examine policy options for acid rain, national forests, fisheries, and river systems management. In the river systems management case, the relationship of efficiency to institutions is explored in detail. Externality and equity issues are common to all four cases.

Chapter Six

Acid Rain
An Issue in Canadian-U.S. Relations

David Freshwater

Concern exists that man-made emissions of sulfur dioxide and/or nitrous oxides are causing environmentally damaging levels of acid rain. Consequences include loss of aquatic wildlife species, reduced forest growth, and decreased agricultural production. The author examines the economic and political issues arising from the transboundary nature of this problem between Canada and the United States. Opportunity costs associated with emissions dilution, capture, and reduction are analyzed for electricity and nonferrous metal producers, the chief sources of acid rain. The analysis incorporates a review of regulations in Canada and the United States and negotiations between the two countries. This chapter provides insights about policy options other than moral suasion for natural resource and environmental issues that span political boundaries.

Acid rain[1] has recently become a widely debated environmental issue that has affected relations between Canada and the United States. Although acid rain problems exist in many areas of the world, this analysis focuses on the impact of the problem on eastern North America. In the process of providing the reader with a general overview of the acid rain debate, the concept of transboundary effects as externalities is introduced. In addition, the differing magnitudes of cost of emission control are demonstrated, showing why it is less onerous a burden for Canada to reduce emissions than the United States. Various emission control technologies are discussed, and the regulatory process for acid rain control in Canada and the United States is reviewed. Joint Canadian-U.S. negotiations are the only practical means to address the transboundary effects of acid rain. The current state of these negotiations is presented, and some concluding comments are offered on the probable course of future events.

WHAT IS ACID RAIN AND WHY IS IT A PROBLEM?

Popular concern with acid rain originated with the Swedish government's report to the United Nations Conference on the Human Environment in 1972. However, the earliest reference to acid rain as a distinct phenomenon occurred 100 years earlier. In 1872 British chemist Robert Angus Smith published *Air and Rain: The Beginnings of a Chemical Climatology,* in which he coined the term *acid rain.* Smith discovered that the acidity of rain in urban areas was almost entirely caused by sulfuric acid resulting from the combustion of high-sulfur coal. At the time of Smith's research, cities such as London and Glasgow experienced acid loadings in their rain that rival the most highly acidic precipitation experienced today. In addition to defining the term, Smith's research determined the causes of acid rain and its method of distribution. These premises form the basis of current scientific views.

A Definition of Acid Rain

In general terms, acid rain refers to rain that has a pH of less than 7.0. Most rain is somewhat acidic as a result of carbon dioxide in the air dissolving in rain to form a dilute carbonic acid (H_2CO_3) solution with a pH of approximately 5.6. Thus rain is inherently acidic. The presence of various dusts or gases in a particular environment can alter the composition of rain, making it more or less acidic. The presence of ammonia or alkaline soil dust can neutralize the inherent acidity of rain, leaving it with a pH greater than 7.0. Similarly, the presence of acid sulfate or acid nitrate can cause highly acidic rain.

Acid sulfate and acid nitrate are both naturally occurring compounds arising from forest fires, lightning, volcanoes, and decaying vegetation. Sulfur dioxide (SO_2) and/or nitrous oxides (NO_x) are emitted by these natural phenomena, and the oxygen in the atmosphere combines with these compounds to form acid sulfate and acid nitrate. These acids eventually precipitate out of the atmosphere and are converted by plants and bacteria into elemental substances. Thus there is a natural sulfur and nitrogen cycle in which acid rain plays an important part in distributing these compounds over the earth's surface. The concern with the acid content of rain is that the loadings of SO_2 and NO_x currently observed at particular locations are often far in excess of the ability of an area's plants, bacteria, and geology to assimilate or buffer the local environment. The particular concern is that these loadings are the result of man-made emissions, not natural processes, and that the resulting loadings are causing major deterioration in the environment. The environmental damage associated with rain of a particular pH cannot, however, be stated in the form of a general rule. The magnitude of the damage from a given level of deposition depends on the nature of the local environment in terms of its natural geological buffering capacity, the susceptibility of the area's plants and animals to acidic conditions, and the frequency and magnitude of the acid loadings.

The United States National Research Council (USNRC) study of acid rain in eastern North America suggests that although more than half the acidity in precipitation throughout the globe may be due to natural causes, there are particular areas where man-made sources dominate natural sources (USNRC, 1983). In eastern North America, 90 to 95 percent of the acidity in precipitation is attributable to human activities. Sources of SO_2 emissions in Canada and the United States, and the distribution of sulfate deposition in the two countries overlap considerably, but there are also differences that exacerbate management problems.

Deposition Processes

There are two basic mechanisms by which SO_2 is transported through the atmosphere to its deposition point. The first involves dry deposition resulting from a variety of processes by which pollutant gases and aerosol particles are directly deposited without undergoing chemical transformation. Traditionally, dry deposition has been considered a local phenomenon having little to do with atmospheric conditions and chemical transformations. The USNRC study suggests that such assumptions may be too simplistic. As dry deposition is thought to account for one-third of sulfur emissions in the northeastern portion of the continent, understanding the distribution mechanism of dry deposition is vital to understanding sulfur loadings.

Wet deposition accounts for another third of eastern North America emissions. The final third is carried out to sea without affecting the North American land mass. In the wet deposition process atmospheric pollutants attach themselves to water molecules and reach the earth's surface as rain, fog, snow, or other forms of precipitation. Unlike dry deposition, chemical reactions may take place in this attachment process.

Although emission sources affecting the northeastern portion of the continent include natural emissions arising in the southern portion of the United States, the primary focus of attention is on major man-made point sources, consisting primarily of coal- and oil-fired thermoelectric power plants and nonferrous metal smelters. For North America, thermal power plants are estimated to account for 57 percent of emissions, fuel combustion for 14 percent, nonferrous smelters for 12 percent, and all other industrial processes account for the remaining 17 percent. Two-thirds of the SO_2 emissions in the United States come from thermal power plants while nonferrous smelters account for 40 percent of Canadian emissions (Appin Associates, 1984). Understandably, the focus of concern in the United States has been on control of emissions from power plants whereas in Canada it has been on the nonferrous smelting industry. Unlike acid sulfates, which result primarily from large, point source emitters, acid nitrates are almost equally likely to come from mobile emitters (vehicle exhausts) or point sources such as power plants or smelters.

The Physical Effects of Acid Rain

The effects of acid rain depend on the nature of the receptor area. To this date the focus of concern has been the impact of acid rain on lakes in areas that have little natural buffering capacity. Large numbers of these lakes are found throughout the Canadian Shield area of Ontario and Quebec and in the mountainous areas of the northeastern United States. In the last few years concern has also risen over the impacts of acid rain on the health of forests in these regions (Gould, 1985), which constitute the prime recreational areas for several of the major urban centers of eastern North America. The effect of acid precipitation in these areas appears to range from a reduction in the quality and diversity of aquatic species in lakes, to complete eradication of virtually all aquatic life-forms. Forest effects appear to range from a slowing of growth rates of trees to the death of many plant species (Gorham, 1982; U.S. Office of Technology Assessment [OTA], 1985).

Forestry effects, particularly in areas with inherently acidic soil, are not readily quantifiable. Gould (1985) suggested that acid precipitation can reduce growth, damage leaves and roots, and lead to heavy metal poisoning of trees. The long life span of trees and the difficulty in obtaining measurements of the magnitude of damages have to date precluded estimates of the damages to forests.

In addition to the concern with aquatic and forest effects, efforts to measure the impacts on agriculture are increasing. Forster (1984) has recently attempted to measure the effects of acid deposition on agriculture in Ontario. Although he noted the tentative nature of his results, it appeared that for corn production alone, approximately Can$100 million (approximately US$75 million) in damages can be attributed to acid deposition per year. A recent United States Department of Agriculture (USDA) literature survey suggests that the effects of acid deposition may vary enormously from area to area making it impossible to generalize about the effects on agriculture (Barse, Ferguson, and Whetzel, 1985).

Although the current literature on acid rain typically does not focus on damages to buildings and human health, these effects have been historically significant. Robert Angus Smith noted in his 1872 work the damage to buildings caused by acid precipitation and argued that some share of the illness in major English cities was attributable to the effects of acid rain and fog. A recent Organization for Economic Cooperation and Development (OECD) study made some appraisal of the various damages caused by acid rain in western Europe (1978). This analysis suggested that health effects are potentially an order of magnitude more costly than the damage to buildings and other structures. Aquatic and crop damages by comparison are significantly less than building damages. While conditions in western Europe are considerably different from those in eastern North America in terms of the population exposed, the value of buildings, and the prevalence of lakes and crops at risk, it is clear that health-related effects of acid precipitation cannot be ignored in North America.

KEY ECONOMIC CONCEPTS IN ASSESSING
ACID RAIN CONTROL

Opportunity Cost

Because sulfur and nitrogen oxides are unwanted by-products of production processes that produce electricity and nonferrous metals such as nickel, copper, and zinc, society faces a dilemma. For purposes of discussion, even if we abstract from the actual world to one in which those receiving the benefits from the production process are the same individuals harmed by acid precipitation, we face a management dilemma. Although acid precipitation can be controlled, it can only be done by raising the cost of producing the commodities we value—electricity, nickel, and so forth. Thus, we are confronted with a situation where part of the cost of production of electricity and nickel is the condition of the environment. The opportunity cost of a cleaner environment is more expensive electricity and nickel. To lower the levels of acid rain requires that we either reduce the amount of electricity and nickel produced or find some new form of production technology that allows us to remove the pollutants from the exhaust gases before they cause environmental damage.

As both the environment and industrial products are valued by society, we are faced with a classic economic trade-off. As a result, society must find a means to make a decision on what constitutes a desirable mixture of environmental quality and industrial products. This process implies the development of some means of valuing the benefits of incremental units of manufactured products versus their incremental costs of production, including environmental damages. Figure 6.1 depicts a simple graphical model of the nature of this decision.

This four-quadrant model incorporates the basic decisions to be made in choosing the mix of output and environmental quality. The upper right-hand quadrant contains the basic information determining supply and demand for manufactured products. The demand curve D is downward-sloping indicating a smaller quantity is desired if price increases. The supply curve S reflects the costs of producing various quantities of output employing a given production technology. The lower right-hand corner reflects the link between levels of output of the manufactured product and levels of emissions associated with the specified production technology. The lower left-hand quadrant indicates the physical damage associated with different levels of emissions. As shown here, the damage levels increase in a linear fashion. Each additional unit of emission causes the same incremental damage. Alternatively, one could draw the damage curve so that incremental damages increase with each unit of emission to reflect lowering of the environment's ability to assimilate pollutants. The upper left-hand quadrant reflects the value society places on the environment. Different societies value environmental quality to different degrees. Thus, one cannot assume that all societies will tolerate the same degree of damages to the same extent. Implicit in

FIGURE 6.1 Conceptual Design of an Environment/Emitter Model

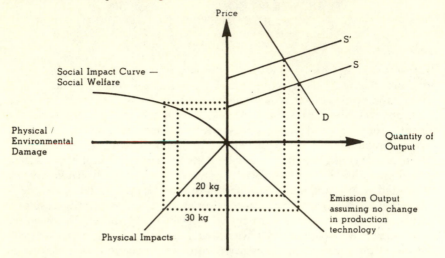

Source: Appin Associates, *Conceptual Design and Economics of a Sulfur Dioxide Abatement Strategy for Canada* (Winnipeg, Manitoba: Appin Associates, 1984), p. 78.

this valuation process, however, is a method for setting a price that measures the value society assigns to the quality of the environment.

By observing an equilibrium in the supply and demand curves of the upper right quadrant, we can trace through the system and find the resulting value assigned to the environment. If the mix of environmental quality and output is not satisfactory then some change must be induced in the system. This can be done by changing either the level of output of the produced good or by changing the production technology. Figure 6.1 indicates how a change in production technology, which reduces emissions but induces a small increase in production costs, changes the level of environmental quality. Although the value of the environment has increased, it has been purchased at a cost of fewer and more expensive manufactured products. As a result, it is impossible to say whether social welfare has improved.

The problem we have currently defined is one in which a single group chooses the mix of environmental quality and cost of manufactured goods it wishes to tolerate. As this group is the direct recipient of any pollution produced in the manufacturing process, it is in the group's interest to determine the correct mix. Even in this simple world it can be seen that changes in production technology or the relative value of the environment or manufactured goods can lead to new decisions. Because sulfur and nitrous oxides are unavoidable by-products of the production of nonnuclear thermoelectricity and nonferrous metals, it is impossible to have the latter without the former. Although technologies exist to control the amounts of harmful by-products that escape into the environment, these technologies are not costless.

Transboundary Externality Effects

The simplifying premise that individuals responsible for producing acid rain are also the only ones who experience its effects has been employed to this point. Clearly, the facts of the matter are otherwise. Perhaps the feature that distinguishes air pollution problems from other environmental problems is the predominance of transboundary flows associated with the long-range transport of atmospheric pollutants (LRTAP). The long distances possible between emitter sites and receptor sites both increase the probability that emitters will make decisions about emission levels without considering their impact on receptors and decrease the probability that receptors will have a means of either compelling emitters to consider these impacts or of receiving compensation. When receptors and emitters are in different countries, there is great difficulty in resolving the arising externality.

In the case of transboundary externalities, when the emitting industry is beyond the influence of the government of the receptor country, there are very few means to induce the emitter to modify its behavior. The acid rain problems of eastern North America are an example of the difficulties inherent in resolving transboundary pollution flows. As Canada and the United States are both emitters and receptors for themselves and each other, a greater potential would seem to exist for a common solution than when one country is the sole receptor and the other the sole emitter.

Transboundary problems also exist within a country. Emissions within one state or province can affect other states or provinces. In these instances, although compliance with national government requirements ensures some means of addressing externality problems, the existing set of rules and distribution of powers is typically not sufficiently sensitive to the needs of particular receptors in their effort to control acid precipitation. Efforts to control local pollution problems, such as dry deposition, can result in increased wet depositions in surrounding jurisdictions.

This point has been particularly important in the negotiations between Canada and the United States. Efforts in the United States to reduce local emissions have often focused on taller smokestacks increasing the dispersion of the pollutants and compounding LRTAP effects.

EMISSION CONTROL TECHNOLOGY

A number of approaches exist for control of sulfur dioxide and nitrous oxide emissions. The first technique relies on dilution of emissions and the assimilation capacity of the environment. A second approach employs capture devices that prevent emissions from leaving the stack and entering the atmosphere. The third involves reducing the actual volume of emissions produced by changing raw materials or production processes. Depending on the type of industry and the magnitude of its emissions, different applications of these approaches have been employed.

Dilution

Historically, the most prevalent form of control strategy has been the use of siting decisions and stack heights to reduce the impact of emissions. This approach was founded on the belief that emissions are a local irritant, and that by taking advantage of prevailing wind patterns and dispersal effects, loadings can be reduced to levels that cause no significant damage. Both power plants and nonferrous smelters in Canada and the United States have relied heavily on this approach. In Canada the principal nonferrous smelters are located in areas of low population, and their stacks have been constructed to ensure wide dispersion of their emissions. Thermal power plants in Canada are also sited in a manner that ensures prevailing winds carry emissions away from population centers. In the United States the focus on local air quality standards has resulted in major incentives for emitters to take advantage of tall stacks as a primary means of complying with air quality requirements. For the operator of the emitting facility, and those in its immediate vicinity, an increase in stack height provides a relatively low-cost form of relief. To the extent that the assimilative capacity of the environment can deal with dispersed loadings, such an approach may also be acceptable from an environmental perspective.

Recognition of the LRTAP problem has tended to limit the acceptability of tall stacks and siting as control measures. If dispersion is not a viable means of reducing loadings to an environmentally safe level, then the effect of dispersion is to place more locations at risk and perhaps increase the damage beyond the level that would exist if pollution loadings were localized. This case is particularly true where the environment's buffering capacity varies widely from area to area. If an emitter of SO_2 and NO_x is located in an area of high-buffering capacity, then local emissions may do little damage relative to the damage caused by allowing that emitter to disperse its emissions into areas with minimal buffering capacity.

Emissions Capture

The other principal means of dealing with emissions once they have been produced employs either mechanical or chemical processes to capture pollutants before they escape into the environment. Flue-gas scrubbers of various types are the primary means of capturing pollutants. In certain cases the scrubbers are designed to produce a useful by-product, generally sulfur either in elemental form or as a compound that has a viable market. Although the installation and operating costs of regenerating scrubbers exceed those of wet or dry scrubbers that produce nonrecoverable sulfur compounds, the existence of a potential market for sulfur or sulfuric acid may make them more profitable in terms of total returns and costs.

Reduced Production of Emissions

Several options exist for reducing the level of pollutants produced by industry. One option is to use raw materials that have a lower quantity of the pollutants. For coal-using power plants or smelters this can be accomplished by the use of low-sulfur coal. Such coal can either be purchased directly or high-sulfur coal can be processed to reduce the sulfur content. For coal users located long distances from sources of low-sulfur coal, the costs of substituting such coal for locally available high-sulfur coal may be prohibitive. Coal cleaning is already a viable option for coal that has high concentrations of inorganic sulfur that can be removed by simple mechanical washing and separation techniques. When the sulfur occurs in any organic form chemical processes are required to break the sulfur from the carbon molecules. Such chemical processes are not currently commercially viable (U.S. OTA, 1985).

Alternatively, production technologies can be modified to reduce the level of pollutants produced. Such modifications result in fewer emissions that have to be removed in the stack.[2] Even though the technology exists to remove large amounts of existing emissions, the capital and operating costs of applying this technology are considerable. Even where recoverable by-products such as elemental sulfur or sulfuric acid can be produced, the lack of local markets or of excess supplies of the product could result in very low receipts from the by-product.

THE COSTS OF EMISSIONS CONTROL

It was estimated in 1981 that reducing acid rain levels to a 20 kilogram per hectare (kg/ha) maximum loading at receptor sites in eastern Canada would require North American expenditures on the order of US$3.8 billion, with approximately US$3.2 billion of this expenditure required in the United States (Appin Associates, 1984). The vast bulk of these expenditures are not associated with either increased revenues from the sale of by-products or increased physical efficiency of plants in the sense of increasing the ratio of outputs produced to inputs used. Consequently, there has been a great reluctance on the part of those firms involved in the production of sulfur and nitrous oxides to undertake investments to reduce emissions, as the benefits of those expenditures accrue primarily to individuals and groups outside the local political and economic boundaries of the emitter. Because many of the associated costs such as reduced employment, higher electricity costs, and possible increases in local environmental damage occur within these boundaries, there has not been strong local pressure to bring about adoption.

Because emitters have little incentive to undertake emission controls, some restructing of incentives will be needed if abatement is to take place. It is this requirement that makes acid rain abatement an interesting economic policy issue. The externality associated with sulfur and nitrous oxide emissions is not trivial in terms of its effects on a segment of society and the environment, yet both its abatement and the formation of institutions to bring it about are also expensive propositions (Regens and Rycroft, 1986).

Sharing the Burden of Control Costs

A major distinction among the various control options identified is the magnitude of the cost of abatement. In all cases some mechanism for identifying a desired emission level is required. Once this step has been taken a process for identifying the amount of each firm's emission reduction, the cost of reduction, and the source of funds for the reduction is required. This latter point is a major issue in developing an operational acid rain abatement strategy.

Emitters uniformly argue that their production processes at the time of initial installation met all applicable standards and that requiring them to modify these processes would impose an unfair burden on them and indirectly on others. The thermal power industry of the midwestern United States argues that compelling it to use low-sulfur coal or flue-gas scrubbers will increase its costs, requiring rate increases that will harm both industrial and residential power users (U.S. OTA, 1985). Similarly, the coal industry of the eastern United States, which mines high-sulfur deposits, argues that the displacement and transport costs of switching to low-sulfur western coal would be vast (Poundstone, 1982). The Canadian smelter industry argues that it is already caught in a cost-price squeeze as a result of low-cost competition from developing countries, excess global supplies, and low demand. The industry maintains that increased expenses for abatement would price it out of the market causing major unemployment problems and hurting exports (Energy Mines and Resources Canada, 1984).

Emitters further argue that only in the case of certain freshwater lakes has a link been made between acid loadings and environmental damages. In all other instances there has been insufficient scientific evidence to establish strong causal relationships. Critical to the success of advocates of acid rain control through emitter abatement is an ability to demonstrate that particular emitters are responsible for acid rain at a given receptor. In a study conducted by the USNRC a team of distinguished atmospheric scientists concluded that acid deposition has potentially harmful environmental effects, but that the available knowledge to link emissions and deposition through LRTAP processes is inadequate to assess causes and effects (USNRC, 1983).

The Effects of Emission Abatement Requirements
on Smelters and Thermal Power Plants

Although smelters and thermal power plants are the two major emitter types in North America, there are differences in their ability to pay for emission controls, as well as differences in their abatement costs. Smelters have relatively low abatement costs but a limited ability to absorb these costs without major effects on profit and output, whereas thermal power plants have higher costs but a greater ability to pass the costs on to consumers who are the beneficiaries of the power.

The Ontario Ministry of Environment (1984) has analyzed the cost of reducing the emissions of the large emitters in the eastern part of Canada to achieve a maximum 20 kg/ha loading at sensitive receptors. Table 6.1

TABLE 6.1: Estimated Costs and Levels of Emissions Reduction at Selected Major Canadian Emitters of Sulfur Dioxide

Sources Affected	Source Number[a]	Total Current Emissions[b]	Percentage Reduction From Source[c]	Reducible Emissions[d]	Unit Charge[e]
MANITOBA					
Thompson	S1	359	90%	40	10.5
Flin Flon	S2	212	26%	120	21.8
ONTARIO					
Falconbridge	S3	122	93%	600	53.1
INCO	S4	866	75%	2020	31.1
Wawa-Algoma	S5	141	85%	920	76.7
Lakeview	P1	91	90%	2420	295.1
Lambton	P2	160	90%	2360	163.9
Nanticoke	P3	155	55%	1740	204.7
QUEBEC					
Noranda	S6	538	67%	940	26.2

[a] s denotes a smelter and P a thermal power plant.

[b] Estimated actual emissions in late 1983 in metric tons.

[c] Amount of reduction resulting from implementing a "least cost" abatement strategy.

[d] Estimated quantity of emission reduction in millions of kg.

[e] Unit cost of reduction in emissions in cents per kg., Canadian dollars.

SOURCE: Appin Associates, Conceptual Design and Economics of a Sulfur Dioxide Abatement Strategy for Canada (Winnipeg, Manitoba, 1984), p. 55.

indicates the costs of compliance for six smelters and three power plants. Figure 6.2 graphs the corresponding unit costs of abatement. These illustrations demonstrate that the costs of control vary greatly by type of industry.

The main area of divergence between the two industries is in the nature of their relationship with the purchasers of their product. This affects their ability to pass expenses associated with acid rain abatement on to customers and affects demand. The nature of the price determination mechanism is critical to this question.

Power plants operate in a highly regulated environment where they are required to meet specific peak power demands. In return they are compensated at a rate determined by a regulatory body and are shielded from competition. Thus the price they receive is determined not by market forces but administratively. In principle, expenses incurred for abatement are likely to be viewed by the rate-setting body as a legitimate charge that can be passed on to customers, thus allowing abatement to take place without impacting unit profit.

The demand curve for a thermal power producer can be expected to be fairly inelastic by virtue of its position as a monopoly and the absence of substitutes for electricity. The supply curve for the power producer is by definition the marginal cost curve of the firm because it is a monopoly. Although in the long term individuals can substitute other sources of energy for electricity, it is unlikely that other firms will be allowed to challenge a power producer's monopoly as a supplier of electricity. Consequently, changes in the firm's cost structure will not result in the same output changes as in the nickel industry.

Although the nickel smelting industry in Canada is certainly not perfectly competitive, a significant degree of competition does exist. As a result the demand curve is somewhat price elastic, indicating that changes in price will affect sales in the short run. This reflects the global nature of nickel markets. Smelters will be confronted with the choice of absorbing abatement costs out of earnings, thereby lowering profits, or of raising their selling price to pass costs on, thereby causing a decline in sales and a reduction in receipts.

Assume for the moment that the supply curves of the two industries are similar so that marginal costs of production are roughly equivalent. Any emission charge or abatement program will be reflected in an increased cost of production. In the simplest case, this can be represented as a shift up in the supply curve, which is indicated as S' in Figures 6.3a and 6.3b. Clearly, equivalent increases in the costs of production will result in major differences in equilibrium outputs and prices when applied to the individual firms from the industry level, reflecting the different nature of the economic markets in which they operate. As a result we might expect the smelting industry to be far more resistant to pressures for abatement than the thermal power industry.

In addition, one must also consider the different impacts that the emissions associated with these two facilities have on their respective target environ-

FIGURE 6.2 Total Emission Levels Versus Unit Costs of Abatement for Selected Emitters

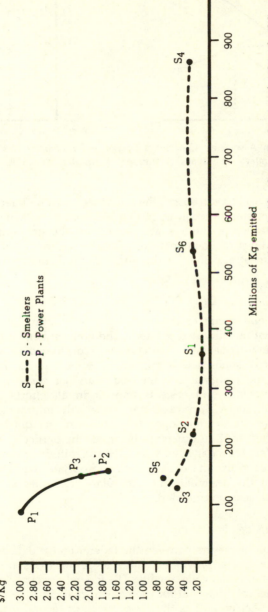

Source: Appin Associates, *Conceptual Design and Economics of a Sulfur Dioxide Abatement Strategy for Canada* (Winnipeg, Manitoba: Appin Associates, 1984), p. 57.

FIGURE 6.3 Industry Supply/Demand Curve

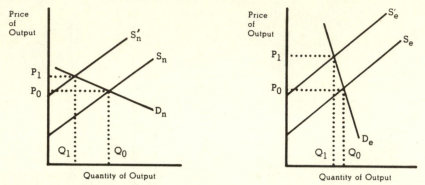

Source: Appin Associates, *Conceptual Design and Economics of a Sulfur Dioxide Abatement Strategy for Canada* (Winnipeg, Manitoba: Appin Associates, 1984), p. 75.

ments. While the ability to absorb the costs associated with reduced emissions is an important consideration in setting environmental standards, so is the impact that particular emitters are having on the environment. It is not clear that loadings of pollutants are adequate indicators of environmental damage; one must also look at the effect of the loadings.

EFFORTS TO CONTROL ACID RAIN

From an economic point of view, the optimal quantity of acid rain to be produced is that quantity that results in the greatest benefit to society when the costs of environmental degradation are considered as are the benefits of manufactured goods and employment opportunities. This evaluation requires equating marginal benefits and marginal costs. A weighing and balancing of benefits and costs is implicit in all efforts to regulate the quantity of acid rain. At the present time we lack the information to determine an appropriate mix of emissions and environmental quality. As different control strategies result in different outcomes, the particular strategy chosen has a great effect on the incidence and the magnitude of costs and benefits. Thus to a great extent the debate over appropriate regulatory methods is as much about the desirability of particular techniques as it is about the correct level of acid precipitation.

Regulatory Activities in Canada

The distribution of powers between the federal and provincial governments in Canada leaves the provinces with the primary responsibility for the maintenance of environmental quality. The federal government is responsible for international relations and for the general maintenance of public health. The Clean Air Act of 1971 is the major piece of federal legislation dealing with air quality. It sets national air quality objectives with respect to tolerable, acceptable, and desirable ranges of pollutants. Only when emissions pose a serious danger to health or when emissions constitute a violation of a treaty with another nation can the federal government set standards or otherwise enforce behavior consistent with its recommendations. In other instances the implementation of the guidelines developed under the Clean Air Act requires provincial legislation. Although the various provinces have legislation concerning environmental quality, there is little formal coordination of either legislation or programs to implement or enforce the legislation (Johnston and Finkle, 1983).

Acid rain abatement efforts in Canada have, however, resulted in joint federal-provincial activity. This cooperation reflects both the allocation of powers and the availability of resources to limit acid rain. Although provincial governments have the legal ability to implement acid rain abatement legislation, the financial resources of the federal government are significantly greater; therefore, federal participation is generally requested in cost-sharing programs. Although joint Canadian-U.S. negotiations remain important, a unilateral federal-provincial abatement strategy for Canada has been developed. It has as its basic principles the following:

- Establishment of a deposition objective of 20 kg/ha/yr of wet sulfate to protect moderately sensitive receptor areas.
- A 50 percent reduction of SO_2 emissions from 1980 levels in eastern Canada (Manitoba, Ontario, Quebec, and the Maritime provinces) to a total of about 2.3 million tons by 1994.
- Basing abatement strategies on a receptor-targeted, least-cost approach. These emissions sources are principally nonferrous smelters and utilities.
- Letting the federal government take the lead in order to take advantage of new and existing government financial programs to assist the smelting industry.
- Allowing provincial governments to assume the lead responsibility for electric utilities by coordinating appropriate emission reduction programs (LRTAP Incentives Work Group, 1984).

This strategy suggests that Canada has opted for administrative mechanisms supplemented by a market subsidy program to decrease the emitters' resistance to pollution abatement. Nonferrous smelters comprise the major domestic source of acid precipitation in Canada. These smelters are typically operated by multinational corporations that have other production facilities in other countries. Previous attempts to lower emission levels at Canadian smelters have resulted in suggestions by the smelters' management that, should their costs increase as a result of emission abatement requirements, they would have to consider closing their operations and transferring them to their foreign facilities. As these smelters provide the major source of employment in areas otherwise deficient in job opportunities, as well as significant export earnings, there has been a reluctance by both levels of government to compel the adoption of high-cost abatement strategies.

This federal-provincial agreement does mark a major change in abatement strategy in Canada because it rejects the use of dispersal approaches and promotes emission reduction techniques. Canadian abatement procedures historically have relied primarily on dispersal through the use of siting restrictions and tall stacks. Most major emitters are located in virtually unpopulated areas of the country, and it was previously believed that, if local pollution loadings could be controlled by the use of tall stacks, emissions problems could be resolved. Even the thermal power plants were located in areas where prevailing winds carried the bulk of emissions away from major population centers.

Existing Canadian legislation deals with the quality of the environment at receptor sites not the quality of emissions that are produced. The agreement's focus on abatement techniques to limit emissions in a manner that will result in major reductions in emissions is an implicit recognition that long-range transport phenomena require strategies that deal with emissions directly, rather than relying on strategies that clearly demonstrate the links between loadings and emitting sources. When a multitude of emitters contribute to an equally large number of receptors, sorting out the damages explicitly identifiable with a particular emitter is virtually impossible.

Regulatory Activities in the United States

The primary air quality control legislation in the United States is the Clean Air Act of 1970 as amended. This act specifies air quality standards to be met in the various states. The primary focus of the act is local air quality, which it regulates by specifying limits on levels of airborne pollutants.

The Environmental Protection Agency (EPA) administers the act and must approve state implementation plans for achieving mandated standards. The act specifically requires that no state's actions should allow behavior that would prevent the achievement of the air quality standards in another state. Although the original focus of the act was on localized interstate pollution flows, three states—New York, Pennsylvania, and Maine—have sought control of acid rain in their territories through this provision. These states charge that emissions in the Midwest are being transported into their territory (U.S. OTA, 1985).

In addition, the act also provides that the EPA not permit emissions in the United States that endanger public health or welfare in foreign countries if the countries in question have similar legislation prohibiting actions that harm the United States. Canada has established such a reciprocal relationship, and the EPA has recognized its existence (Carroll, 1985). The current position of the EPA is that knowledge of LRTAP processes is not sufficiently developed to allow the act to be applied to other than local interjurisdictional disputes (Gould, 1985). To this date there has been no formal action by the EPA to implement the provision, and there is pressure within Congress to repeal this provision.

An interagency task force with a ten-year mandate to carry out research on and assess the impact of acid rain was created by the Acid Precipitation

Act of 1980. Effective action to reduce emissions remains a local decision undertaken on a state by state level, with those states experiencing the greatest acid precipitation loadings exhibiting the greatest efforts at control. No strong state and federal working groups have been formed at this time to establish procedures for acid rain control. Various states have identified the need to undertake such controls and are moving toward regulating local emitters in an effort to reduce loadings. In particular, the states in the northeast have formed a coalition of governors to press for abatement. This action resulted in a suit filed in federal court to require the EPA to impose emissions restrictions in the Midwest. This suit was dismissed in September of 1986 on procedural grounds after being upheld in a lower court.

Canadian-U.S. Negotiations

In addition to their domestic abatement activities, the United States and Canada have recognized the desirability of joint action on acid rain. While both nations recognize the potential for significant damage from acid precipitation, they have yet to reach a consensus on the actual magnitude of damages and an appropriate control strategy. Carroll (1983) argued that there appeared to be both a greater public and government concern with acid rain effects in Canada than in the United States. This greater concern is understandable as the negative effects of acid rain are more directly experienced by a greater proportion of the Canadian population than the U.S. population. In addition, the control costs of acid rain are both lower in Canada and likely to be directly experienced by a smaller proportion of the population than in the United States.

The peak in cooperative activity occurred in the late 1970s and the early 1980s during the Carter administration. In 1978 a bilateral research group on LRTAP was established. This venture was followed by the signing of a Memorandum of Intent on Transboundary Air Pollution on August 5, 1980. In the memorandum the two countries agreed to work toward the development of an agreement that would combat transboundary air pollution, including acid rain, by enforcing and strengthening domestic air quality legislation to limit emissions. Formal negotiations commenced in 1981 but by 1982 had come to a virtual halt as a result of Canadian pressure for an immediate committment to a 50 percent reduction in emissions and the U.S. insistence that additional research was required before expensive actions be undertaken.

Current cooperative action is limited. Canada continues to lobby within the Congress and executive branches of the U.S. government for action. In addition, Ontario and Quebec have attempted to use U.S. administrative and judicial procedures to limit emissions by midwestern utilities. The two provinces joined in the suit noted above that was filed by the northeastern states. Under Section 115 of the U.S. Clean Air Act of 1970 foreign countries have the right not to be harmed by emissions from U.S. sources providing they have granted similar rights to the United States. This provision has been found applicable to Canada as Canada's Clean Air Act provides similar rights to the United States. In 1984 New York initiated suit to compel the

EPA to enforce the provisions of Section 115. Although direct Canadian use of U.S. legislation is potentially a means of dealing with transboundary problems, there are concerns over the subordination of national interests to foreign concerns. Consequently, litigation of international issues in national courts does not appear to be a likely means of resolving the issue.

In 1986 acid rain was a major issue in the meeting between President Ronald Reagan and Prime Minister Brian Mulroney in Quebec. This meeting resulted in an agreement to establish a bilateral investigation of the effects of acid rain and a commitment to a major research program. Following the report of the two envoys, there was pressure in Canada for immediate action but continued resistance in the United States. It was not until the 1987 meeting between the two leaders that President Reagan agreed to ask that funds be appropriated to carry out the research agreed to a year earlier.

Joint agreement on an appropriate abatement strategy for Canada and the United States does not appear to be imminent. This lack of agreement reflects a major difference in opinion over the major issues involved in acid rain control. The U.S. government and a major portion of its research appear to view acid rain as primarily a national issue that pits interests of two regions against each other. Damages outside the United States are considered incidental to resolving the magnitudes of the burden that would be relieved in the Northeast by abatement imposed on the coal mining and power generation activities of the Midwest. Canada, by contrast, is confronted with emissions loadings in sensitive areas that are often primarily the result of U.S. emissions. For Canada, domestic control of emissions, although helpful, is often inadequate to ensure the viability of susceptible environments. Thus in the international bargaining process Canada has a vital interest in reaching an agreement, whereas the United States will agree to abatement primarily on the basis of weighing the balance of domestic costs and benefits.

The United States may adopt a more international perspective on acid rain control after the construction of a major copper smelter in Mexico just south of the Arizona border. Given the prevailing wind pattern, the rudimentary pollution abatement processes in place at the plant, and the susceptibility of the receptor area, major effects are likely. If the United States is to pressure Mexico for abatement, significant admission of similar effects being caused in Canada may have to be accepted.

COMMENT: THE DILEMMA OF REGULATION

The inability to link emitters to damages and the nature of current legislation in both countries that focuses on ambient air quality, not deposition effects, restricts the ability to control emissions for the purpose of acid rain abatement. Imposing a workable regulatory system for acid rain abatement would require considerable changes to existing legislation or the introduction of new legislation. Even if this were accomplished, the transboundary problem would remain because compliance with one country's laws could still result in excessive acid deposition in another. Given the lack of consensus on the need to abate emissions, legislation to require abatement is problematic.

Market incentive schemes, particularly subsidies, have been proposed by emitters as a fallback position if controls are required. Both smelters and power plants note the major capital costs required for them to reduce emissions and argue that those reaping the benefits of reduced emissions should be willing to pay for them. Because society collectively benefits, they argue, society should collectively pay. This option would reduce the burden on utility ratepayers, smelter workers who might otherwise lose their jobs, and stockholders of the companies.

Other forms of market incentives that reverse the burden of control by requiring emitting companies to pay for pollutants discharged into the environment are understandably less popular with smelters and power companies. Emissions charges or performance bonds transfer the cost of control back to the emitter. The emitter must determine if the costs of control are less than the penalties associated with failure to comply. Even when the current level of charges or bonds is less than the cost of compliance, the company must consider whether failure to comply will stimulate an increase in the charges to a level that will force compliance. In this case the firm will have paid both the initial penalty and will still have to reduce its emissions.

A salient problem of either an administrative or a market incentive program is the need to have the basic scientific knowledge to determine what the damages of acid rain are and the ability to determine how much emissions at particular receptors must be reduced. In the absence of such information neither type of program can begin to allocate emission reductions to individual sources with any degree of assurance that the pattern of abatement will have the desired effect on receptors. Given the massive capital expenditures associated with abatement, an inappropriate system of abatement could impose great costs on particular segments of society for little purpose. This is the fundamental argument of those favoring greater research before acting.

The higher cost of achieving abatement at thermal power plants compared to smelters helps to explain the reluctance of the United States to commence abatement. Conversely, Canada, where the bulk of domestic emissions come from relatively low-abatement cost smelters, is exerting pressure for rapid action. Not only are unit costs of abatement lower in Canada, so is the total expenditure required. These facts, combined with a higher proportion of the population exposed to acid rain effects and fewer regional domestic conflicts, go a long way to explaining attitude differences in the two countries.

Nevertheless, there is also a fear that acid rain damage may be cumulative and at some point irreversible. If this is true, failure to act now could result in levels of damage that cannot be reversed. The knowledge gained from further research may be developed too late to be of any value. Proponents of immediate action argue that even potentially inefficient action is desirable to losing the ability to act.

Looking beyond this fundamental difficulty, once the decision to act is made, how should action be undertaken? Because the LRTAP process is one in which numerous emitters affect individual receptors and conversely individual emitters affect numerous receptors, some form of integrated approach appears necessary. However, different regions within a country, not to mention different countries, may place different values on environments of the same quality. In this situation it could be virtually impossible to meet all of the different objectives; some form of compromise over the appropriate level of abatement in general and at specific sites will be required.

Various factors will limit the ability to resolve this dilemma. First, science is limited in predicting LRTAP processes and the complete effects of acid precipitation in different environments. Second, the transboundary nature of the LRTAP process will require subjugation of individual political authorities to a wider, more global objective. Neither state, provincial, or federal governments, each having particular interests, will find it easy to reach a consensus. Third, the differing interests of the individuals and corporations involved in the process and the magnitude of the costs incurred, irrespective of the level of abatement, will ensure that considerable controversy will arise over the allocation of costs. Costs borne by local economies as a result of abatement efforts could be of the same order of magnitude as the direct costs. Finally, consensus will require a commitment of political will. Acid rain is only one item on a crowded political agenda, and although it is an important issue, it cannot be expected to monopolize the attention of politicians.

NOTES

1. Within the chapter acid rain will be used as a general term to denote all forms of acid precipitation, including rain, snow, sleet, fog, and so forth.

2. For thermal power plants, fluidized bed combustion and limestone-injection, multistage burners are the two most promising means of new technology to reduce pollutants produced in burning coal. For smelters, the available technology includes fluid bed roasters, pyrrhotite rejection processes, continuous smelting processes, and the addition of sulfuric acid plants to converters and reactors.

REFERENCES

Appin Associates (1984). *Conceptual Design and Economics of a Sulfur Dioxide Abatement Strategy for Canada.* Winnipeg, Manitoba: Appin Associates.

Barse, Joseph R., Walter Ferguson, and Virgil Whetzel (1985). *Effects of Air Pollution and Acid Rain on Agriculture: An Annotated Bibliography.* U.S. Dept. of Agriculture Economic Research Service Staff Report AGES850702. Washington, D.C. October.

Carroll, John E. (1983). *Environmental Diplomacy.* Ann Arbor: University of Michigan Press.

——— (1985). "Acid Rain—Acid Diplomacy" in E. J. Yanarella and R. H. Ihara, eds., *The Acid Rain Debate.* Boulder, Colo.: Westview Press.

Energy Mines and Resources Canada (1984). *Canada's Nonferrous Metals Industry: Nickel and Copper.* Ottawa, Ontario: Energy Mines and Resources Canada.

Forster, B. A. (1984). "An Economic Assessment of the Significance of Long Range Transported Air Pollutants for Agriculture in Canada." *Canadian Journal of Agricultural Economics* 32 (3):498–525.

Gorham, E. (1982). "Acid Rain: Questions and Answers" in P. S. Gold, ed., *Acid Rain: A Transjurisdictional Problem in Search of a Solution*. Buffalo: Canadian-American Center, State University of New York at Buffalo.

Gould, R. (1985). *Science and Politics of Acid Rain*. Boston: Birkhauser.

Johnston, D. M., and P. Finkle (1983). *Acid Precipitation in North America*. Calgary, Alberta: Canadian Institute of Resources Law, University of Calgary.

LRTAP Incentives Work Group (1984). *Analysis of Policies to Implement an Acid Rain Abatement Strategy*. Toronto, Ontario. Mimeographed.

Ontario Ministry of the Environment (1984). *The Economics of Acid Precipitation*. APIOS Report 006/84. Toronto, Ontario: Ministry of the Environment.

Organization for Economic Cooperation and Development (1978). *The Costs and Benefits of Sulfur Oxide Control*. Paris: The Organization for Economic Cooperation and Development.

Poundstone, William (1982). "Acid Rain: What We Know and What We Don't Know" in P. S. Gold, ed., *Acid Rain: A Transjurisdictional Problem in Search of a Solution*. Buffalo: Canadian-American Center, State University of New York at Buffalo.

Regens, James L., and Robert W. Rycroft (1986). "Options for Financing Acid Rain Controls." *Natural Resources Journal* 26 (3):519–549.

Smith, Robert Angus (1872). *Air and Rain: The Beginnings of a Chemical Climatology*. London: Longmans, Green.

U.S. National Research Council (1983). *Acid Deposition: Atmospheric Processes in North America*. Washington, D.C.: National Academy Press.

U.S. Office of Technology Assessment (1985). *Acid Rain and Transported Air Pollutants*. New York: UNIPUB.

SUGGESTED READINGS

Gold. P. S. (1982). *Acid Rain: A Transjurisdictional Problem in Search of a Solution*. Buffalo, N.Y.: Canadian-American Center, State University of New York at Buffalo. This book provides a good overview of the political issues that are involved in the controversy between Canada and the United States over acid rain control. It consists of a series of papers by scientists and government officials from both countries.

Johnston, D. M., and P. Finkle (1983). *Acid Precipitation in North America*. Calgary, Alberta: The Canadian Institute of Resources Law, University of Calgary. Although the book has a strong Canadian orientation it does a nice job of reviewing aspects of law in both countries that are applicable to the control of acid rain.

Regens, James L., and Robert W. Rycroft (1986). "Options for Financing Acid Rain Controls" in *The Natural Resources Journal* 26, no. 3. This article examines various methods for determining the costs of acid rain controls in the United States. Although it does address Canadian conditions the primary focus is the United States in terms of identifying both benefits and costs.

United States National Research Council (1983). *Acid Deposition: Atmospheric Processes in North America*. Washington, D.C. National Academy Press. This is the classic report that forms the scientific backdrop for concern with acid rain effects in the United States. Although other reports have taken its conclusions further, it provided important ammunition for those trying to get acid rain onto the agenda for negotiations.

STUDY QUESTIONS

1. Much of the debate over acid rain has focused on the uncertain relationship between cause and effect. How should policymakers take into account the possibility that waiting for clarification of this relationship may result in far greater damages?

2. Are there fundamental political or economic differences between transboundary effects when two countries are involved as opposed to two regions within the same . country?

3. Assess the desirability of abatement programs that result in equal cuts by all polluters versus programs that require cuts by those whose costs of abatement are lowest. Are there ways to make the two approaches equitable?

4. Is there any reason to treat government-owned public utilities in a different manner than investor-owned, profit-maximizing firms when setting performance standards for emissions?

Chapter Seven

National Forest Management
The Issue of Below-Cost Sales

Douglas J. Krieger

Management of national forests entails decisions that affect many, often conflicting, resource uses such as timber production, wildlife habitat, watershed protection, livestock grazing, recreation opportunities, and aesthetic enjoyment. This economic analysis focuses on the sale of timber, especially so-called below-cost sales by the U.S. Forest Service. The case specifically addresses problems with joint production of forest outputs and allocation of associated costs. Multiple-use management of the national forests is related to economic efficiency, market effects, discounting, community stability, and timber supply. Forest management practices such as sustained yield, even flow, and allowable cut are also discussed. Insights are offered on managing forests and other resources that provide multiple-use benefits.

Over the past decade there has been heated debate over the way in which the national forests are managed. Much of this debate has focused on the practice of below-cost sales of national forest timber, sales for which benefits fail to cover costs. Such sales are difficult to identify because of problems with the allocation of joint production costs and inadequate knowledge of forest production functions. Furthermore, there are inherent questions of the distribution of the costs and benefits of management options.

Most forest management activities have an impact on the production of more than one forest output and it is this characteristic of joint production that poses the primary problem for below-cost sale identification. If an activity produces several goods, how can the separate costs of each good be determined so that the "correct" amount of each can be produced? Joint cost allocation will be seen to be necessarily somewhat arbitrary and hence a fundamental source of disagreement between parties on either side of the below-cost sale issue.

NATIONAL FOREST MANAGEMENT

The Forest Reserve Act of 1891 set aside several million acres of forest land for the public domain. The motivation for this action was a concern by conservationists with the "cut-and-run" forestry practices of the time. These practices were rapidly depleting the nation's virgin stands of timber. Several significant additions to this initial land base prior to 1907, when further withdrawals were restricted, established what have become the national forests. Today the national forests encompass some 191 million acres of forest and range land (see Figure 7.1). These forests are managed by the U.S. Forest Service, an agency in the U.S. Department of Agriculture (USDA).

The national forests provide a diverse selection of goods such as timber, wildlife habitat, watersheds, stock grazing, recreational opportunities, and aesthetic pleasures that benefit many different groups of people. The provision of all of these goods is possible and mandated within the existing national forest system, a concept referred to as multiple use. The Multiple-Use Sustained-Yield Act of 1960 directs that the management objectives of national forests be

> the management of all the variable renewable surface resources of the national forests so that they are utilized in the combination that will best meet the needs of the American people . . . [and the] harmonious and coordinated management of the various resources, each with the other, without impairment of the productivity of the land, with consideration being given to the relative values of the various resources and not necessarily the combination of uses that will give the greatest dollar return or the greatest unit output (Clawson, 1976).

Conflicts often arise, however, because of the incompatible-use nature of some of these activities on specific land areas. For instance, it will not be possible to produce timber for eventual harvest and provide wilderness recreation opportunities at the same location. The central management issues facing the Forest Service revolve around the questions of how and where the various outputs of the forests should be produced and how much of each to provide.

Economics in National Forest Management

The National Forest Management Act (NFMA) of 1976 stipulates, in part, that the answers to these questions be sought within an economic framework. The specific wording of the NFMA reveals that economic efficiency in the use of forest resources was one intent of the act (Walker, 1976). Efficiency is basically a measure of how well inputs are combined in the process of forming outputs. Economic efficiency is achieved when more of a good cannot be produced without decreasing the output of another and when the welfare of one individual cannot be improved without reducing that of another. Although efficient outcomes are often held up as the ideal, they are difficult to identify in practice. The calculation of efficient outcomes requires that the conditions for a perfectly competitive market be met and assumes the status quo distribution of income or wealth.

The concept of efficiency most relevant to this analysis is that of allocative efficiency. For the individual, allocative efficiency in consumption is defined in terms of equality between price ratios paid for goods and the ratio of the marginal utilities that they provide. In the aggregate the efficient mix of outputs in production occurs when the social values between outputs and consumption goods are equal to the rate at which one can be transformed into the other at the margin. Given these conditions, the identification of efficient combinations in outputs and consumption requires, among other things, knowledge of (1) the values of goods and services derived from the forests, (2) the costs of providing these outputs, and (3) the production processes that relate inputs to forest outputs.

The valuation of many forest outputs such as wildlife habitat, recreation, watersheds, and so forth presents problems because these outputs are not bought and sold directly; hence the market attaches no explicit price or value to them. Clearly, however, these goods and services do have value. Their valuation needs to be made in terms of some common denominator—in this case, money—if the various forest outputs are to be comparable when evaluating alternative management plans.

The Problem of Joint Costs

The costs of providing many of the products of the national forests are also difficult to determine. It is characteristic of the production processes for many forest outputs that specific inputs often contribute to the production of several goods. A road constructed for removing timber, for instance, may also enhance access to the forest for other uses. When a single input enters into the production of several goods, the question arises as to how the cost of that input should be allocated among the joint products. Without an appropriate allocation of production costs the cost of providing any single good independently of the others may be difficult to determine.

Total costs in the case of joint production can be divided into two categories—separable and joint. The separable cost of one output is the savings that would result from eliminating that output and maintaining the level of production of all other goods. It is the cost attributable entirely to the production of that good. Of the two, only the separable costs can be assigned unambiguously to the production of a single good; the allocation of the joint costs must always be somewhat arbitrary (Eckstein, 1958).

Related to the allocation of costs is the issue of knowledge of the production processes for forest outputs. When goods are jointly produced, changes in the level of provision of any one may alter the level of the others as well. In the case of forest goods, for instance, logging activities on a site may lead to changes in wildlife habitat, water flows, or recreation opportunities on that, as well as adjacent, sites. In order to identify separable costs the production relationships between the various goods must be

FIGURE 7.1 National Forests and Grasslands

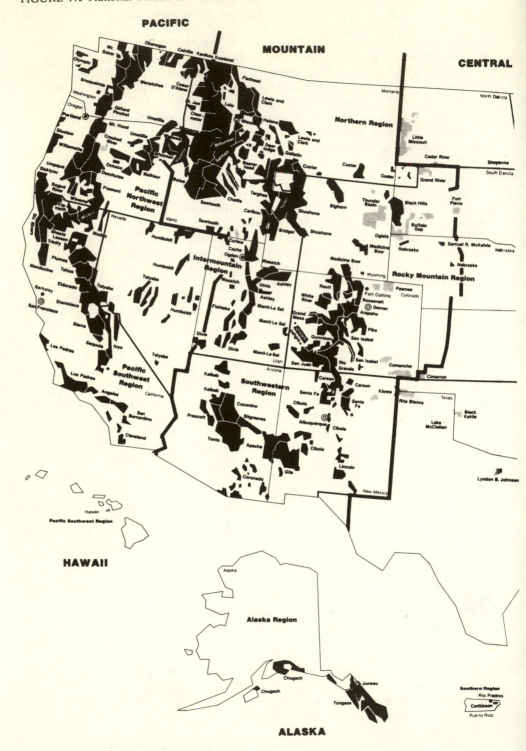

Source: U.S. Forest Service.

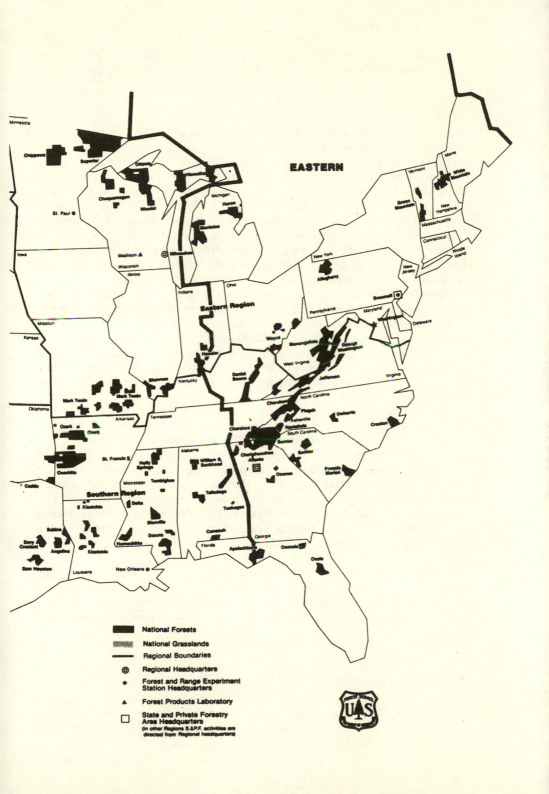

EASTERN

Minnesota

Chippewa

Superior

Ottawa

Hiawatha

Chequamegon

Nicolet

Michigan

Huron

St. Paul

Manistee

Madison

Milwaukee

Wisconsin

Illinois

Indiana

Ohio

Iowa

Eastern Region

Missouri

Kansas

Shawnee

Hoosier

Kentucky

Daniel Boone

Mark Twain

Mark Twain

Oklahoma

Ozark

Ozark

Arkansas

Tennessee

St. Francis B.

Caddo

Ouachita

Mississippi

Holly Springs

Tombigbee

Davy Crockett

Sabine

Kisatchie

Homochitto

Angelina

Kisatchie

Sam Houston

Louisiana

New Orleans

New York

Allegheny

Pennsylvania

Vermont

Maine

White Mountain

Green Mountain

New Hampshire

Massachusetts

Connecticut

Rhode Island

New Jersey

Maryland

Delaware

West Virginia

Wayne

Monongahela

George Washington

Jefferson

Virginia

Cherokee

North Carolina

Pisgah

Asheville

Nantahala

Uwharrie

Croatan

Cherokee

South Carolina

Sumter

Sumter

Alabama

William B. Bankhead

Chattahoochee

Atlanta

Oconee

Francis Marion

Talladega

Tuskegee

Delta

Bienville

Desoto

Conecuh

Florida

Georgia

Apalachicola

Osceola

Ocala

Ocala

Southern Region

National Forests

National Grasslands

Regional Boundaries

Regional Headquarters

Forest and Range Experiment Station Headquarters

Forest Products Laboratory

State and Private Forestry Area Headquarters
(In other Regions S.&P.F. activities are directed from Regional headquarters)

FOREST SERVICE
U S

understood for the forest as a system of interrelated sites. The current state of such knowledge, however, is often inadequate for this purpose.

WHAT ARE BELOW-COST SALES?

Much attention has been focused on the practice of selling timber from the national forests when the revenues from the sale are insufficient to cover the costs of selling the trees, that is, below-cost sales. This definition focuses on short-term cash flows and is consistent with Forest Service practices in the appraisal of proposed timber sales. Considering only short-term cash flows, however, ignores many of the actual costs and benefits associated with timber sales. Costs, for instance, may include those of raising the timber or the opportunity costs of harvest in terms of other forest outputs. Similarly, there can be benefits associated with a sale in addition to timber revenues. A broader definition of below-costs sales, and the one used here, is based on a comparison of all costs and benefits of a sale.

Below-cost timber sales represent an inefficient use of forest resources. In some cases the value of forest outputs that can be produced when a site is managed for timber will exceed the value of outputs when timber management is not an objective. Similarly, on other sites the value of outputs surrendered under timber management schemes will dominate. From the standpoint of efficiency, it is uneconomic to sacrifice a higher valued bundle of outputs from a forest site for one of lower value as would be the case with a below-cost sale.

The Multiple-Use Sustained-Yield Act mandates that the national forests be managed to produce a wide variety of goods, with the mix of these outputs not necessarily determined by the maximization of revenues. Environmentalists, sportsmens' groups, and others, however, contend that Forest Service actions and proposed management plans are not consistent with the spirit of the act (Hanson, 1986). They are angered by the degradation or destruction of forest outputs such as fisheries or de facto wilderness that can accompany logging operations and related development. When timber is sold below cost, forest outputs that have a positive net value are being sacrificed for the purpose of timber production that is not economically justified.

Because below-cost sales are defined in terms of a comparison of sale costs with benefits, the problems of resource valuation, cost allocation, and production function specification make accurate identification of such sales extremely difficult. The factors that affect the level of timber revenues and costs in timber operations can be grouped into three general categories: physical-biological, access costs, and market conditions.

Physical-Biological Factors

Forest land can be classified as commercial or noncommercial depending on its potential to grow timber. Commercial forests are defined as those that are capable of producing more than 20 cubic feet of industrial wood in natural stands per acre per year (Clawson, 1976). The Forest Service further classifies commercial forest land in terms of its site class. Site classes range from class I lands, capable of producing more than 165 cubic feet of wood per acre per year, to class V lands, which can grow between 20 and 50 cubic feet.

From a purely physical standpoint, site productivity depends on such factors as soil type, climate, tree species, and stand density. Raising and selling successive crops of usable timber on a site, however, entails management costs in terms of site preparation, reforestation, fire protection, pest control, stand improvement, and sale preparation. The physical productivity of a site is important in determining the amount and quality of timber that can be removed and hence affects the level of sale revenues available to offset these costs.

Access Costs

In addition to the management costs of raising and selling timber there are also costs associated with physical access to the standing trees. Road construction represents a major portion of the cost of timber harvest on the national forests. For the 1980 to 1984 period about 50 percent of the entire Forest Service appropriation was spent on roads (National Trails Coalition, 1985). Forest roads are funded in one of two ways: (1) directly out of the Forest Service budget—hard money roads—or (2) from the proceeds of the corresponding sale—purchaser credit roads. When the latter method is used the purchaser of the timber usually pays for road construction, and the cost is deducted from the price paid for the timber.

Environmental and multiple-use considerations can also affect the cost of harvesting timber on a given site. On some sites it may be necessary to specify special harvest or site treatment techniques in order to protect other forest outputs. Harvest techniques on sites with highly erodible soils or steep terrain, for instance, may emphasize particularly stringent road building standards or other practices to minimize the impact of logging on watersheds and fisheries. In the Northern Region, for example, an average of $18 is spent to protect nontimber resources for every thousand board feet of timber that is harvested (Risbrudt, 1986).

Access costs can vary considerably depending on the existing network of roads, the terrain, and environmental and multiple-use considerations. When these costs are included with management costs in the costs of producing timber on the national forests, a greater number of sales will appear to be below cost.

Market Conditions

The two categories discussed so far have concentrated on the role of costs in the determination of sale viability. A below-cost sale, however, is defined in terms of revenues as well as costs. Thus, the magnitude of sale receipts will help determine whether timber operations on a given site will yield revenues in excess of costs. Revenues are determined by the market price for standing timber, which is, in turn, a function of the demand for final wood products. A significant amount of the timber harvested in the United States is ultimately used in the construction industry (USDA, 1982), with about 25 percent of the softwood sawtimber supplied from the national forests. Because of the sensitivity of the construction industry to economic conditions the induced demand for construction wood products is quite volatile, and prices for standing timber fluctuate widely as a result. Consequently, economic conditions that shape the demand for final wood products, and hence the price of standing timber, will play a significant role in the profitability of timber sales. A Forest Service study of forests for which costs exceeded revenues between 1979 and 1983 attributes part of the problem to weak markets for timber products (USDA, 1986).

For the purpose of a Forest Service appraisal the revenues expected from a sale are based on expected bid prices, referred to as the sold value. Harvest generally takes place several years after the actual sale, however, so bid prices for timber reflect expectations of future market conditions rather than current conditions. If, at the time of harvest, prices are lower than those that were expected, the harvest value of the timber will be lower than the sold value. When wood product prices fall between the time timber is sold and harvested, the price actually paid is usually adjusted downward by some fraction of the price difference. The Forest Service thus bears some of the risk of such changes in market conditions. Actual timber sale receipts, then, depend on the harvest value rather than the sold value on which the sale is initially evaluated. Therefore a sale that initially appears to be viable may not cover costs if prices fall between sale and harvest. Similarly, a sale that is expected to yield a deficit may be profitable in the future if market conditions improve sufficiently.

A longer range view of market conditions or prices for wood will necessarily consider changing technology in wood use. Technological change, often spurred by market conditions, may alter the pattern of wood use and hence the demand for standing timber. The development of substitutes for wood will tend to reduce timber demand while newly discovered uses will increase demand.

Below-Cost Sales in Perspective

Factors such as climate, tree species, and terrain, which play a large role in the determination of the economic viability of timber sales, are relatively homogeneous over sizable geographic areas. This homogeneity implies that below-cost sales are likely to be more heavily concentrated in some regions and forests than others. A detailed study reveals that, while sale receipts generally exceed costs for the national forests as a whole, there is significant geographic variation in the ratio of receipts to costs (Sample, 1984). Of the nine national forest management regions the ratio of receipts to costs for 1983 ranged from .01 in Alaska to 2.62 in the Pacific Northwest.

In general, of the nine regions (see Figure 7.1), only the Southern, Pacific Southwest, and Pacific Northwest regions yielded receipts in excess of costs.

Of the six remaining regions, Alaska and the Northern Region realized the greatest losses. This kind of study provides only an indication of regional patterns of the ratio of monetary receipts to expenditures; it implies nothing about individual sales. Even in regions or forests that showed a net loss, some sales yielded positive net returns while some sales incurred monetary losses in regions that showed an overall excess of receipts over costs. Because nonmonetary costs and benefits of timber sales are not considered, Sample's study did not identify below-cost sales as defined here. Except in cases where there are substantial nonmonetary benefits to timber harvest, there is likely to be a strong correlation between low-receipt–expenditure ratios and actual below-cost sales. This kind of information may, therefore, be useful in targeting areas where below-cost sales are most likely.

IDENTIFICATION OF BELOW-COST SALES

Although the definition of below-cost sales is relatively straightforward, the identification of such sales in practice is quite difficult. Problems of cost allocation over both joint products and time make it hard to determine the costs associated with timber operations on specific sites. In addition, current Forest Service accounting practices are not adequate to accurately identify costs on the basis of individual sales.

Cost Allocation

A primary obstacle to the identification of below-cost sales, as well as the source of much disagreement, stems from the difficulty in allocating joint costs. Using this argument the Forest Service, in effect, denies that a real problem of below-cost sales exists. When costs are allocated correctly among joint products, they claim very few sales actually fail to cover costs. They argue that commercial timber sales are frequently the most effective method of enhancing other outputs of the forests. For example, sales may be designed primarily to benefit watersheds or wildlife habitat, and logging roads may provide improved access for a variety of other forest uses.

The opponents of Forest Service timber sale policies, on the other hand, claim that the negative external effects of logging and related activities are often overlooked. Part of the costs of timber harvest takes the form of reduced opportunities for outputs that are incompatible with timber production. Increased stream siltation as a result of logging activities, for instance, can damage fisheries, and logging techniques may reduce the aesthetic benefits derived from the forests. Critics of timber sale policies also express skepticism concerning the magnitude of the indirect benefits of timber harvest to other forest outputs that are claimed by the Forest Service (Emerson, 1986). Because the assignment of joint costs is necessarily somewhat arbitrary, it is unlikely that the below-cost sale debate can be resolved through arguments about the "correct" allocation of such costs.

Benefit cost analysis is the appropriate basis for economic choice when evaluating production alternatives, and this technique does not require the allocation of joint costs (Eckstein, 1958). If the net present value of forest benefits with a planned timber sale exceed the benefits for any plan that excludes timber harvest, then the sale is economically justified. To apply this method of evaluation, however, requires considerable knowledge of production relationships and a great deal of analysis. Without such knowledge it will be impossible to obtain reliable estimates of the costs and benefits associated with any proposed plan. Without adequate estimates of production functions for forest outputs, benefit-cost analysis will not help to resolve the issue of below-cost sale identification.

The Distribution of Benefits Over Time

Many of the costs incurred in forest management can be viewed as investments that will yield benefits sometime in the future. If such costs are charged exclusively against current period benefits then total benefits will be understated with respect to costs. The proper way to treat future benefits that arise from costs in the current time period is to discount the benefits to present value terms. Once costs and benefits are expressed in terms of the same time period they can be correctly compared.

A problem with discounting is the choice of the discount rate. This rate defines the relative importance of present and future values; the greater the rate the more heavily weighted are present values relative to those in the future. Ideally, the chosen discount rate should reflect the preferences of individuals for present versus future consumption and the value of benefits to future generations. Individuals place different values on the future, however, and the value of benefits to future generations is unknown. The choice of a particular rate, then, will benefit some—those whose preferences coincide with the rate—and impose costs on others, perhaps in future generations.

Roads, which represent a major portion of the costs of many timber sales, have a usable life that exceeds the time period a site is actively logged. In addition to providing improved access in the current period these roads yield benefits well beyond the time period in which construction costs are incurred. When a road is built into a previously roadless area to access timber, it often substantially reduces road construction costs to adjacent sites that may be logged in the future. If the entire cost of the road is charged to the initial sale it may appear to be below-cost even though subsequent sales in the area are deemed profitable. A proper accounting of costs for a capital improvement, such as a road, would amortize the costs over the expected life of the asset.

Similarly, some sales may be conducted to improve an existing timber stand or to salvage timber killed by fire, disease, or insects. Such sales represent an investment in the long-term capacity of the forest to produce timber, and as such, the costs should be allocated, in part, to future benefits. Whether such an investment really yields benefits is largely a function of the productivity of the site and the demand for timber. On the less productive sites it may not be possible to grow timber quickly enough or of high enough quality to justify investments in stand improvement. On these sites the first harvest of a natural stand, even if not below-cost, is referred to as "timber mining" because the timber, in this case, is not an economically renewable resource (Hyde, 1984). On the other hand, the future benefits of stand improvement on a more productive site may justify a sale that would otherwise be below-cost. The General Accounting Office (GAO) reports, however, that below-cost sales made to improve existing timber stands are not often justified by future revenues (GAO, 1984). The present value of these revenues is likely to be small because of the length of time over which the income is discounted. For example, a sale made to establish a better stand of trees on a site may take 40 or more years (the amount of time to grow trees to maturity) to yield significant revenues. When values are discounted over such a time span they are substantially reduced unless very small discount rates are used.

Accounting

The allocation of costs presents one obstacle to the identification of below-cost sales, but perhaps a more significant problem is the yearly cash flow accounting system used by the Forest Service. This system, implemented forestwide rather than site by site, compares costs with receipts for each year. Receipts from timber sales, however, are paid at harvest, which can be up to seven years after the sale. When an accounting system compares costs and receipts on an annual basis, sale revenues in any given year will not be matched with the costs of those particular sales but, rather, with costs incurred on current sales that may not be harvested for several years. Ideally costs and receipts should be compared for each sale in terms of the present values of those costs and receipts. Data collection costs, however, prevent the Forest Service from tracking the costs and receipts of individual sales necessary for present value calculations.

Concern with the below-cost sale issue resulted in a provision in the appropriations bill for 1985 that requires the Forest Service to develop an accounting system capable of determining the costs of producing timber. Some see this as wasted effort (Bowes, Krutilla, and Stockton, 1987). Because the allocation of joint costs necessary to such an accounting scheme is to some extent arbitrary, the resulting determination of timber production costs will be arguable. However, given the problem of joint-cost allocation, it is difficult to analyze timber operations as separate from other management objectives. There are also those who, while they hold no illusions that such an accounting system will eliminate below-cost sales, see the effort as a necessary first step in making the Forest Service more accountable for its timber operations.

One way to determine the total costs of providing forest outputs is to apply capital accounting procedures (Bowes, Krutilla, and Stockton, 1987). Capital accounting dictates that changes in the asset value of the forests, which influence the future flow of outputs, be included in the costs and benefits attributable to current actions. Timber sales that remove timber or improve existing stands, roads that enhance forest access, and practices that damage other forest resources all affect the future output potential of the forests. The present value of these asset changes, either positive or negative, is properly included in current comparisons of the costs and benefits of forest management alternatives. The focus of the study by Bowes, Krutilla, and Stockton (1987) is on measuring the separable costs of timber in the context of capital accounting. These costs include the impacts of timber harvest on the future flow of other forest outputs. FORPLAN, the Forest Service's linear programming forest planning model, although imperfect, supplies the necessary information concerning the production processes for forest outputs.

OUTCOME CONSIDERATIONS IN TIMBER SALE POLICY DESIGN

The below-cost sale issue has received so much attention largely because of the range and magnitude of the possible consequences of any decision concerning timber sale policy. Many organizations and groups have taken positions on the issue reflecting their own diverse interests in the management of the national forests. The choice of management policy will ultimately benefit some of these interests while others will lose. With respect to below-cost sales, three areas of concern have emerged as the primary forums of debate over the distribution of costs and benefits: (1) multiple use, the use of forest outputs other than timber; (2) community stability; and (3) timber supply.

Multiple-Use Considerations

Timber harvest, while it can enhance some forest outputs, may destroy or diminish others. If a sale is actually below cost and total costs exceed total benefits, then timber harvest is not justified and the site is best suited to the provision of other goods. Environmentalist and sportsmen's groups often use the below-cost sale argument in trying to protect forest outputs provided in roadless or other areas. The value of such sites to society is, they argue, greater when timber harvest is forgone. One point of debate between these groups and their opponents stems from the problems of accurately identifying below-cost sales. Another arises from questions of equity, the distribution of costs and benefits to individuals. The question of equity cannot be resolved by economics; the fairness issue is an ethical or political concern. Economic analysis, however, can identify the distributional consequences of policy alternatives thereby providing valuable information to the political decision process.

The analysis of below-cost sales as defined here compares the total costs and benefits to society as a whole; the question of their distribution among individuals is not addressed. For some individuals the benefits resulting from timber harvest may exceed the costs even on sales that are below-cost from a societal perspective. Similarly, on sites where timber sales are economically justified, timber harvest may impose costs in excess of benefits for some individuals. Forest management policy concerning below-cost sales will affect the entire range of forest outputs, including specific sites. Discontinuation of below-cost sales would result in increased production of forest outputs that are incompatible with timber harvest. Society as a whole will gain from such a policy as will those individuals who place a higher value on outputs other than timber at the affected locations. The losers will be those who place a higher value on timber production at those sites.

The benefits and costs of current timber harvest policies are not limited to present generations. The time frame involved in timber growth and the irreversibility of some management decisions imply that future generations will be affected as well. Many forest policy actions have irreversible, or only slowly reversible, consequences. A road constructed into a previously roadless area would, for instance, degrade the wilderness potential of that land. To evaluate policy alternatives in terms of a comparison of costs and benefits in such a case requires knowledge of the value of forest outputs to future generations. Because we know very little about these values, caution is dictated when making policy decisions with intergenerational consequences.

Community Stability

The equity issue is relevant to the regional distribution of costs and benefits as well as to the distribution of costs and benefits among individuals. The national forests are concentrated in the West where the vast majority of land is owned by the government (see Figure 7.1). The geographic distribution of national forests and the productive sites within the forests imply that the residents of some regions will be more directly affected by forest policy than those living elsewhere. Furthermore, given this distribution, below-cost sales represent a subsidy with unequal regional impacts. Such a subsidy encourages timber production in regions where the cost of raising timber is relatively high. To the extent that the subsidy shifts timber harvest from low-cost to higher-cost lands, an inefficient pattern of timber production is represented: Timber is not being produced at the lowest cost. A complete economic analysis must consider these regional impacts in evaluating policy alternatives.

Many small communities in forested regions have developed around timber harvesting and processing industries. The economic health of these communities, in terms of employment, income, and other factors, is often closely tied to that of the wood products industry. In regions where timber is supplied primarily from the national forests and few alternative timber sources exist, the industry is particularly susceptible to timber supply fluctuations resulting from changes in national forest timber sale policy. Recognizing this dependence, the promotion of community stability has been stated explicitly as one objective of national forest management in the Sustained-Yield Forest Management Act of 1944. Specifically, the act authorizes sustained-yield management in order to "promote the stability of forest industries, of employment, of communities and taxable forest wealth, through continuous supply of timber" (Daniels and Daniels, 1986). Although the concept of community stability may be interpreted in a variety of ways, in general it means the preclusion of wide fluctuations in employment tax revenues, or other indicators of community economic health.

The national forests also impact regional economies by in-lieu-of-tax payments. These payments are made to local governments to compensate for taxes that would be paid if the lands were privately held; the payments are used to fund schools and roads. The magnitude of these transfers is tied primarily to timber harvest receipts. Thus, counties with significant national forest harvest will face a loss of revenues if harvest volumes are reduced. Depending on the size of these reductions, residents of affected communities may experience a decrease in the quality of life attributable to a reduced level of governmentally funded infrastructure.

The application of sustained-yield and even-flow policies, which ensure a stable, sustainable supply of timber, reflects the concern for community stability. In addition, a portion of national forest timber sales are reserved for small businesses, which often are located in small, timber-dependent communities. These sales, referred to as the small business set-aside, provide a less competitive environment in which small firms have a better opportunity to acquire timber that is near their processing facilities. A consequence of reduced competition is that prices at these sales are generally lower than those obtained at other sales. Furthermore, a disproportionate share of below-cost sales are included in small business set-asides.

The forest products industries and the Forest Service claim that the withdrawal of forest land from timber production for wilderness expansion or other multiple-use considerations will restrict timber supply and adversely affect the economic health of timber-dependent communities. For example, in investigating the consequences of an expansion of Redwood National Park through government acquisition of private commercial forests, McKillop (1978) found evidence of substantial costs in terms of local employment in the timber industry and related jobs. When the multiplier effect is considered, the economic ramifications could extend beyond the initial loss of jobs.

Demand Considerations in Community Stability

Current forest policy and the arguments of the wood products industries seem to focus on timber availability as the key to community stability. Such reasoning, however, reflects only part of the problem. Demand considerations play a much more significant role. The market for wood products is highly volatile because of its dependence on the construction industry, which is, in turn, influenced largely by general economic conditions. Demand-induced fluctuations in the timber industry may be more important in determining timber industry employment, tax revenues, and other measures of community stability than is an adequate timber supply. In the early 1980s, for example, the wood products industry, despite a three-year backlog of purchased but uncut federal timber, was suffering a severe slump resulting from a decline in the demand for wood, which was brought about by the general downturn in economic conditions. The high unemployment figures and related hardships faced by timber-dependent communities were not, in this case, the result of inadequate timber supply.

Demand instability in timber-dependent communities is a cyclical phenomenon influenced by fluctuations in the general level of economic activity. Two other developments are expected to have important implications for employment in wood products industries and the regional pattern of wood production. Forests in the Southeast, because of their high productivity, have an absolute advantage over those in the Northwest in wood production. As the old growth forests of the Northwest are harvested, it will become necessary to invest in more intensive forestry practices to meet wood demand. Investment in such practices will take place where it will yield the greatest returns, primarily in the Southeast. Most projections of future timber supply predict that the Southeast will become the major timber growing region of the country by the year 2030 (Emerson and Helfand, 1983). Secondly, technological innovation is expected to reduce the work force required in the wood products industries by 36 percent in the next 15 years. These developments will require significant adjustments in timber dependent communities and the associated work force in the future.

It is argued that current forest policy, although it may contribute in some circumstances to short-run stability, may increase transitional costs by inhibiting a community's ability to respond to the predicted long-run changes in the timber industry. Given the demand-driven, cyclical nature of the timber industry, it is conceivable that current policies aimed at stabilizing timber supply actually encourage potentially unstable community structures. Diversification of a local economy will generally improve stability by diluting the effects of fluctuations within a single sector. A community assured of a reliable supply of low-cost timber, however, has little incentive to pursue diversification and may thus be more vulnerable when supply or demand considerations, technological innovation, or regional shifts in wood production create hardships for the local timber industry. With substantial changes predicted for the forestry sector, government policy should focus on easing the inevitable transition in timber-dependent communities rather than in perpetuating an inefficient timber production system.

TIMBER SUPPLY

Sustained Yield, Even Flow, and Allowable Cut

The provision of an adequate supply of timber and other forest outputs in the present and in the future, has been an issue in forest management since the early twentieth century when the possible consequences of deforestation became apparent in the United States. The issue is evident in the wording of the Multiple-Use Sustained-Yield Act where it is translated into the concept of sustained yield. The act defines sustained-yield management as "the achievement and maintenance in perpetuity of a high level annual or periodic output of the various renewable resources of the national forests without impairment of the productivity of the land" (Clawson, 1975). This policy, in effect, constrains timber harvest levels to be no higher than those consistent with sustained-yield management, referred to as "even flow."

Sustained yield implies that, in the long run, timber harvest levels are restricted by the capacity of the forest to grow wood. The amount of wood grown on a forest will depend on the physical-biological potential of the land, the age and condition of existing stands, and the level of management for timber production that is practiced. Changes in timber-growing capacity will affect the quantity of wood that can periodically be removed from the forest under sustained-yield management, referred to as the "allowable cut," and hence the supply of wood available from the national forests. Furthermore, calculations of allowable-cut harvest levels consider only lands used for commercial timber production; wood growth in areas set aside for wilderness or other uses that preclude timber harvest are not included. The potential quantity of timber that can be supplied by the national forests under sustained-yield management is thus determined by both the amount of land considered suitable for commercial timber operations and the productivity of that land.

Below-Cost Sales and Timber Supply

The Roadless Area Review and Evaluation (RARE II) identified approximately 64 million acres of national forest land for possible wilderness designation. These areas generally represent land that is not well-suited to timber production. Only 26 million of these acres are classified as commercial forestland and hence correspond closely to areas where below-cost sales would be expected. The results of the Rare II study, along with recent withdrawals of forestland for wilderness expansion, have fostered concern within the timber industry about the supply of timber that will be available from the national forests.

Land withdrawn from consideration for commercial timber production, for whatever reason, reduces the base upon which allowable cut is calculated and may result in less timber being offered from the national forests. Allowable cut, however, is calculated on timber growth rather than on the land area included in the base. By their very nature, forest areas that are considered for wilderness inclusion, and many of those for which below-cost sales are an issue, are old growth forests. They have not previously been harvested. Furthermore, these forests are generally of relatively low productivity. On many such forests the annual addition to wood volume may be very small and may actually be outweighed by loss to disease and decay. In their present state such forests contribute very little to annual wood growth, and their withdrawal from the timber base will have little effect on the allowable cut. For instance, the effect on annual allowable cut of seven newly designated wilderness areas in Montana have been examined (Bolle 1986). The study did not find a reduction in the allowable cut in any of these cases that was attributable to the withdrawal of land for wilderness inclusion. For the more productive of these sites, however, harvest of old growth timber and replacement with younger, faster growing trees, will have an immediate effect on allowable cut—the "allowable-cut effect." The question then becomes on which sites should intensive forestry efforts be concentrated in order to increase timber output from the national forests.

Supply Potential of the National Forests

Capital, rather than land, may be the limiting factor in timber production on the national forests (Behan, 1977). To maximize output under such conditions requires that returns to the scarcer factor of production be maximized, resulting in the efficient mix of the factors of production. This implies that, in order to maximize wood output, capital should be applied to those sites where it will yield the greatest returns. In spite of this wisdom, claimed Behan, the Forest Service applies capital fairly evenly over forests and regions without regard to differences in wood-producing potential. The objective of the Forest Service, however, is not the maximization of wood output; rather, the current distribution of capital may contribute to the production of other goods. It has been estimated that timber production on the national forests could be increased to 6 or 7 billion cubic feet annually, two or three times the current level, if timber management activities are concentrated on the more productive sites (Clawson 1975). At the same time the production of many other forest outputs could be increased on those lands found economically unsuitable for timber production. These studies suggest that the withdrawal of marginal timber-producing sites, such as those where below-cost sales are likely, and the reallocation of capital to more productive sites may ultimately increase, rather than decrease, the supply of wood available from the national forests.

Supply Potential of Private Forests

Sale policy on federal lands will also affect another important component of the national timber supply picture—the private forests. These forests, held by both forest industries and private individuals, yield about four-fifths of the nation's timber (Emerson, Stout, and Kloepfer, 1984). Nonindustrial private forests account for about 59 percent of commercial land and have a productive capacity about equal to the average on all other forests, but somewhat less than that for forest industry lands (USDA, 1982). In general these forests are poorly stocked and the timber is of relatively inferior quality (Clawson, 1975). Investment in these forests, where economically feasible, has the potential to make a substantial contribution to national timber supplies and remove some of the burden from the national forests. Investments in timber production on such lands is restricted, however, by a number of factors such as small parcel size, ownership objectives, and inadequate returns (Clawson, 1977).

One criticism of below-cost sales is that they depress timber prices and make private investments in forestry less attractive. The withdrawal of national forest land from timber production, when it restricts supply relative to demand, will push timber prices up and increase returns to forest investments. Although the actual response of rising timber prices is uncertain (in terms of investment in private forests), it is estimated that the output from private forests could meet total domestic demand by the year 2030 if landowners could realize a 10 percent return on their investments (Forest Industries Council, 1980). Thus, below-cost sales, while they also may contribute to the short-run timber supply, may in fact have a detrimental effect on long-run supplies by depressing stumpage prices, the price of standing timber.

In the context of stimulating private investments in forests, the congressional Office of Technology Assessment (OTA) stresses that uncertainty about future timber markets is the greatest deterrent to intensified timber management (U.S. OTA, 1983). This uncertainty implies that policies that stabilize timber prices may contribute more to eventual timber supplies than those that increase returns to forest investments. Hagenstein (1985) suggested that federal timber policies have indeed helped stabilize timber prices and that, initially, one of the rationales behind the sustained-yield policy was to bolster prices.

The Effects of Timberland Withdrawal

Withdrawing forestland from timber production where below-cost sales are predicted will certainly have relevant short-run impacts on timber supply in some regions. Depending on the productivity of the remaining land and the pattern of forest ownership in the region, it may be possible to maintain supply through more intensive management of federal lands or by bringing private lands into production. In many regions, particularly in the West, however, these options will not be available. Supply restrictions would be expected to result in stumpage price increases. Faced with higher prices for their raw materials the timber industry would have to increase the price of wood products or accept a reduction in profit.

The demand for final wood products and for national forest timber has been found to be inelastic (Jackson, 1984), implying that total revenue will increase as product price rises. Thus, if the wood products industry finds it necessary to increase prices as a result of the withdrawal of federal timberland, total revenues may rise. As prices rise, however, demand will become less inelastic and finally elastic, implying that at some point total revenue will begin to fall. The point at which the demand changes from inelastic to elastic is an empirical question.

To illustrate this point consider the graphs of Figure 7.2. Graph 7.2a is a demand curve for timber; it describes the relationship between price and quantity demanded. Total revenue is given by price times quantity or, for any price-quantity pair on the demand curve, the area of the rectangle bounded by the axes and this point (for example, the shaded area). As price is increased and the quantity demanded decreases, total revenue at first becomes larger, reaches a maximum, and then decreases as shown in graph 7.2b. The range over which revenue rises as price rises is the inelastic portion of the demand curve; in this range the increase in price is pro-

FIGURE 7.2 Demand and Total Revenue Functions

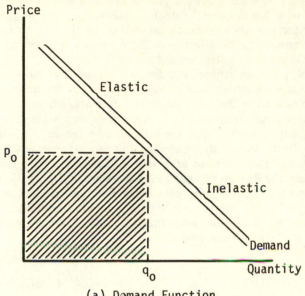

(a) Demand Function

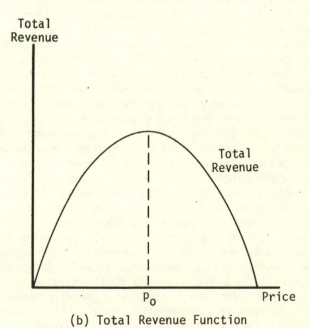

(b) Total Revenue Function

portionally greater than the decrease in quantity demanded. As the price continues to rise the decrease in demand becomes proportionally greater until the added revenue from the price increase is exactly offset by the fall in revenue from the decreased demand. This is the point of maximum total revenue. If the price is increased past this point, the effect of the decrease in demand outweighs the effect of rising price and total revenue falls. This is the elastic portion of the demand curve.

The implications of an inelastic demand for national forest timber apply to the federal government as a seller of timber. As the quantity of timber offered for sale from the national forests is curtailed, total revenue from sale activities would be expected to rise, other things being equal. At the same time, with a reduction in the number of sales on the less productive forests, sale costs would fall, narrowing the gap between costs and receipts for the national forest system as a whole. Concerned with the expanding federal deficit, the Reagan administration has endorsed expansions in harvest levels in order to increase the contribution of the national forests to the U.S. Treasury. Given the current situation in timber markets, however, a policy of harvest reduction rather than expansion is more consistent with an objective of deficit reduction.

CONCLUSIONS: THE FUTURE OF BELOW-COST SALES

Below-cost sales represent an inefficient use of the national forest resource. Evaluating timber sales on the basis of short-term cash flows, which is the Forest Service practice for sale appraisal, ignores many of the costs and benefits relevant to a complete economic analysis. To decide on the efficient use of forest resources requires knowledge of the total costs of providing each of the various outputs as well as the value of these goods. As this chapter emphasizes, however, many forest outputs are jointly produced, and the allocation of costs among such products is to some extent arbitrary. Furthermore, many of these goods are difficult to value in monetary terms. These difficulties imply that there can be no real resolution of the debate over below-cost sales. There will always be argument over the appropriate allocation of costs and the value of outputs. If below-cost sales are to be more clearly identified, however, effort could be productively expended in improving information about the production relationships among the various forest outputs and in the valuation of those that are unpriced.

The costs and benefits of timber sale practices considered here have been microeconomic in nature and restricted to those that occur in a closed economy. Timber and wood products, however, are internationally traded commodities, and changes in prices brought about by timber sale policies would be expected to have repercussions in trade markets as well. Increased federal stumpage prices, for instance, may lead to greater imports of Canadian lumber, which currently accounts for about one-third of all lumber used in the United States. Such trade shifts affect the international balance of payments and can subsequently affect domestic welfare through employment, interest rates, or currency values. The effect of higher stumpage prices may also be multiplied through the domestic economy beginning with their effect on industries that use wood products.

Continued public concern with below-cost sales and national forest management issues in general has prompted more legislative involvement in national forest management. Public involvement in the planning process has been solicited, and, predictably, much conflict has resulted. Whether these actions will affect timber sale policy will depend on the behavior of the Forest Service in response to public and legislative pressures. Most Forest Service employees are trained foresters, and many see their job as raising timber. In several cases forest managers continue to pursue timber production goals primarily despite outside pressures. There is enough flexibility in present appraisal practices that these actions can be disguised. For instance, the cost of hard money roads is not considered in appraising timber sales; therefore, an uneconomic sale may appear profitable on paper if appropriated funds are used to construct access roads. Although the timber production emphasis within the agency is changing, it will not be rapid. Consequently, changes in Forest Service policy regarding below-cost sales should not be expected overnight but will occur gradually as the agency adjusts to a new set of values.

REFERENCES

Behan, R. W. (1977). "National Forest Management and the Economics of Mule Hitching." *American Forests* (January):20–23.

Bolle, Arnold W. (1986). "Below-Cost Timber Sales and Montana's Long-Term Timber Supply." *Western Wildlands* (Spring):35–38.

Bowes, Michael D., John V. Krutilla, and Thomas B. Stockton (1987). *Below-Cost Timber Sales and Forest Planning*. Baltimore: Johns Hopkins University Press, for Resources for the Future.

Clawson, Marion (1975). *Forest for Whom and for What?* Baltimore: Johns Hopkins University Press, for Resources for the Future.

———(1976). *The Economics of National Forest Management*. Baltimore: Johns Hopkins University Press, for Resources for the Future, Working Paper EN-6.

———(1977). *Decision Making in Timber Production, Harvest and Marketing*. Washington, D.C.: Johns Hopkins University Press, for Resources for the Future, Research Paper R-4.

Daniels, Steven E., and Barbara J. Daniels (1986). "The Impact of Below-Cost Timber Sales on Community Stability." *Western Wildlands* (Spring): 26–30.

Eckstein, Otto (1958). "Water Resources Development: The Economics of Project Evaluation," *Harvard Economic Studies*, vol. 104.

Emerson, Peter M. (1986). "The Below-Cost Timber Sale Issue: Going Against the Grain." *Western Wildlands* (Spring):16–21.

Emerson, Peter M., and Gloria E. Helfand (1983). "Timber Supply, Community Stability and the Wilderness Scapegoat." *Western Wildlands* (Winter): 14–19.

Emerson, Peter M., Anthony T. Stout, and Deanne Kloepfer (1984). *Wasting the National Forests: Selling Federal Timber Below Cost*. Washington, D.C.: The Wilderness Society, September 1984.

Forest Industries Council (1980). *Forest Productivity Report.* Washington, D.C.: National Forest Products Association.

Hagenstein, Perry R. (1985). "Comments," in Roger Sedjo, ed., *Investments in Forestry: Resources, Land Use and Public Policy.* Boulder, Colo.: Westview Press.

Hanson, Dennis (1986). "The Rise and Demise of Forest Planning," *Sierra* (January/February):40–46.

Hyde, William F. (1984). "The Federal Preserve in the West: Environmental Champion or Economic Despoiler?" in George M. Johnston and Peter M. Emerson, eds., *Public Lands and the U.S. Economy: Balancing Conservation and Development.* Boulder, Colo.: Westview Press.

Jackson, David H. (1984). "Divestiture, Harvest Expansion and Economic Efficiency: The National Forests in the Early 1980's" in George M. Johnston and Peter M. Emerson, eds., *Public Lands and the U.S. Economy: Balancing Conservation and Development.* Boulder, Colo.: Westview Press.

McKillop, William (1978). "Economic Costs of Withdrawing Timber and Timberland from Commercial Production." *Journal of Forestry* (July):414–417.

National Trails Coalition (1985). *Our National Forests: Lands in Peril.* Washington, D.C.

Risbrudt, Christopher (1986). "The Real Issue in Below-Cost Sales: Multiple-Use Management of the Public Lands." *Western Wildlands* (Spring):2–5.

Sample, Alaric V., Jr. (1984). *Below-Cost Timber Sales on the National Forests.* Issue Brief, Economic Policy Dept., the Wilderness Society (July).

U.S. Department of Agriculture, Forest Service (1982). "An Analysis of the Timber Situation in the United States, 1952–2030." *Forest Service Report,* no. 23 (December).

————(1986). *Analysis of Costs and Revenues in the Timber Programs of Four National Forests.* Washington, D.C.

U.S. General Accounting Office (1984). *Congress Needs Better Information on Forest Service's Below-Cost Timber Sales.* Report GAO/RCED-84-96. Washington, D.C.: General Accounting Office.

U.S. Office of Technology Assessment (1983). *Wood Use, U.S. Competitiveness and Technology.* Washington, D.C.: Office of Technology Assessment.

Walker, John I. (1976). "Economic Efficiency and the National Forest Management Act of 1976." *Journal of Forestry* (November):715–718.

SUGGESTED READINGS

Bowes, Michael D., John V. Krutilla, and Thomas B. Stockton, (1987). *Below-Cost Timber Sales and Forest Planning.* Baltimore: Johns Hopkins University Press, for Resources for the Future.

The focus of this paper is primarily on the development of an accounting system capable of identifying potential below-cost sales. The separable costs of timber production are isolated in a capital accounting framework that stresses the temporal aspects of forest management expenditures and the interdependence of forest uses. The paper provides a good discussion of the problems encountered in identifying below-cost sales from an accounting standpoint.

Clawson, Marion (1975). *Forest for Whom and for What?* Baltimore: Johns Hopkins University Press, for Resources for the Future.

Although this book is not *about* below-cost sales it provides an excellent background and reference to the general problems of national forest policy. Clawson discusses the problems of designing public forest policy in the context of conflicting and incompatible uses. The book provides a good discussion of the issues of public forest management, with primary focus on the development of criteria by which forest policy should be determined. The economic analysis is largely positive in nature; Clawson's own views are apparent, but the real emphasis is on the distribution of costs and benefits of alternative policies.

Frome, Michael (1984). *The Forest Service*. Boulder, Colo.: Westview Press.
In this sympathetic, yet constructively critical assessment of the Forest Service, Michael Frome sketches its growth from its inception to its current position as an agency struggling to meet often conflicting demands. He also traces the history of the U.S. attitude toward its forests, examines global forestry concerns, and looks at the programs designed to deal with human as well as natural resources in the future. The book includes chapters on mining laws, timber harvesting, wilderness issues, environmental forestry, deforestation, the impact of government energy programs on forests, endangered wildlife and plants, and resources education.

Johnston, George M., and Peter M. Emerson, eds. (1984). *Public Lands and the U.S. Economy: Balancing Conservation and Development*. Boulder, Colo: Westview Press.
Three chapters in this book deal with timber issues on federal lands. Although the focus is primarily on the feasibility of private ownership of federal timberland, issues related to the below-cost sale issue such as the nature of timber demand and community stability are explored as well. The analyses presented are both empirical and conceptual and draw from institutional as well as neoclassical economics.

McKillop, William (1978). "Economic Costs of Withdrawing Timber and Timberland from Commercial Production," *Journal of Forestry* (July):414–417.
In this paper an economic approach is taken to identifying the costs of restricting timber harvests on private and public lands, and emphasis is given to the selection of criteria that can be used to assess such costs. The framework, once developed, is used to estimate the effects of the expansion of the Redwood National Park in California. This piece represents the views held by groups such as the forest products industry who oppose policies that appear to restrict timber supplies; the work outlines some of the economic foundations of their arguments.

Western Wildlands (1986). Missoula: Montana Forest and Conservation Experiment Station, Univ. of Montana, vol. 12, no. 1.
This special issue contains eight articles covering a range of issues related to below-cost sales. Although the point of view of these pieces is generally that of those who are critical of current timber management policies, they do present the views and arguments of one side of the controversy over public land management. The empirical and conceptual works presented here cover topics ranging from the nature of the market for timber products to the political and policy problems in dealing with below-cost sales.

STUDY QUESTIONS

1. Under what circumstances can sales of timber at below cost be justified?
2. The selling price of harvested timber has a critical role in assessing the benefits of cutting forests. If timber prices are volatile, the determination to cut or not cut can be shown to be correct or incorrect depending on the price used. As forest management requires long-term planning, what is an appropriate price to use for

planning purposes? Possible candidates include the current price, a five-year average price, and the price expected to prevail at the time of harvest.

3. Evaluate the argument that in any multiproduct production process the allocation of joint costs among the products is an arbitrary exercise.

4. How do you respond to the argument that choosing a discount rate for future forest benefits and costs is a political rather than an economic choice?

Chapter Eight

Economic Rationale in the Development of Fisheries Management
Atlantic Striped Bass

Ivar E. Strand, Jr.

Excessive harvesting has often been blamed for the drastic decline in certain fisheries as well as for the potential extinction of some fish. As a result, some governments have attempted to regulate fisheries. In this case study, The author presents the standard economic analysis of fisheries and applies the model to the Atlantic striped bass fishery. Both biological and economic objectives in fisheries management are discussed. The common property traits often found in fisheries management are reviewed along with the applications of economic efficiency, the role of stochastic physical processes, and the potential existence of irreversibilities. This chapter surveys the conventional economic theory of fisheries and demonstrates how the theory can be applied to specific policy issues for a certain species, especially the issue of species preservation.

In the last 20 years, government agencies have substantially increased their role in the harvest of seafood products. The traditional role of government as a passive trustee for fisheries resources in inland and international waters has yielded to active management of the seafood industry. Two obvious cases are the Magnuson Fisheries Conservation and Management Act (MFCMA; Public Law 94-265, 1976), which regulates fishing in waters from 3 to 200 miles from the U.S. coastline, and the emergency moratorium on the 1985 harvest of striped bass imposed by the state of Maryland.

The primary reason for the increased intervention has been the dramatic declines in certain fisheries resources, with excessive harvest usually cited as the cause. Figures 8.1 and 8.2 illustrate the harvest associated with two resource bases and the dramatic collapse of the resources. Haddock production and stocks on Georges Bank, a traditional New England offshore fishery, reached a peak in the mid-1960s and has since collapsed to a level about one-twentieth of that peak (Figure 8.1). Similarly, after a peak harvest of

FIGURE 8.1 Georges Bank Stock Size and Harvest, 1963–1985

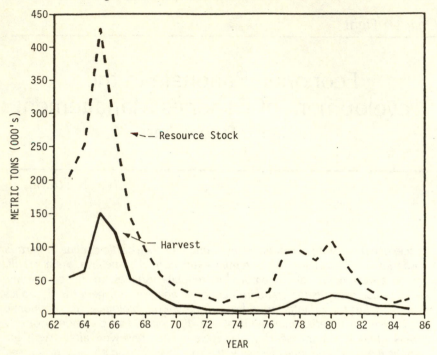

Source: U.S. Department of Commerce, *Status of Fisheries Resources Off the Northeastern United States for 1986*, NOAA Technical Memorandum NMFS-F/NEC-43, 1986.

Atlantic Coast striped bass in the early 1970s, its recruitment (new fish entering the harvestable population) and stock has since fallen (Figure 8.2). In both cases, there is an indication that a record harvest prior to the collapse was at least partially to blame for the current level of the resource stock.

Additional public involvement in fisheries resources has meant new public management decisions. Management agencies have been forced to determine the goals of regulation and the regulatory strategy to achieve those goals. Three management goals are often proposed:

1. Maximum sustainable yield (MSY)—the greatest level of production possible on a sustained basis;
2. Maximum economic yield (MEY)—the level of production yielding the greatest economic return to producers and consumers;
3. Optimum yield (OY)—maximum sustainable yield as modified by relevant biological, economic, and social considerations.

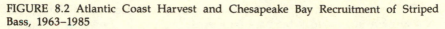

FIGURE 8.2 Atlantic Coast Harvest and Chesapeake Bay Recruitment of Striped Bass, 1963–1985

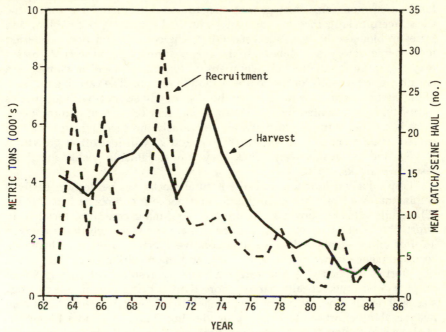

Source: U.S. Department of Commerce, *Status of Fisheries Resources Off the Northeastern United States for 1986*, NOAA Technical Memorandum NMFS-F/NEC-43, 1986.

Unfortunately, a statement of goals does not ensure a successful management program. The strategies to achieve the objectives are critical links between what exists and what could be. Strategies are needed that cope with unusual characteristics of specific fisheries. The process that determines strategies is evolving as are the institutions that manage the resources. Initial insights about fisheries management are provided by conventional economic theory of fisheries.

ECONOMIC EFFICIENCY IN FISHERIES PRODUCTION (MEY)

The Economic Argument for Regulation

The literature on the economically efficient level of fishery production is extensive and thorough (e.g., Gordon, 1954; Scott, 1955). Authors have concentrated on management to achieve either the economically efficient level of fishing input (effort) or output (production). Although inputs are discussed here, later arguments address the efficient level of output rather than input. This development is more easily related to the concept of the sustainable yield.

The underlying biology of the ecosystem is represented in Figure 8.3. Net growth in the stock biomass (aggregate weight) is shown as a concave function of stock size. Net growth constitutes new biomass entering the stock (recruitment), increase in the weight of the existing population, and losses in biomass due to natural mortality. The concave function is referred to as compensatory growth because the average growth of the stock decreases over the entire range of stock. Competition for limited food or cannibalism are among the reasons for the compensation in growth. The carrying capacity of the environment, how much stock the system will support without species mortality, is represented by B_{CC}. When production or harvest is introduced, there is another form of mortality, and obviously the carrying capacity will no longer be attained. Harvests of Y_A, Y_B, and Y_S will just offset growth at B_A, B_B, and B_S, respectively. Thus they are sustainable yields for those respective stocks.

The production function from the natural stocks can be derived easily if we assume fixed proportions in inputs and hence a composite input, effort (E), results. This is shown in Figure 8.4. Assuming constant efficiency in effort, the level of output that can be sustained indefinitely with a given level of effort—sustained yield—is a concave function of effort. There is a correspondence between a level of effort and the resulting stock size. When no effort is applied (E_0), the carrying capacity results. Extreme levels of effort (E_D) will theoretically harvest more than is being grown, a zero stock size will result, and the output sustainable at E_D will be zero. Additional insights about effort can be obtained by viewing Figures 8.3 and 8.4 together. High levels of effort (E_B) can result in diminished stock (B_B) but a sustainable stock (Y_B). The maximum sustained yield or harvest is obtained with E_S effort and resulting stock size B_S. At all of the sustainable yields, the net growth in the stock is equal to harvest, the condition necessary for sustaining the harvest level.

In a production sense, notice that as effort has increased in the interval E_0 to E_S, its marginal product falls. The source associated with the decline in marginal productivity is the lower size of stock as effort increased. Thus, there are really three elements contained in Figure 8.4, with the third representing the equilibrium stock. The reason it is possible to obtain the same level of output (Y_A) with different levels of effort ($E_A < E_B$) is because the higher effort has led to a smaller stock ($B_B < B_A$). Larger stocks of fish make it easier to harvest fish. The fish stock has productivity in the sense that it makes harvest easier.

Comparison of yields associated with effort E_A and E_B illustrates another point—negative marginal productivity of effort. After level E_S, effort has negative productivity. Increases in effort, although increasing short-term production, will deplete the stock so that the long-run sustained yield will be lower than the initial yield. If stock were a controlled input, this possibility would be precluded. Rising stock scarcity would raise the price of access to stock and prevent effort from exceeding E_S. However, in many fisheries, access is not controlled and negative marginal productivity of effort can result.

FIGURE 8.3 Compensatory Biological Growth

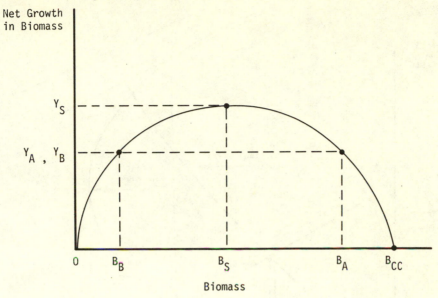

FIGURE 8.4 Sustained Yield–Effort Relationship

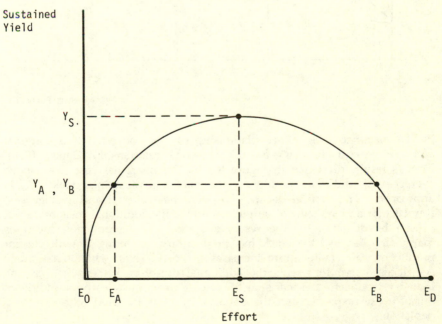

FIGURE 8.5 Average and Marginal Cost Curves for Fishery

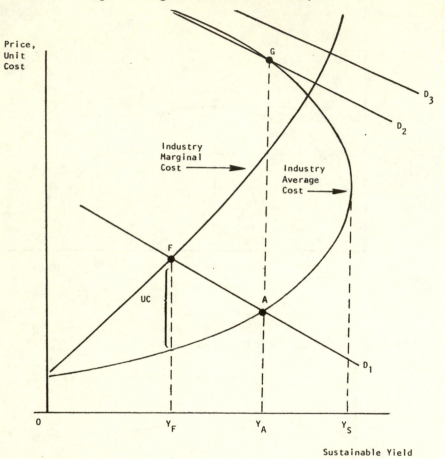

The sustained yield–effort relationship can be converted into marginal and average costs by using a total cost–effort relationship (Copes, 1970). Copes's result, presented in Figure 8.5, is that marginal cost rises above average cost and rises rapidly as the maximum sustained yield (Y_S) is approached. The vertical distance between the marginal and average cost (say UC) for a given level of output represents the additional costs of output caused by depletion of the resource stocks when production increases marginally. Because the stock has productivity, depleting it with current production can create future increases in costs. Thus, while the average social cost curve represents the additional out-of-pocket expenses of the industry producers, the marginal social cost curve includes both additional out-of-pocket expenses and the opportunity costs incurred with increased depletion.

The parabolic shape of the average cost depicts a possibility that normally is not considered in economic production—an industry operating with a negative marginal product of inputs. Average costs of producing Y_A can be as low as $Y_A - A$ and as high as $Y_A - G$, depending on the size of the resource stock. Trying to expand production beyond Y_S causes production costs to rise but output to fall because of stock depletion. Clearly, no rational manager of the industry would attempt to expand production beyond Y_S but the institutional arrangement may cause *individuals* within the industry to be motivated so that the sum of individual effects exceed Y_S.

This can be illustrated by examining the situation at the intersection of D_1 and the average cost curve (point A). Here, the industry revenues are equal to industry costs (including normal profits), and thus there is no incentive to exit or enter the industry. This competitive equilibrium can be contrasted with the economically efficient level where price equals marginal social cost (point F). Without fishery management, the higher future costs of smaller stocks cannot be taken into consideration by the individual fisherman. Thus the user costs are external to the firm, and the industry is led to overexploit the stocks. The economic loss arises because fish stocks as an input are too small, and thus some of their productivity is lost. If demand rises sufficiently (say to D_2), each firm will try to expand production by adding new inputs. Price is in excess of average costs so entry may occur. The long-run result may be no increase in yield although higher prices and costs result (point G).

Economists have argued that either taxation or property rights changes are needed to achieve the economically efficient level of production, Y_F. The argument is subtle because there are a number of approaches that can force production to be at Y_F. For example, a simple dictum that the fishery will be closed once a quota of Y_F is reached will achieve the desired level of production. The problem with this solution is that it will not be achieved in a manner that minimizes costs to society. Quotas normally cause the entire average cost curve to shift. When there is a profit margin caused by the difference between price and average cost (UC at Y_F), firms in the industry will be driven to try to harvest more of the quota or firms will enter the industry through transfer or construction of vessels. The inefficiencies of the new effort are exhibited in higher average costs, hence the shift in the average cost curve. Additional new efforts cease once the difference between price and average cost are eliminated at the quota level of production. The inefficient effort with new investment represents lost opportunities for the nation in other sectors.

The distinction between regulations preserving efficiency and an open-access quota system can be seen easily. A tax of UC will increase the average cost of production to such a level that no new entry will be entertained. Likewise, property rights with quota Y_F will take on a value to the holder of the right equal to UC. In both cases, average costs rise to prevent new entry, yet the schemes do not draw resources from the rest of the nation to achieve production of the quota. Thus, there may be substantial gains from using taxes or property rights to achieve the desired level of production.

Biological and Economic Objectives

A biologist might argue that maximum economic yield (MEY) is not the appropriate harvest objective in a fishery. Often, biologists view the objective as obtaining the most food from the sea. Maximum sustained yield (MSY) is the commonly espoused harvest goal, and, surprisingly, it is consistent with MEY in certain circumstances. Those circumstances are enumerated below. Also it is shown that although MEY and MSY may be the same value, strategies to reach them can be efficient or inefficient.

Take, for example, MSY, shown as point Y_S in Figure 8.5. Clearly, as demand increases (say D_1 to D_2), the intersection of the demand curve and the marginal cost curve (point F) approaches production level Y_S. In the limit, the output level for MEY is the same as for the MSY objective. Thus, MEY and MSY objectives converge under conditions of increasing demand. Another circumstance that will equate MSY and MEY occurs when the opportunity costs of fishery labor and capital are low. In this case, the actual expenses of fishing may not be a good indicator of the social cost of fishing. The social cost is lower, drawing the social marginal cost curve lower and its intersection with demand (point F) toward the right and MSY (Y_S). Extreme immobility of the resources leads to an MEY that equals MSY.

In both instances, however, the same objective does not imply the same means or regulations used to achieve it. Cutting back production requires a rise in a firm's average cost. Regulations such as quotas do not immediately raise average cost enough to ensure that more expenditures are not undertaken on new vessels or inputs for existing vessels. To ensure that resources are not wasted, transferable property rights for parts of the quota or a taxing scheme must be employed. Only in this way will the incentives to increase production or to enter the fishery be lowered.

Stochastic Considerations

Thus far, we have treated fishery production as completely deterministic, with no uncertainty in either the biological or economic system. This model is far from the reality of these systems. One has to consider how uncertainty and randomness alters the management problem.

One important point made by Hanneson (1984) is that the uncertainty that exists in the mind of the individual fisherman can contribute to less investment, and therefore production can come closer to the MEY (in some average sense). Each fisherman, in comparing income from alternative employment or investment, may consider not only the average payoff from fishing but also how much the income will vary from year to year. In general, a person or firm will prefer a career or enterprise that has a steady income to a career or enterprise whose income fluctuates. This preference has been established for fishermen also (Bockstael and Opaluch, 1983). There are therefore fewer participants in the industry than there would be if riskiness were not present. The riskiness of the business thus reduces the potential for overharvest. One clear implication is that one must not lessen the risk for fishermen if the common property nature of fishing is not removed. Income subsidies or guaranteed loan programs do nothing more than attract more unwanted effort.

Another impact on fishery production is the effect of randomness. McKelvey (1983) has argued that randomness can lead to inappropriate types of vessels, especially in a common property, multiple species fishery. Consider two fisheries, each with specialized boats. As demand grows, the resource bases are depleted, and the advantages of specialization diminish. When growth (e.g., recruitment) is random, it may pay to develop a general, all-purpose vessel that can switch between the two stocks. The strategy would be to redirect away from the relatively poor stock. Thus, common property and randomness combine to reduce the advantages of specialization. Too many general vessels result.

Management, therefore, should be aware of the necessary change in the multipurpose and specific fleet mix as the resource stock is rebuilt. Either incentives for proper capital structure could be introduced or the need to allow more specialized vessels over time could be acknowledged directly. This is not to say that multipurpose vessels should be excluded. They play a critical role relative to the uncertainty. Anytime an unusually large stock occurs (because of random processes), the multipurpose vessels help to harvest it before natural events, such as mortality, cause it to decline. Thus there is a role for both types of vessels, but the amount of each will vary depending on whether the resource is managed.

Extinction and Irreversibility Considerations

The potential for irreversible effects from management decisions influences rational strategies for harvesting renewable resources (e.g., Berck, 1979; Arrow and Fisher, 1974; Spence, 1973). In fisheries, there are two distinct situations in which irreversible decisions are potential: the entry of vessels into a fishery and the extinction of a species. Each will be considered separately.

The first potential irreversibility results from the nature of capital invested in fisheries and the typical political regime associated with fisheries management. The capital stock (vessels) tends to depreciate in an extremely slow fashion. There are vessels currently operating that were built shortly after the Civil War. The political reluctance to remove vessels from a fishery and the stochastic nature of recruitment can cause management problems. Unusually good recruitment can rapidly attract investment in an open access fishery. The investment does not exit with the speed that it entered. The result can be a continually declining or lower than desired resource base.

To appreciate the second potentially irreversible decision, consider Figure 8.5 under open access conditions and with demand D_3. There is no circumstance (level of stock) under which average costs are greater than or equal to price. It always pays individuals within the fishery to continue to harvest until the stock is driven to an irreversible size of zero—extinction. Without a parent population, there is no natural growth. As the natural system will not change from this state, it is biologically irreversible. The condition that caused the irreversible change and extinction was the open access nature of the fishery.

Reproductive characteristics of certain species suggests a growth relationship different from the usual concave (compensatory) growth relationship shown in Figure 8.3. For these species, the average growth of the stock is not always decreasing as stock size increases. Average growth might be expected to increase with increasing stock at low levels of stock, a condition referred to as depensatory growth. Costs of searching for a mate or propensity to spawn in groups might lead to this phenomenon. The effect of increasing average growth is to heighten the potential for stock extinction. If harvest is in excess of growth, stocks will decline at a more rapid rate than they would with compensatory growth. Small reductions in harvest, while potentially reversing a decline in stocks with compensatory growth, will be inadequate to halt a decline with depensatory growth. Without a radical, quantum decrease in harvest, stocks will be driven to extinction.

Finally, it is possible that growth is characterized by a range in which net growth becomes negative. If, for example, reproduction became extremely small at small stock size, natural mortality could make net growth in stocks negative. Allowing stocks to reach the critical threshold of negative growth implies extinction and an irreversible decision in the most tragic sense of the word. Once stocks fall in this range, nothing can be done to prevent extinction.

The possibility of extinction can evoke resource values not discussed previously. Objects can have value separate from consumption. A major tenet of Western culture is that despoiling nature is bad. Extinction represents the extreme spoilage. Thus, we value the existence of a species even though we do not personally use it. The willingness to pay to avoid loss of a resource is referred to as existence value.

The importance of nonconsumptive values in the presence of potential extinction lies in the costs associated with certain courses of action. Without nonconsumptive values, it might make sense to harvest the last fish of a species. However, if nonconsumptive values are present, the cost of consuming the last unit of the resource includes all of the future nonconsumptive values that would be forgone. It seems implausible that the value from present consumption of one fish could exceed these costs.

Unfortunately, the potential for extinction is normally clouded with uncertainty. The causes of declining fishery resources are often open to debate and the effects of different courses of action are known only in an extremely general sense. The comparative static analysis is of little usefulness here, and the economic analysis necessary to determine an "efficient" solution is shrouded with very limiting caveats.

Bishop (1978) suggested that economic rationality in the presence of grave uncertainty might be obtained using game theory (Luce and Raiffa, 1957).

Rather than trying to obtain MEY, the manager is cast in a game of chance with nature as the opponent. A conservative course of action (e.g., severe restrictions on production) may economically damage present producers and consumers, but it may also maintain stocks or increase stocks greatly. A more liberal course that imposed few restrictions has a higher current return, but stocks might be lost entirely. If the manager chose to avoid the maximum possible loss, then the conservative course of action would be taken. There are, of course, more refinements possible in the game structure, but the notion of avoidance of maximum losses has its appeal, particularly in the political arena. People would much rather be known for actions that maintain a status quo than for inaction that leads to disaster. One could consider this approach as an optimal yield (OY), given the uncertainties of the biological system and the motives of the political system.

THE MANAGEMENT OF ATLANTIC STRIPED BASS:
A CASE STUDY

The concepts introduced above, particularly the difficulty of managing a fugitive resource that is subject to extinction, are directly applicable to the management of the Atlantic striped bass fishery. Management takes place at a state level, but the habitat of the fish is not set by political jurisdictions. For a state such as Maryland, where the fishery is important for both sport and commercial reasons, there are strong incentives to manage the resource. However, local efforts are limited in their effectiveness by an inability to control access to the fish while it is in other jurisdictions and the resulting uncertain impact of state programs on the stock of striped bass and the welfare of local fishermen. In addition, limited knowledge of the behavior of the fish adds more uncertainty to the problem.

Rapid declines in the striped bass population, with an associated increase in the effort required to catch the fish, suggested that overfishing was taking place and that extinction was a possibility. The need for an integrated management program by all jurisdictions where the fish were harvested was apparent if the population of striped bass was to be rebuilt. This requirement necessitated coordinated action to limit harvests, especially in Maryland as it manages the main spawning area.

The moratorium on the 1986 harvest in Maryland waters represents the culmination of a process lasting more than a decade. Prior to 1978, there had been eight years of poor recruitment in the Chesapeake Bay (Figure 8.2), and consideration was being given to the enhancement of stocks through hatchery activities as well as through increased management. The following section provides background on the striped bass resource and traces the history of intervention by state and federal agencies since 1978. Where appropriate, the economic aspects of problems and policies are given.

Background Biology

The striped bass is native to the Atlantic and Gulf coasts of North America. In the north, it is generally referred to as a striper or linesider. In the south it is commonly called a rockfish. The species was artificially stocked on the West Coast in the late 1800s and is still present there. The striped bass is an anadromous species, spawning in freshwater rivers but living much of its life in the coastal saltwater. Adults will go upstream to spawn in the early spring and return to coastal saline waters in the late spring. The bays, river mouths, and ocean are all potential habitats for overwintering stripers.

There are currently three major stocks of striped bass on the Atlantic Coast: the Chesapeake Bay, the Hudson River, and the Roanoke River stocks (Figure 8.6). The Chesapeake Bay offers spawning and nursery grounds for a distinct striped bass population that yields up to 90 percent of the commercial catch taken on the Atlantic. Stripers that are less than two years old and some three- and four-year-olds, live solely in the Chesapeake, whereas nearly all of the older females and some of the older males migrate to the waters off of New England in the late spring. The age of maturity of striped bass varies, but a conservative estimate is that males are mature by age four and females by age six. The size of a mature male will be in excess of 15 inches, the female in excess of 20 inches.

The Hudson River and Roanoke River stocks each contribute less to the coastal stock than the Chesapeake, but they can be important in certain years, especially with low Chesapeake stocks. The Roanoke River stocks tend to be more provincial, staying largely within the confines of Albemarle Sound during their adult life. There is also some evidence that the migratory range of Hudson River stocks is not as extensive as the Chesapeake stocks (from Delaware Bay to Cape Cod). Thus, the range of the Chesapeake stock exposes the migratory age classes to exploitation from more fishermen in more Atlantic Coast states than other states.

Markets

Large wholesale markets perform an important role in the distribution of striped bass. New York's Fulton market is critical in distributing striped bass into the New York metropolitan area and the Baltimore market into the Baltimore-Washington metropolitan area. Between 1972 and 1978 these two markets distributed between 50 percent and 75 percent of the total reported Atlantic Coast landings of striped bass. It is generally believed that the Fulton market establishes the "industry price" for striped bass, the price from which middlemen will compute marketing margins. The central markets therefore facilitate price establishment and the transmission of critical economic information.

Central markets also increase the competitiveness among fishermen in different states. That is, a 12-inch striped bass not caught by a Maryland gill netter may migrate to Massachusetts waters and be caught by someone there. Now, in addition to not catching the fish, the Maryland fishermen further suffers as the Massachusetts's catch enters the Fulton market and depresses prices throughout the region. A 10 percent increase in northern landings was found to decrease the Maryland price by about 10 percent. A similar transmission occurs from Maryland landings to northern prices.

FIGURE 8.6 Major East Coast Spawning Areas for Striped Bass

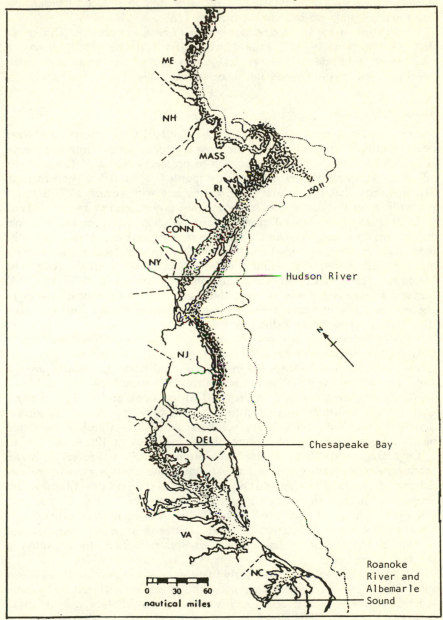

Source: U.S. Department of Commerce, *Biological and Fisheries Data on Striped Bass,*
Morone saxatilis *(Walbaum),* U.S. National Marine Fisheries Service Technical Series
Report No. 4, May 1977.

In fact, it was found that 60 percent of the doubling of the Rhode Island price between 1973 and 1979 could be attributed to reduced Chesapeake Bay catch (Strand, Norton, and Adriance, 1980).

Growth in per capita income was found to be an important "shifter" of demand during the 1970s (Strand, Norton, and Adriance, 1980). Maryland, New Jersey, and Rhode Island were found to have positive income elasticities. The increasing income raised the price substantially during the period.

Management Issues

Striped bass, like most fish species in the United States, traditionally have been controlled through state fishery management groups although there is a trend for a more regional approach to problems. The U.S. Constitution affords to states all powers not explicitly granted to the federal government. The authority that the federal government has with regard to fish arises primarily from the commerce, treaty-making power, and property clauses.

Until 1976, most federal management was expressed in international agreements to which the United States was a cosignatory. In addition, the federal government provided funds through grants to facilitate state management for species that could not be managed by a single state. The Magnuson Fisheries Conservation and Management Act of 1976 (MFCMA) initiated a more active role for the federal government by establishing eight regional councils to manage fisheries stocks predominately caught within the 3–200 mile exclusive fishing zone.

Because striped bass are not predominantly caught within the exclusive fishing zone, regulations have been decided at the prerogative of Atlantic Coast states. Table 8.1 shows the myriad of regulations that existed around 1980. Essentially, the fishermen in northern states from New York to Maine capturing migrating stocks were required to use hook and line (normally a gear used by sportfishermen) and to keep fish only in excess of 16 inches. Southern states from New Jersey southward to North Carolina permitted nearly all gear and allowed capture of fish in excess of 12 inches.

Organized in 1972 by federal legislation, the State/Federal Fisheries Management program exists to facilitate interstate management of inshore fisheries. A program was established around 1978 (Striped Bass Management Project) to manage the striped bass on a regional basis. The organization consisted of a board composed primarily of individual state managers, a scientific and statistical committee, and a citizen's advisory board. It was through this organization that the problem was brought to the attention of the U.S. Congress.

The U.S. Congress recognized early that research was necessary to address several questions. The regional nature of the resource suggested that greater federal intervention was necessary. Why, after all, should Maryland undertake to research the problem when the northern states would derive many of the benefits from the acquired knowledge and subsequent action? To help the states address the problem, an Emergency Striped Bass Study was funded in 1979, which provided funds to examine the status of stocks, to identify

TABLE 8.1:   Summary of Size Limit Regulations for Atlantic
             Striped Bass Harvest

| Management Unit | Size Limit (in inches) | | Additional Information |
	Min.	Max.	
Massachusetts	24	None	---
Rhode Island	16	None	---
Connecticut	16	None	Sport fish only -- sale of fish caught outside state water permitted
New York	16	None	---
New Jersey	18	None	---
Delaware	12	None	20 lbs. maximum size in Delaware Bay
Maryland[a]	12	32	Some closed seasons in spawning areas
Potomac River	12	32	Two fish greater than 32" may be caught per day per person -- no sale of these allowed
Virginia	14	40	One fish greater than 40" may be caught per day per person -- no sale of these allowed
Washington, D.C.			All fish sold must have been legally harvested
North Carolina	12	None	---

[a]   North of Howell Point, the Taylor Island line, the minimum is
     14 inches.

the causes for the observed declines in catch, and to analyze the economic effects of the declines.

What was not known was the cause of the decline. From Figure 8.5, one could easily have argued that demand increased, raising price and decreasing stocks and their growth. That line of argument stressed overfishing as the cause. This conclusion, however, is still not defensible after eight years of research.

The problem is that changes in the environment occurred coincidentally with the increasing demand. Substantial increases in nutrient-loading in the 1970s is held responsible for a dramatic decline in the abundance of Chesapeake Bay submerged aquatic vegetation. The vegetation is the nursery grounds for striped bass, and its loss may have increased mortality for juvenile striped bass. Thus, the appropriate value for MEY and MSY is not known, nor is it necessarily the right concept to be using in this circumstance. The concept of optimal yield was considered a better one to apply in this case.

The economic effects were addressed directly because of existing data and regional models. One study (Norton, Smith, and Strand, 1983) concluded that the 1979–1980 fishing activity related to striped bass generated nearly 12 million dollars of economic benefits to users, two-thirds of which was associated with recreational activity. The investigators also determined that over 200 million dollars in economic activity and 7,500 jobs were lost as the result of the decline in the resource from 1974 to 1980. These figures clearly established the economic importance of the resource.

Management Approach

The question still remained as to the appropriate course of management, both with regard to what was to be done and who was to do it. In 1981, the Striped Bass Board recommended to the participating states a plan that raised the minimum size limit to 14 inches in the producing areas of Albemarle Sound, Chesapeake and Delaware bays (and their tributaries), and the Hudson River. It also raised the limit to 24 inches in the coastal fishery. Furthermore, the spawning areas were closed to fishing during spawning season, and any maximum size limits imposed by states would remain in effect.

With the limited adoption of the recommendations, spawning success in the Chesapeake remained at a minimal level (see Figure 8.2). The survey index exceeded five only twice (1978 and 1982), and the recruitment average from 1979 to 1984 was the lowest for any five years on record. The only bright spot was the 1982 age class, which was about the 20-year average for recruitment.

The absence of successful spawning led the state/federal group to recommend greater restrictions on harvesting. Additional measures were proposed to reduce total fishing mortality by 55 percent and eliminate 95 percent of the fishing mortality on the 1982 age-class females. States were encouraged to apply any regulations to achieve the goal and to raise the minimum size limit on stripers to keep a fisherman from harvesting the 1982 age class. Typically, a state would have to have a 20-inch limit in 1985, a 24-inch limit in 1986, a 31-inch limit in 1987, and so forth.

In order to provide an additional incentive to states, Congress passed legislation in 1984 (Public Law 98-613, the Atlantic Striped Bass Conservation Act) enabling the federal government to impose a complete ban on striped bass harvest in states found not in compliance with the recommendations. To date, there has only been the implied threat of sanctions but that has been sufficient to compel states into active management.

Some states have taken rather dramatic action. Maryland has had a complete ban in effect since January 1985. The justification for the action was based on the state's endangered species legislation. In addition, it is illegal to possess striped bass in Maryland, which halts any attempt at striped bass aquaculture or importation into Maryland. The legislation appears to minimize the likelihood of extinction of striped bass and also the cost of enforcement.

AN ASSESSMENT

Looking back on the evolution of striped bass management, the determination and commitment of the participants is impressive, even if the results are not. It has been a controlled process that has afforded states their constitutional right while preserving the important role of the federal government. Many now believe the stage is set for a major comeback in spawning success.

Economics functioned in shaping the policies in several ways. First, economic analysis was used to justify the intervention. There appeared to be significant economic gains to make the issue worthy of government intervention. Secondly, the economic competition among states made independent intervention by state governments unlikely and unworkable. If intervention was to be undertaken, the federal government had to intercede to facilitate the actions. Finally, the dramatic actions taken by some states to eliminate harvest suggests a strategy to avoid maximum potential losses.

The process, however, is not over and a most difficult period remains. To date, the regulations have been enacted in an emergency, when stocks were low and no one had too much to lose. The regulations hurt everyone slightly, and the issue of how to allocate the stocks was easy to determine: No one received much. As stocks return, however, we face a tougher "allocation" question.

In an efficiency sense, the allocation decision may be the one to which economics offers the greatest contribution. User charges and property rights to a fixed quota have been suggested as efficient strategies to achieve management objectives. Resources will not be wasted if these strategies are employed. Economic efficiency also would require relatively fewer part-time or all-purpose vessels and more specialized vessels.

However, the irony may be that the interpersonal economics of the allocation decision makes the logic of economic efficiency irrelevant. Whose ox is being gored becomes more important than questions of wasted resources in the economy. The political process that worked reasonably well when no one had much to lose may not work well when there are many rivals for a potentially valuable resource. Thus, even though the striped bass resource will be conserved by government intervention, it is unlikely that efficient methods of management will follow when the emergency passes. The strategy to manage the striped bass fishery will likely be a political compromise with economic efficiency having only marginal significance.

If this prediction is realized, the striped bass management process will be even more representative of the fishery management process. A resource base collapsed, causing hardship among the users but also causing profits to be sufficiently low for management to be accepted. Economics is used to justify the intervention. However, once the regulations have returned the resource to a safe level, economic efficiency arguments become secondary to the political agenda.

REFERENCES

Arrow, K. J., and A. C. Fisher (1974). "Environmental Preservation, Uncertainty and Irreversibility." *Quarterly Journal of Economics* 88:312–319.

Berck, P. (1979). "Open Access and Extinction." *Econometrica* 47:877–882.

Bishop, R. C. (1978). "Endangered Species and Uncertainty: The Economics of a Safe Minimum Standard." *American Journal of Agricultural Economics* 60:10–19.

Bockstael, N. E., and J. J. Opaluch (1983). "Discrete Modelling of Supply Response Under Uncertainty: The Case of a Fishery." *Journal of Environmental Economics and Management* 10:125–137.

Boreman, J. (1983). "Simulation of Striped Bass Egg and Larva Development Based on Temperature." *Transactions of the American Fisheries Society* 112:286–292.

Copes, P. (1970). "The Backward Bending Supply Curve of the Fishing Industry." *Scottish Journal of Political Economy* 35:69–77.

Gordon, H. S. (1954). "The Economic Theory of a Common Property Resource." *Journal of Political Economy* 62:124–142.

Hanneson, R. (1984). "Fisheries Management and Uncertainty." *Marine Resource Economics* 1:89–97.

Kohlenstein, L. C. (1980). "Aspects of the Population Dynamics of Striped Bass (*Morone saxitilis*) Spawning in Maryland Tributaries of the Chesapeake Bay." Ph.D. diss., Johns Hopkins University, Baltimore, Md.

Luce, R. D., and H. Raiffa (1957). *Games and Decisions*. New York: John Wiley and Sons.

McKelvey, R. (1983). "The Fishery in a Fluctuating Environment: Coexistence of Specialist and Generalist Fishing Vessels in a Multipurpose Fleet." *Journal of Environmental Economics and Management* 10:287–310.

Norton, V. J., T. P. Smith, and I. E. Strand (1983). *Stripers: The Economic Value of the Atlantic Coast Commercial and Recreational Striped Bass Fishery*. University of Maryland Sea Grant, UM-SG-TS-83-12, 54 pp.

Scott, A. D. (1955). "The Fishery: The Objectives of Sole Ownership." *Journal of Political Economy* 63:116–124.

Spence, A. M. (1973). "Blue Whales and Applied Control Theory" in H. W. Gottinger, ed., *Systems Approaches and Environmental Problems*. Gottingen, F.R.G.: Vandenhoeck and Ruprecht.

Strand, E. E., V. J. Norton, and J. G. Adriance (1980). "Economic Aspects of Commercial Striped Bass Harvest." *Marine Recreational Fisheries* 5:51–62.

U.S. Department of Commerce (1977). *Biological and Fisheries Data on Striped Bass, 'Morone saxatilis' (Walbaum)*. U.S. National Marine Fisheries Service Technical Series Report no. 4.

U.S. Department of Commerce (1986). *Status of Fisheries Resources Off the Northeastern United States for 1986*. NOAA Technical Memorandum NMFS-F/NEC-43.

SUGGESTED READINGS

Acheson, James (1975). "The Lobster Fiefs: Economic and Ecological Effects of Territoriality in the Maine Lobster Industry." *Human Ecology* 3(3):183–207.

This paper offers an interesting description and analysis of unsanctioned property rights. The argument is offered that Maine "harbor gangs" enforce two different types of implicit property rights around islands in the Gulf of Maine. The effects on lobster populations and prices of the two types of rights are examined.

Anderson, Lee G., ed. (1981). *Economic Analysis for Fisheries Management Plans.* Ann Arbor, Mich.: Ann Arbor Science Publ., Inc. 318 pp.

This compendium of readings is directed toward problems inherent in managing specific fisheries. A breadth of problems, analyses, and issues is presented. Students will obtain an appreciation of the need to understand specifics of a fishery in order to assess policy alternatives.

Bell, Frederick (1972). "Technological Externalities and Common Property Resources: An Empirical Study of Northern Lobster." *Journal of Political Economy* 80:148–158.

This paper presents another look at the Northern Lobster industry. The author assesses the losses inherent in what he assumes is an open access fishery. He finds the harvest to be close to MSY and shows that a 50 percent reduction in effort would cause only a 20 percent reduction in catch. It is interesting to compare his results with the results in Acheson.

Norton, V. J., T. P. Smith, and I. E. Strand (1983). *Stripers: The Economic Value of the Atlantic Coast Commercial and Recreational Striped Bass Fishery.* University of Maryland Sea Grant, UM-SG-TS-83-12. 54 pp.

This report gives a thorough discussion of the economic importance of Atlantic Coast striped bass. Economic valuation and impact analysis procedures are presented and applied to the Atlantic Coast striped bass fishery. The effects of major policy changes are examined.

STUDY QUESTIONS

1. Under what circumstances is maximum sustainable yield equivalent to maximum economic yield?

2. How do the problems of managing an essentially nonrenewable resource compare to managing renewable resources like fisheries? Draw examples from earlier chapters.

3. Relate the conflicting interests of sport and commercial fishermen in the striped bass fishery to the issues of multiple use and sustained yield discussed for forest management in Chapter 7.

4. The parabolic average-cost curve in Figure 8.5 is not typical of most industries. Why is it relevant to a fishery and not relevant to industries such as manufacturing or agriculture?

Chapter Nine

Dividing the Waters
Designing Management Institutions
for the Columbia River

Philip Wandschneider

Allocating the water from rivers entails choices that can affect hydroelectric power, commercial and recreational fishing, agricultural irrigation, transportation, and recreational uses and other resource decisions. The author analyzes the conflicts that have arisen over some of these alternative uses in the Columbia–Snake River system. An economic analysis of water allocation institutions that incorporates the concept of efficiency is applied to centralized and decentralized management systems. The chapter provides a framework for analyzing institutional alternatives for managing a complex natural resource with multiple, often conflicting, user groups.

A major river system can be the lifeblood of a region. Such is the case for the Columbia–Snake River system in the Pacific Northwest (see Figure 9.1). Its waters are used to produce agricultural products on more than 5 million acres, generate three-quarters of the electricity in the Pacific Northwest, and provide habitat for a large commercial and recreational fishery. Its waters also form a highway for commerce to ports in central and eastern Washington and 465 river miles inland to northern Idaho. Finally, the river system and its environs directly sustain numerous aesthetic, recreational, and, for some, even religious experiences. Dividing the waters of such a major river system among its various uses has serious social and economic implications for a region.

ALLOCATING WATER

River Characteristics and Allocation Problems

The procedure for allocating the stream flow of the Columbia or any other river among its various uses can be viewed as a two-stage process. Consider the problem of allocating one year's streamflow. First, it must be determined

FIGURE 9.1 Columbia/Snake River Basin: Hydropower Projects and Primary Future Irrigation Areas

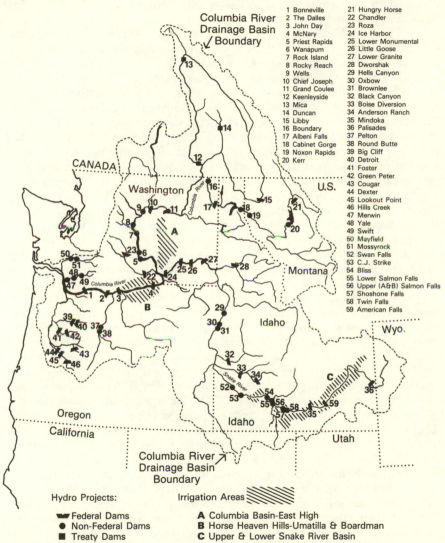

1	Bonneville	21	Hungry Horse
2	The Dalles	22	Chandler
3	John Day	23	Roza
4	McNary	24	Ice Harbor
5	Priest Rapids	25	Lower Monumental
6	Wanapum	26	Little Goose
7	Rock Island	27	Lower Granite
8	Rocky Reach	28	Dworshak
9	Wells	29	Hells Canyon
10	Chief Joseph	30	Oxbow
11	Grand Coulee	31	Brownlee
12	Keenleyside	32	Black Canyon
13	Mica	33	Boise Diversion
14	Duncan	34	Anderson Ranch
15	Libby	35	Mindoka
16	Boundary	36	Palisades
17	Albeni Falls	37	Pelton
18	Cabinet Gorge	38	Round Butte
19	Noxon Rapids	39	Big Cliff
20	Kerr	40	Detroit
		41	Foster
		42	Green Peter
		43	Cougar
		44	Dexter
		45	Lookout Point
		46	Hills Creek
		47	Merwin
		48	Yale
		49	Swift
		50	Mayfield
		51	Mossyrock
		52	Swan Falls
		53	C.J. Strike
		54	Bliss
		55	Lower Salmon Falls
		56	Upper (A&B) Salmon Falls
		57	Shoshone Falls
		58	Twin Falls
		59	American Falls

Hydro Projects:

⚓ Federal Dams
● Non-Federal Dams
■ Treaty Dams

Irrigation Areas ▨

A Columbia Basin-East High
B Horse Heaven Hills-Umatilla & Boardman
C Upper & Lower Snake River Basin

Source: P. R. Wandschneider, "Who Controls the Water? Managing the Columbia–Snake River," Bulletin PNW 249 (Pullman, Wash.: Washington State University Cooperative Extension, 1985), p. 2.

how much water is allocated to consumptive uses such as irrigation and municipal and industrial water supplies, and how much is to remain in the stream to be allocated to nonconsumptive uses such as hydropower production, fish habitat, recreation, and waterborne transport. Next, the water allocated to consumptive and instream uses must be divided among the individual uses and users.

Dividing the block of water assigned to consumptive uses is relatively straightforward and similar in many ways to dividing the annual output of corn or coal. The water can be subdivided into parcels of any desired size and allocated for the exclusive use of a particular individual or group. One complication is that the total block of water is available in a fixed quantity. It cannot readily be augmented in the way production of coal can be increased through increased effort in response to increases in demand. It is similar in this respect to the annual output of a crop such as corn, except that corn output can be changed from year to year, if not within a year. A more fundamental problem with streamflows is that water is available at predetermined sites and is quite expensive to transport. These two circumstances combine to place strict limits on how much water is available and at what location. Finally, water diverted for consumption has one more characteristic that complicates allocation: Not all water diverted is totally consumed. Some proportion of the water seeps through the ground and emerges in some downhill location at some later time. These return flows, which are usually of altered quality, become available for allocation to additional consumptive or instream uses.

The block of water allocated for instream flows poses a different set of problems partly because instream uses are largely nonconsumptive. For instance, use of the streamflow for fishery habitat leaves it available for hydropower, recreation, and transportation. The streamflow possesses the quality of a joint-impact good: Use for one purpose does not reduce quantity available for other uses. One might think at first that this joint-impact nature would eliminate conflict among instream users. On closer examination one finds a number of allocational issues. The first is that annual streamflow is allocated over time by adding and withdrawing from storage reservoirs. This intertemporal allocation occurs on an annual, seasonal, weekly, daily, and even hourly basis. Different instream uses have different requirements for streamflow at different times. For example, in the Northwest, demands on streamflow for hydropower production are greater in the winter (for electric heating) than the summer, on weekdays than on weekends, and during the day (especially the early morning) than at night. In contrast, fishery flow requirements are at a maximum during the spring outmigration of juvenile anadromous fish, mostly salmon and steelhead. Anadromous fish are those that live in the ocean but migrate to freshwater streams for spawning. The juvenile fish ride the seasonal floodwaters out to sea. Also, their weekly and daily migration patterns do not follow the rhythms of hydropower.

One final complication in water allocation concerns the quality and other attributes of the water itself. Both instream and consumptive uses may have different requirements for biological and physical qualities of the water. For instance, human consumption demands high standards of purity, while fish habitat requires its own particular levels of temperature and water quality. Hydropower production requires that the streamflow be dammed up and dropped through a series of turbines, which is harmful to fish.

In summary, allocation of yearly streamflow requires the balancing of water supply against many different demands. For many years, this balancing act was relatively easy in the Pacific Northwest because of the huge volume of streamflow in the Columbia River. Someone observing the huge outflow of water at the mouth of the Columbia River might even now find it difficult to think of the river as a scarce resource. However, in recent years major conflicts have emerged between three of the most economically and socially significant users: hydropower, irrigation, and fishery habitat.

Columbia River Water Use Conflicts

Hydropower-Irrigation Conflicts. Until the mid-1960s the enormous size of the streamflow of the Columbia River, the Snake River, and their tributaries made the conflict between the hydropower and irrigation a moot issue.[1] However as energy demand increased, the best, environmentally acceptable dam sites were fully developed. Turbines were installed to use virtually all river flow, and the Northwest for the first time had to turn to coal, gas, and nuclear power for the production of electricity. The harnessing of the entire streamflow, plus the large increases in energy prices in the 1970s, increased the value of hydropower dramatically. What was produced for 2.5 mills (1 mill = 0.10 cent) per kilowatt hour (kwh) was now worth fifteen, twenty, even thirty times more. Therefore, the opportunity cost of new diversions of water for irrigation became quite high. Water diverted does not drive turbines. Water diverted high up in the stream could have gone through as many as eight dams and produced vast amounts of energy.[2]

Today an acre-foot of water diverted at Grand Coulee is worth $36, and an acre-foot diverted in southeastern Idaho is worth $64 annually, assuming a value of $0.035 per kwh (Butcher, Wandschneider, and Whittlesey, 1986). Very few new agricultural endeavors could pay $36 to $64 an acre-foot for water and be profitable. Prices above $7 or $8 are often considered onerous. Therefore, by almost any measure, it is more efficient to continue to use the water in hydropower than it is to open new lands for irrigation. Whether or not land will or should continue to be developed for irrigation is therefore a key question in the region. It should be noted that the analysis for lands already irrigated is somewhat different since infrastructure investment has already been made.

Fishery-Hydropower Conflict. Development of the Columbia River and its environs for other river uses has generally sacrificed the indigenous anadromous fishery. The fish were adapted to the free-flowing stream. The simple construction of dams and reservoirs harmed the fishery by blocking adult upstream migration and degrading spawning grounds. Water impounded for irrigation, flood control, navigation, and hydropower turned the free-flowing stream into a series of lakes. As the juvenile fish employ the natural streamflow to carry them to the sea, the slower flow increased the time of migration and thereby increased mortality, usually due to disease or predation.

The construction of the dams and reservoirs is a fait accompli, but the degree to which streamflow is slowed can be altered by management. The greater the volume of the water through the system, the faster the streamflow. Therefore recent conflict between hydropower and fishery uses of the Columbia River has centered over how much water is to go through the system at what times. Hydropower operators want to store spring floods and increase flows in winter to produce electricity for heating. Fishery interests want to allow large spring floods to transport juvenile fish.

The historical manner of river control was to shape riverflows to maximize hydropower subject to the largely complementary requirements of navigation and flood control, and the requirements of safety, facility maintenance, and other uses (Blumm, 1981; Wandschneider, 1984). In the late 1960s and the 1970s increasing demands for more recognition of fish habitat needs were made by environmental interests, commercial and recreational fishery interests, and Indian tribes. Fishery interests had little direct representation or authority among managers of streamflow. There was, however, a considerable, if sometimes vague, body of law mandating recognition of fishery concerns. These included the multiple-use management provisions of the acts that authorized most federal projects, as well as some laws explicitly requiring consideration for fish by federal water management agencies. The Fish and Wildlife Coordination Act of 1934 is an example. Also four Indian tribes had treaties dating to the 1850s with strong fishery provisions. In response to this legal structure and increasing demands, in 1976 the Army Corps of Engineers initiated a "fish-flow" program that attempted to give some consideration to juvenile downstream migration in streamflow management. However, fishery managers had little authoritative standing among the managers of the streamflow except the general mandate of federal agencies for multipurpose management of their projects. According to fishery defenders this fish-flow program was relatively weak; during periods of water scarcity, energy production was always maintained (Blumm, 1981).

COLUMBIA RIVER MANAGEMENT

The institutional rules and framework that guide water allocation between irrigation, hydropower, and fish, and within each use category, begin at the highest level in the United States—the Constitution. The Constitution does not explicitly grant authority over water allocation to the federal government, therefore it is assumed to be one of the residual powers vested in the states. But according to various rulings of the U.S. Supreme Court, other powers granted to the federal government (control of interstate commerce, general welfare, and so forth) authorize federal control over certain aspects of water allocation. Therefore, control over water in the United States, including the Northwest, is subject to the shared authority of federal and state governments.

Instream and Consumptive Uses

Roughly speaking, authority is divided so that states control allocation of water to consumptive uses, while the federal government oversees instream uses. Each state has a water code setting the rules by which individual users may obtain and use water. In the Northwest, state water law follows the appropriation doctrine. Establishing rights according to the appropriation doctrine requires that one actually put the water to beneficial use; except for the federal government, no one can claim water and hold it for future use or sale. The appropriation doctrine also includes the principle of prior appropriation: When water is insufficient for all users, the individual holding the senior or oldest right has the right to his or her entire appropriation. Water rights are administered through a system of state-granted permits or certificates. States also retain the right to set aside or appropriate water for the public interest and to regulate water use under the permits.

In contrast to the states the federal government has no unified water code, but rather a disparate collection of laws that (1) charter certain federal water development agencies; (2) authorize specific water development projects and water resource related programs; and (3) regulate certain types of water use, especially regarding water quality.

Consider the question of allocating water between the instream and consumptive use categories. The supremacy clause of the Constitution dictates that, when federal and state laws conflict, federal law prevails. Because federal law generally pertains to instream use one might infer, therefore, that the Supremacy Clause implies that instream water users will prevail when conflicts exist. In fact, the situation is often the reverse; instream users must be satisfied with whatever streamflow is left after consumptive users have taken what they wish. The reason is that Congress has generally constrained itself to relatively specific and limited water use issues. In the 1800s the federal role was limited to navigation and flood control. This was followed by some federal development of specific irrigation projects (beginning in 1903) and federal licensing and development of hydropower sites (1920). Gradually other uses such as recreation and wilderness expanded. A limited role in water quality was expanded in the 1960s. Even now Congress rarely assumes complete control over water allocation of a river segment. An example of an exception is the setting aside of some wild and scenic rivers for exclusive, natural flow uses.

Within the structure of state and federal law, a myriad of state and federal agencies and private enterprises and organizations operate, each with its own role and authority. Decisionmaking tends to be made in clusters oriented toward specific water uses.

Irrigation

Water use for irrigation is allocated under state law according to the appropriation doctrine described above. State laws also govern irrigation associations, districts, and companies. Federal reclamation and other state and federal land and water use laws affect irrigation. The key water use decision is the determination to develop land for irrigation. Three different types of irrigation investment decision processes can be identified, each with its own set of actors and rules: federally developed irrigation projects under the Bureau of Reclamation; federally subsidized programs such as the Desert Lands Act and various soil conservation programs; and commercial projects.

Hydropower

Federal authority over hydropower is expressed directly in the development of hydropower projects by the Army Corps of Engineers (Corps) and the Bureau of Reclamation (the Bureau), and through the regulation of nonfederal power producers by the Federal Energy Regulatory Commission (FERC). (The Corps also has primary responsibility for flood control and navigation.) Nonfederal entities include both investor-owned utilities and local government-owned utilities usually called public or municipal utilities. There are over 100 utilities in the Northwest, virtually all of which participate to some small degree in hydropower planning and operations. About two dozen of these either own or lease most of the hydropower and other electrical energy production capacity. The largest utility is the federal Bonneville Power Administration (BPA), which owns and operates no generation equipment, but markets virtually all of the power produced at federal projects as well as some power resources owned and operated by other entities, for instance the Washington Public Power Supply System (WPPSS).

The utility industry is linked by a number of contracts and voluntary associations. Voluntary associations operate in the area of power planning, while complicated reciprocal contractual agreements and an international treaty govern operations. In 1980 a new agency was added in the field of power planning. The Pacific Northwest Power and Conservation Planning Council (Power Council) operates under the charter of a federal law specifying its authority, but it is constituted by an interstate compact between four northwestern states (Idaho, Montana, Oregon, Washington).[3] Each governor appoints two members to the council. The Power Council is charged with developing a regional power plan and a fish and wildlife program. With some exceptions, the Bonneville Power Administration is required by law to conform to the plan in its acquisition of new power resources, and to finance the fish and wildlife plan from power revenues.

Fish, Wildlife, Recreation, and the Environment

In the general area of environmental use, state and federal laws are intertwined. The federal government regulates certain areas deemed to be of national significance. Examples include the Endangered Species Act (1973); the Wild and Scenic Rivers Act (1968); regulation concerning discharges in navigable water; and the various clean air, clean water, and toxic substance regulations. Certain federal agencies have operational as well as regulatory functions. Examples include the fishery research and operations activities of the U.S. Fish and Wildlife Service, the Corps of Engineers, the Bureau of Reclamation, and the BPA. Of course, the federal government also owns and manages certain facilities (dams and reservoirs) and resources, especially land, that have major environmental implications. National parks, forests, and Bureau of Land Management land occupy large portions of the Columbia River watershed. Finally, various federal laws control the spending of federal money and those actions of federal agenciees that have environmental implications. A central example is the National Environmental Protection Act (NEPA), which requires the preparation of an Environmental Impact Statement (EIS) for any federal program or project that has potentially significant environmental impacts.

State agencies set basic fish and game laws, although federal law obtains beyond the three-mile ocean limit. States operate most fish hatcheries, though federal agencies finance much of the Columbia River hatchery program. States also have laws regulating environmental uses with state versions of federal environmental protection legislation.

In summary, fishery habitat protection is an amalgam of state instream flow programs, Indian treaty fishing rights, Indian and other federal reserved water rights, Federal Energy Regulatory Commission licensing regulations on nonfederal power producers, the multiple-use management planning laws of federal water and land management agencies, and federal laws such as the Endangered Species Act.

ECONOMIC ANALYSIS OF WATER INSTITUTIONS

Judging Outcomes

The concepts of externality, efficiency, and equity are useful in examining outcomes. Allocative efficiency is clearly related to the river water use problem: How can river water be allocated to obtain the highest valued output of goods and services? However, efficiency has limitations for evaluating institutional performance. One of these limitations is that allocative efficiency is an ambiguous concept. The value of a bundle of goods and services depends on prices, and prices can change over time as scarcity, institutions, and distribution change. An example of this change of value was described earlier—the 20- to 30-fold increase in value of hydropower. What was efficient in an era of 2 mils per kwh is not efficient in an era of 40–60 mil/kwh. To the degree that what is efficient depends on the nature of institutions, it is circular to try to judge institutions on whether or not they are efficient.

Another limitation of efficiency is that, if used alone, it is simply too narrow. Society requires more of its institutions than that they be efficient. Society also requires that they be fair. Fairness, is however, an even more ambiguous category than efficiency. There may be as many conceptions of fairness as there are people, though certainly there are some broad principles to which many, most, or nearly all would agree. Instead of entering the lengthy debate about what justice criteria society might impose, the approach taken here will be to explore the conflict resolution characteristics of the water institution and leave the reader to apply his or her own principles of justice.

The term *conflict resolution* is used because it includes the decision process as well as the outcome. Economists usually use the concept of distributional equity to describe and analyze the fairness or justice aspects of economic problems. Distributional equity is an outcome category: How fair is the resulting distribution of goods and services? But when social decisions are at stake the process is often as significant as the outcomes. Sometimes the issue is whether the way in which the decision was made violated the perceived rights of certain parties, rather than whether they have obtained their just share. One most often sees concern over *procedural* justice in legal proceedings. But in economic decisions about who will get what, it is also important that procedural rights be protected: that the process appear fair to winners *and* losers.

Some aspects of procedural fairness are closely related to the idea of externality. Externality is usually thought by economists to be related to efficiency: An outcome that results from decisions in which some party is not represented is inefficient. But on close examination it almost invariably turns out that some party affected by a decision is left out of the decision process. Therefore, it may be that the procedural question of who has a right to be represented is more important than the question of the efficiency of the outcome.

Economic Organization and River Systems

Suppose that we analyze a particular river allocation and decide that it is inefficient or unfair and that an alternative division of the waters would be better. How should such a judgment be implemented? Should we simply decree a change? We as individuals have, of course, little to say over water allocation; but we as a collective, a society, do have the prerogative and, in fact, the inevitable job of deciding how the water should be allocated. But it is not practical to constantly gather information and vote on what the water allocation should be for each river each day and hour of the year. Instead we must choose an institutional structure to continually gather information, decide on the best allocation, and implement that decision. The key question then becomes, Are there any organizational forms that can be trusted to consistently produce socially desirable water allocations?

Efficiency and Economic Systems. To many economists the ideal economic system is the perfectly competitive market (PCM). Perfectly competitive markets have a number of remarkable economic properties. First, when economic actors behave according to theoretical assumption, PCMs will allocate resources so as to balance supply and demand (production and consumption) automatically. Shortages and overproduction will not occur. Second, economic actors generally will be motivated to act in reality in the way they are assumed to act in theory. People are simply required to act in their own best interest, an assumption that, while not universally met, is certainly a believable approximation of reality. Finally, the allocation obtained by the PCM will be economically efficient, where efficient means that it will be impossible to find any alternative allocation of resources that will make any group of people better off without harming some other group. In short, PCMs will produce economic outcomes guaranteed to exploit every potential area of mutual advantage. In the language of welfare economics, the outcome is Pareto Optimal.

Given this list of characteristics, the perfectly competitive market seems to be an attractive candidate to allocate river water. The PCM does have, however, a number of problems. One is that, while efficient, there is no guarantee that the resource uses (allocation) determined by a PCM will be equitable or just, depending, of course, on one's concept of equity and justice. Moreover, PCMs are impossible to implement in the real world. A PCM requires that all resources be nonunique, divisible, and reproducible at constant or decreasing costs. The PCM also requires the absence of externalities, free or open access commodities, and joint-impact goods. Where such imperfections exist, market failure is said to occur, and the outcome of the (no longer perfectly) competitive market cannot be guaranteed to be efficient (Pareto Optimal). Indeed, in general the market allocation *will be inefficient.* In cases of extreme market failure, markets simply cannot exist.

Returning to the case of Columbia River management, it is immediately apparent that many of the assumptions needed to guarantee existence of a PCM are violated. Consider some specific examples. Large dams and other water development projects are unique and indivisible. Streamflow and river amenities are joint-impact goods: If available to one, they are available at little or no incremental cost to others. Hydrological interdependence and the joint-impact nature of streamflows imply that decisions made by those controlling streamflow at one point will affect all lower water users. Salmon and steelhead are open access, fugitive resources.

In summary, adoption of a perfectly competitive market as the institutional framework for water resource use decisionmaking is infeasible. Moreover, the PCM may, or may not, meet other social objectives.

Given that a perfectly competitive market is not feasible, there are two directions one could pursue. One could keep the economic system as close to the market structure as possible—a decentralized system—or one could introduce a central management agency to coordinate all resource decisions. The central management agency can be visualized as a single authority in charge of all water development and owning and selling all water services in the river basin. The Tennessee Valley Authority is an example of an agency that controls many aspects of water development and water use in a river basin. A more decentralized economic system would be characterized by a large number of organizations owning and controlling water at many different geographic locations and many different points in the chain, from resource ownership to resource use for production, and to delivery and distribution of some water-based product like energy or farm goods.

Centralized Economic Systems. Economists, political scientists, and sociologists have developed a number of hypotheses about the types of outcomes that can be expected from more decentralized or more centralized organizations. First, consider arguments suggesting that more centralized management agencies would be more efficient. Recall the earlier discussion of the idea that market failures lead to inefficiency and that river systems possess many instances of market failure. It is sometimes argued that such market failures could be corrected by creating a single, merged agency that would internalize all the various market failures. The central management agency would consider the full consequences of different water allocation schemes and so be able to determine the most efficient allocation.

For example, imagine that water flows through two dams owned by two separate utilities. Suppose the upstream utility, A, has an increase in demand, and in response it increases the flow of water from its reservoir to increase power production. If downstream utility B has no storage and no market for increased production, it will have to spill the water, thereby wasting potential energy production. Unified management of the utilities would allow this externality to be internalized. Facility A would release water in amounts such that facilities A and B together would produce the energy required to meet the increased demand. In the Columbia River case, this simple relationship can be extended to more than 50 hydroelectric production sites with 12 major storage reservoirs.

Centralizing the authority to gather information, decide the cost allocation, and implement that decision raises, however, a number of questions. Although a central agency might be more efficient in theory, in practice such a central agency would have its own flaws. For instance, it would be difficult for the central planners to know all the details of operations needed to oversee such a vast system. Moreover, what is to guarantee that the central decisionmakers will be motivated to make efficient decisions? Central decisionmakers will have their own motives, including security and bureaucratic empire-building, that may lead to a bloated, costly bureaucratic structure.

Finally, there is an issue of who is to exercise this central authority. Central control is, in a sense, dictatorial and therefore seems contrary to the democratic traditions of the United States. On closer examination, however, the polity of the United States is replete with central control by elected representatives and their appointed officers. Democratic centralism features the indirect control by the majority voters. In a sense, then, democratic centralism is a dictatorship by the majority. This "dictatorship" is limited, however, by the Bill of Rights and the division of the society into spheres in which family, markets, churches, and so forth are the dominant institutional form.

Decentralized Economic Systems. Because centralized economic systems have a number of potential problems, and centralization implies the existence of rule by the majority, the potential virtues of decentralization need to be reexamined. True, perfect competition is not possible, but some economists and political scientists argue that decentralized systems can still do a reasonable job. For instance, decentralization proponents argue that problems of externalities can be solved by clearly specifying property rights and establishing a structure for negotiations among the various organizations. Also, decentralization allows part of the system to be operated by private, profit maximizing firms that are usually more cost conscious than state-owned enterprises. And competition is believed to sharpen the economic performance of both private and public enterprises. Finally, decentralization allows one to establish many small consumer units tailored to the tastes and needs of particular groups, while larger production units are able to capture economies of size.

An example from the utility industry illustrates the possibilities of de-centralized river management. Suppose in the earlier example of utility A and utility B, the utilities simply negotiated an agreement whereby they bought and sold power from each other or, equivalently, traded power at various times, and at the end of the accounting period the net user paid the net provider. That is, the upstream utility A, facing an increase in demand, negotiates so that production from both utilities is used to meet the demand and less water is released. Later, the downstream utility may call for an increase from both utilities. At the end of the month or year accounts are settled.

In terms of decisionmaking a decentralized approach also has some virtue. A common decision rule in decentralized institutional structures is consensus. All decisions require unanimity, and compliance may even be voluntary. (Compliance may be mandatory, once all have agreed. An example is the legally binding contract.) The unanimity rule protects all represented interests from unfavorable change as any party can veto a proposal. This is the primary virtue and the primary defect of the unanimity rule. It is a virtue because it tends to promote efficiency—as any mutually advantageous proposal will win acceptance—and to protect existing rights holders.[4] It is a defect because any current rights holder can veto change. For instance, slaveholders can veto the abolition of slavery and monopolists can veto antitrust legislation. The choice between centralization and decentralization is therefore, in part, a choice between rule of the majority versus the veto power of the elite, and a choice between openness to change versus continuity of the status quo.

Economic Behavior and Institutional Change

A final set of conceptual issues concerns how institutions change in response to changing circumstances. One approach to institutional change would be to say that real world decisionmakers rationally weigh costs and benefits of alternative institutional forms and choose the best one. This view of institutional decisionmaking would be reassuring provided (1) we could be sure all appropriate costs and benefits were considered, and (2) costs and benefits (i.e., efficiency) were the only or dominant social concern. If decisionmakers do dispassionately weigh costs and benefits, we can be sure that they mostly weigh the ones bearing on them. Only if their private costs and benefits are the same as the social costs and benefits would this be a happy outcome. In the view of some scholars, decisionmakers are rational, and private and social costs and benefits are usually in line. Institutional change is, in this case, (1) rational and (2) good, in the sense of efficient. A major exception is seen to occur when actors seek to make economic gains by capturing the rents from government regulatory activity.

Consider an example of institutional change from this perspective. At the start, water is viewed as a good that is equally and freely available to all. But as time goes by some people want to use a large amount of water for farming, mining, and power generation. If these uses exceed the quantity of water, uncertainty and fights would ensue. It is argued that everyone would be better off if rights to water were clearly assigned to individuals. The individual could then use it, sell it, or buy more. Investments in agriculture, mining, and power could be made uncluttered by uncertainty with regard to the accessibility of water.

This story illustrates some strengths and weaknesses of the efficient, rational view of institutional change. Clearly, potential for economic gains will motivate people to try to work out problems and achieve mutually advantageous results. This view of institutional change is therefore somewhat related to the consensus, decentralized approach to institutional design described earlier. It envisions the promotion of efficiency and the protection of established rights. However, promotion of efficiency is restricted by the veto power of the currently powerful, and fairness is attenuated by the weak rights held by some parties. In the real world issues of coercion, habit, tradition, and the community's sense of justice play a role. Rationality and efficiency are highly modified for good and ill. Inefficient outcomes are chosen because they are fair or conform to traditions. And sometimes outcomes that are unfair and inefficient will be forced on the general populace by those with sufficient power.

ANALYSIS OF WATER ALLOCATION CONFLICTS

It is clear that there is no central management agency for the Columbia River, but neither is the system totally decentralized. There are certain significant actors at key stages in the decision process who exercise a great deal of authority. In the next pages we examine the relative degree of centralization and decentralization of management and the manner in which conflicts have been resolved.

Hydropower-Irrigation Water Allocation

Hydropower. Hydroelectric power in the Northwest is produced by dozens of enterprises, public and private, but operations are coordinated almost as if they were a single, merged utility through various voluntary and contractual agreements. Moreover, the various utilities are divided into large producer enterprises and many smaller retail utilities, many of which are rural electric cooperatives and other public utilities.

Energy planning is also partly decentralized. Each utility is separately responsible for its own customer base, though the Bonneville Power Administration is in a unique position of wholesaling power to many of the small retail utilities. Until 1980, electricity planning was solely the province of the individual utilities with coordination through their voluntary planning organization, the Pacific Northwest Utilities Conference Committee (PNUCC). Each utility could accept or reject the plan as it chose. With the creation of the Power Council this decentralism has been modified. The Power Council makes 20-year forecasts and fashions plans to meet the forecasted demand. The act that created the Power Council also made the BPA responsible for meeting these projected demands. It must meet its own customer needs and any utility in the region can apply to the BPA to obtain energy for future needs.

Irrigation. Irrigation corresponds approximately to the decentralized model. There are three significant areas of irrigation water control: (1) specification and regulation of rights, (2) irrigation development plans, and (3) ongoing operation of irrigation infrastructure. Specification and regulation of rights are the province of government in all types of economic organization. Control over water is split between state and federal governments.

Three general patterns of irrigation development were listed earlier: Bureau of Reclamation projects, federally subsidized programs, and commercial development. Commercial development basically follows the rules of the marketplace in land and agriculture except that water is generally a free, though rationed, good, and states often have their own irrigation subsidy programs. The most significant federal irrigation subsidy programs in the Northwest have been the cheap land programs of the Carey Act and Desert Land Act. In those programs, federal authorities, in cooperation with the states, certainly have overall goals regarding water use, but these goals are not directly implemented. Instead cheap federal land is made available to promote irrigation development.

The Bureau of Reclamation projects are more centrally managed. In 1980 Bureau projects constituted 39 percent of the total irrigated acreage in the Northwest (54 percent in Washington, 23 percent in Oregon, and 42 percent in Idaho). While this would seem to indicate a large degree of central planning in irrigation development, Bureau irrigation development is not entirely a top-down affair. Bureau projects evolve through a political process requiring local support as well as agency sponsorship. Local support is, admittedly, strongly encouraged by the historically favorable terms accorded under reclamation law. The major subsidies are that the government provides interest free loans for project construction and that resources from hydropower revenues are used to pay back a high proportion of the principal on the project loan. Project participants therefore pay operations costs and a portion of the principal of the loan calculated by the Bureau of Reclamation as their ability to pay. Since the 1950s, federal water projects, including those of the Bureau, have been subject to a benefit-cost analysis. The benefit-cost analyses have been much criticized but appear to be becoming significant factors in the approval of projects. Benefit-cost analysis is a very direct application of the teachings of market-failure type welfare economics to water resource management.

The third phase of irrigation water use, the ongoing operation of the irrigation infrastructure, is largely up to the individual farm operators according to the rules of any irrigation district, corporation, or association of which they may be members. Recently, states have attempted to introduce laws that would allow some year-to-year management of water allocatioin. State minimum flow programs attempt to ensure that water withdrawals do not endanger instream water uses. However, these programs have more impact on the future allocation of water then they do on current water decisions because a water right, once granted, is considered to be the property of the license holder. A law that makes one's right subject to minimum flows is a taking of property in the eyes of most water permit holders. Although new licenses may be issued with provisions making them subject to a state's minimum flow program, the large number of existing rights are exempt from such programs.

In summary, irrigation presents a mixed model that leans toward the decentralized model. There are, however, strong elements of central control in basic water allocation and in irrigation investment and increasing elements of central control in yearly water allocation.

Most observers would probably agree that historically the mostly decentralized management structures of the hydropower and irrigation sectors have been reasonably fair and efficient (however measured) within their sectors, especially hydropower. This can best be seen in the well-integrated, single-utility, day-to-day operation of the system. However, the sectors have not been without their problems. The consensus requirement has often meant protracted and sometimes bitter negotiations before consensus emerged. For instance, in the early years there were arguments about access to hydropower sites between advocates of public power and private (investor-owned) power. The Snake River dams were eventually built by an investor-owned utility after years of planning and debate, and a change in federal policy from encouraging public power under the Roosevelt and Truman administrations to support for private enterprise under Eisenhower. The most dramatic example of prolonged negotiation concerned building storage for the Columbia system. In addition to the usual upstream versus downstream conflicts, the negotiations were international in character as many of the best reservoir sites are located at the headwaters of the river in Canada, but most of the energy production occurs downstream in the United States. Difficult questions included the financing of the reservoirs, payment to storage entities by energy producers, compensation for flooded land, and technical design issues influencing where and how much energy would be produced (Krutilla, 1966). In both the Snake River and Canadian storage cases, and more generally throughout the system, the total quantity and the operation of storage reservoirs are almost certainly not at the maximum potential for hydropower production due to the negotiating strengths and veto power of various entities.

Still another example of a breakdown in energy management was the regional decision to build expensive nuclear power plants that were apparently poorly managed but more importantly were unnecessary. The lack of a central planning and development agency may well have contributed to these management errors, though it should be noted that the centrally controlled Tennessee Valley Authority also built costly and redundant nuclear power plants.

Irrigation Versus Hydropower. The decentralized system of protected, individual rights has promoted the secure development of irrigation and probably facilitated the use of water by those most knowledgeable about needs at the farm level, the farmers. However, the rigidities of the appropriation system keep water in inefficient uses (transfer of rights is inhibited) and provide little incentive for conservation. These rigidities are even more significant when attention is turned to the allocation of water between hydropower and irrigation. Irrigators can effectively ignore the impacts of their withdrawals on instream users. Irrigators do not have to compensate fishery or hydropower users for the losses the depletion in streamflows cause. This uncompensated diversion ignores potential values of water ranging up to 50 to 60 dollars per acre-foot per year.

In recent years several developments have diminished the flow of water for consumptive uses. First, lower commodity prices and higher input prices, especially electricity pumping costs, have made agricultural expansion uneconomical even with free water. Even though farmers don't pay for water, they do build and operate water delivery and pressurization systems. Second, in Idaho, the state supreme court has ruled that hydropower operators with valid water permits are to be treated the same as other water rights holders. It had been assumed that even when hydropower facilities possessed paper rights, these were temporary, subject to the water being claimed by consumptive users. Finally, states have begun to develop water use plans and instream flow protection plans that reserve a certain amount of water for nonconsumptive uses. These instream flow programs are intended primarily for fishery and wildlife uses but also protect flows for hydropower.

Applying Economic Concepts. Using the analytic concepts developed earlier, several lessons can be drawn. First, the decentralized aspects of the institutional structure operate reasonably well within the subsectors of irrigation and hydropower for narrow allocation issues. Seasonal and daily hydropower operations and farm-level irrigation decisions seem relatively efficient. When issues broaden or major changes occur, in prices, for instance, the decentralized system's responses are sometimes perceived to be inadequate and central planning is called upon. An example is the establishment of the Power Council to coordinate energy planning.

When the agenda is broadened to consider hydropower versus irrigation, this weakness is magnified. When one party is left out, hydropower, for example, inefficiency will result, the consequence of an externality. In terms of conflict resolution the decentralized unanimity structure protects the rights of those who are represented. Because hydropower had few rights, it was not protected. Whether this exclusion is fair depends on whether one believes consumptive users *should have* an absolute right to "free" water. For many years and for many people, irrigation development was (and is) perceived to be the foundation of a rural society. This ideology would lead one to reject the rational benefit-cost calculation that irrigators should compensate hydropower interests for any water taken. But today some groups think that their rights as energy consumers and utility stockholders are at least equal to the rights of potential irrigators.

Institutional change has moved in the direction predicted by the rational change model—toward more rights for energy—but it has done so in fits and starts. As long as the free water, family-farm ideology retains some of its strengths, its adherents resist rational institutional reform. For *existing* irrigators this resistance poses a direct trade-off between ideology and their pocketbook. The potential for sale of water to hydropower offers the possibility of a lucrative windfall. To existing irrigators continuation of free water for new irrigators would mean an increased supply of agricultural commodities. Increased supply would lower the price of the product and therefore the income of existing irrigators.

Fishery-Hydropower Water Allocation

Historically, anadromous fishery management was parceled according to species and to life phase. For instance, hatcheries might be run by state fishery departments but funded by the U.S. Army Corps of Engineers. Natural propagation depends on spawning habitat whose vitality is the outcome of agricultural, forestry, and water development management. Harvest is regulated by the separate states, the fishery councils, and the Indian tribes. Conditions for upriver and downriver migration were the province of the various project operators.

Fishery Management Versus Other Uses. Even in early years efforts were taken to mitigate the deleterious effects of river development on upstream migration. Fish ladders were built, and, for those cases in which dams completely blocked passages (Grand Coulee and Hells Canyon), hatcheries were built. These measures had two significant defects. First, the hatcheries were generally located below the lowest dam, Bonneville. Besides changing the mix of salmonid stock, this policy of substituting downriver runs for upriver runs discriminated against Indian tribes with Columbia River fish treaty rights whose rights applied to harvest *above* Bonneville. The second problem is that little attention was given to downriver migration. It has since become a more significant issue as the tribes have asserted their rights, and the cumulative impact of converting the free-running Columbia-Snake to a series of dammed up pools has become apparent (Blumm, 1981).

Beginning about 1976, efforts were made to assist downriver migration by manipulating streamflows to help flush the juvenile salmonids out to sea. However, it was not until the implementation of the Northwest Power and Conservation Act of 1980 that major efforts occurred. The act requires that damages inflicted on the fishery in the course of developing the river for hydropower be rectified. Financing is from hydropower revenues, essentially BPA. Since 1980 programs to improve spawning, enhance downstream dam bypass, and regulate streamflow have been strengthened considerably. the fish flow has been institutionalized, and an already existing corps fish transportation scheme was strengthened. The juveniles are collected and barged or trucked past the dams. Mechanical bypass systems are being developed or have been installed on major dams so that the juveniles don't have to go through the turbines.

In summary, fishery management was historically not so much decentralized as disconnected and fairly weak vis-à-vis other uses. Since the passage of the 1980 Northwest Power Planning and Conservation Act, fishery policy has been better linked and given added stature relative to the other water users.

Application of Economic Concepts. The case of water management for the anadromous fishery provides some illustrations of the potential pitfalls of a decentralized resource management system. The decentralized approach to managing the Columbia River places a premium on the strength of voice resource users have in the negotiation arena. Weak or nonexistent representation for a resource use implies inefficiency due to the externality of leaving out a relevant cost or benefit, and potential injustice due to the lack of rights. The fishery resource possesses characteristics that tend to disperse and weaken its advocates. The open access quality dilutes the incentive for any one party to invest time and effort in defending the resource. The idiosyncrasy of the fish's life cycle and its migratory patterns places the resource in many different jurisdictions at different life stages.

The changes that have recently increased the standing of fish habitat in the competition for water have been largely imposed by the courts and the federal government. These changes have modified overall Columbia River management in two significant ways. First, the creation of the Power Council increases the centralized elements of Columbia River management. The Power Council has become a powerful mechanism for bringing together all of the many parties concerned with fishery habitat management. Second, the Power Council, the act which created it, and recent court decisions have increased the authority of the fishery managers vis-à-vis the managers of the other resources. Therefore those changes have increased coordination within the fishery use management (through centralization) and for fish habitat as compared with other uses (through increased rights).

Finally, the recent changes in fishery management contradict a pure efficiency explanation of institutional change. Although changes in environmental and recreational values certainly have increased recently, the value of hydropower has also increased enormously. It is highly probable that most efficiency measures would find it inefficient to reallocate water and other resources from hydropower to fish habitat.[5]

Social values, issues of justice, seem to have driven the recent shift in the balance of power and rights to fish, not a change in relative economic values. The role of social values is illustrated by the manner in which relative rights were shifted toward fishery habitat. The rights shift did not materialize from a negotiated consensus. Rather, the change came through two centralized channels. A major avenue has been a series of court decisions resulting from lawsuits by the four Columbia River Treaty tribes and other Native Americans with treaty rights to fish and hunt (Blumm, 1981). The other major avenue was insertion of fish and wildlife protection and enhancement measures in the Pacific Northwest Regional Power and Conservation Act, an act that started solely as an energy act. Therefore, in these cases, institutional change came because of issues of justice (court decisions) and political power, respectively.

TAKING STOCK: OVERVIEW AND CONCLUSIONS

In this chapter we have reviewed the nature of a river resource, the Columbia River management structure, and some economic concepts with which to understand and judge the consequences of applying particular management systems to river systems. What lessons have been learned?

First, there is no optimal or ideal management system. The lack of an ideal management system is due in part to the complexities of the problem and in part to the lack of unanimously acceptable criteria for judging what is best. In theory and in practice relatively decentralized and relatively centralized management systems have their virtues and their defects.

Second, we have learned that we cannot easily predict institutional change. We investigated the idea that institutions might change in a rational way to increase the efficiency of use. In line with this hypothesis, people are clearly motivated to change the rules that guide resource management when there are costs to be borne or profits to gain. But the example of the resistance to changes in water laws to facilitate transfers of water from irrigation to hydropower, and the example of the change in rules to promote the rights of fishery habitat, contradict efficiency predictions. Rather, issues of power, ideology, and social justice play a large role.

Given the first two lessons, is there anything remaining? I think the answer is yes. Although we may not be able to choose one ideal management system nor to predict changes over time, we can use the tools of economics to understand and explain resource management systems. We can understand potential consequences of using more or less decentralized management systems in different situations. We found, for instance, that management within resource categories—hydropower, irrigation, fish habitat—achieved apparently different levels of efficiency. The hydropower system is relatively efficient: The water rights system has facilitated expanded agricultural production but is marred, for example, with regard to inefficiencies due to lack of transfer; fish habitat management was anarchic rather than decentralized. We see that as the resource commodity approximated a normal market good, coordination and efficiency problems were lower in a decentralized system.

We also saw that decentralized systens break down in terms of efficiency and justice when an important party is left out of the decisionmaking. A decentralized consensus system tends to perpetuate such an exclusion because it is not in the interest of present rights holders to diminish their rights. In these cases change must be imposed, if it is to come, from higher central authorities.

In summary, analysis of resource management is an imprecise but rich endeavor. There are no golden rules or bottom lines, but there are many smaller lessons to learn and apply.

NOTES

1. For fuller treatment of the hydropower-irrigation conflict, see Butcher, Wandschneider, and Whittlesey (1986).

2. Some water seeps back to the river downstream from its point of diversion (return flow), and therefore may go through some of the lower dams.

3. Pacific Northwest Electric Power Planning and Conservation Act of 1980, Public Law 96-501, 94 Stat. 2697, codified at 16 U.S.C. 839 (1982).

4. Efficiency in this context is more restricted than the Pareto Optimality concept mentioned earlier. This concept of efficiency is termed Pareto Safety and excludes outcomes that are efficient in the Pareto Optimality sense, if an existing rights holder would be harmed.

5. There are many efficiency concepts and measures, some of which have been cited in this chapter. Moreover, a particular efficiency concept, such as benefit-cost analysis, will give different results depending on assumptions regarding technology, income distribution, and tastes.

REFERENCES

Blumm, M. C. (1981). "Hydropower vs. Salmon: The Struggle of the Pacific Northwest's Anadromous Fish Resources for a Peaceful Coexistence with the Federal Columbia River Power System." *Environmental Law* 11:212–300.

Butcher, W. R., and P. R. Wandschneider, with N. K. Whittlesey (1986). "Competition Between Irrigation and Hydropower in the Pacific Northwest" in K. D. Frederick with D. L. Gibbons, eds., *Scarce Water and Institutional Change*. Washington, D.C.: Resources for the Future.

Krutilla, J. V. (1966). "The International Columbia River Treaty: An Economic Evaluation" in A. V. Kneese and S. C. Smith, eds., *Water Research*. Baltimore: Johns Hopkins University Press.

Wandschneider, P. R. (1984). "Control and Management of the Columbia–Snake River Systems." *Agric. Res. Ctr. Bulletin* XB 0937. Pullman, Wash: Agricultural Research Center, Washington State University.

——— (1985). "Who Controls the Water? Managing the Columbia–Snake River." Bulletin PNW 249. Pullman, Wash.: Washington State University Cooperative Extension.

SUGGESTED READINGS

Blumm, M. C. (1983). "The Northwest's Hydroelectric Heritage: Prologue to the Northwest Electric Power Planning and Conservation Act." *Washington Law Review* 58:175–229.

A readable, well-documented, historical survey of major developments in Columbia

River policy. A good place to start for anyone wishing to learn more about Northwest energy, fishery, and water law and policy.

Butcher, W. R. and P. R. Wandschneider, with N. K. Whittlesey (1986). "Competition Between Irrigation and Hydropower in the Pacific Northwest" in K. D. Frederick with D. L. Gibbons, eds., *Scarce Water and Institutional Change.* Washington, D.C.: Resources for the Future.
A more detailed, but accessible, account of hydropower-irrigation trade-offs in the Northwest that advocates institutional reform to facilitate water transfers. Other chapters in the book contain case studies of water management issues in California and Virginia. The introductory chapter is a good introduction to water problems and policies.

Krutilla, J. V. and A. C. Fisher (1975). *The Economics of Natural Environments.* Baltimore: Published for Resources for the Future by the Johns Hopkins University Press.
Although parts of this book use sophisticated economic tools and concepts, much of it is accessible to the economic newcomer. The analysis applies and extends standard economic reasoning (that is, externalities) to problems of valuing and managing natural environments. Case study/applications include Hells Canyon of Idaho-Oregon, recreation in the Sierras of California, and the Trans-Alaska pipeline.

Randall, A. (1983). "The Problem of Market Failure." *Natural Resource Journal* 23:131–148.
A review and critique of the concept of market failure. The treatment is accessible to the noneconomist, yet outlines sophisticated concepts bearing on the problem of allocation of resources when the economist's perfect market cannot exist.

Wandschneider, P. R. (1984). "Managing River Systems: Centralization versus Decentralization." *Natural Resources Journal* 24:1043–1066.
This article discusses in detail the institutional structure described in this chapter; it also uses the Columbia River as the case study.

STUDY QUESTIONS

1. The Columbia River's multiple-use characteristics are the focus of this chapter. Of the uses identified by Wandschneider, which are clearly mutually compatible, which are clearly incompatible and which may be compatible at current use levels?

2. Identify, by reference to examples, how divided authority among two countries, one province, and six states has complicated management decisions in the Columbia Basin. For one of your examples, consider how more centralized and more policentric management would likely affect outcomes.

3. In Chapter 3, concerning groundwater allocation mechanisms in Florida, effective solutions were found for problems similar to allocation problems described in Chapter 9. How do the differing resource characteristics of groundwater and streamflow influence the ability of policymakers to resolve allocation problems?

4. Compare and contrast Wandschneiders's analysis of economic efficiency with the approaches of Freshwater, Krieger, and Strand.

Part Three

Policy Analysis Using
Mathematical Models

Models are important tools for analyzing natural resource and environmental problems and for developing policies to resolve them. By using models, analysts can determine key components of problems and study the interactions among components. Models provide policymakers with insights about the probable consequences of their options.

Chapters 10 through 12 use mathematical and empirical models to analyze pest management, the greenhouse effect on the Canadian prairies, and energy policy. Model components include examination of individual behavior, efficient allocation of limited resources, and market equilibrium.

Each chapter in Part 3 describes a modeling process in the context of a case study and demonstrates how the analysis of the issue affects model development. Examples are given of mathematical simulation, econometric, linear programming, and input-output models. The models are presented clearly and simply, with relevance drawn to policy and analysis. A common theme of the chapters is that the increased mathematical rigor and quantification inherent in modeling requires a thorough knowledge of the interdependencies of physical, institutional, and economic factors.

Chapter Ten

Pest Management
Factors Influencing Farmer Decisionmaking

Karen Klonsky

Attempts by farmers to increase crop production by the use of pesticides have raised concerns about a number of environmental issues, including the quality and safety of the food supply. This chapter focuses on the application of economic analysis to individual farmer pest management decisions, especially integrated pest management. The collective results of individual decisions regarding inputs to production ultimately determine pesticide use. This chapter introduces the concepts of economic injury and thresholds (marginal analysis), reviews current laws and regulations, and explains several mathematical models of pest control.

Our chemically oriented, high-energy-use agriculture has increased productivity. At the same time it has created perplexing problems concerning the quality and safety of the environment and food supply. Some of the chemical inputs that the farmer finds profitable to use are considered toxic substances in a broader context. Their use by the farmer to reduce crop loss results in damages to other elements of society.

A basic goal of commercial farmers is to maximize the difference between the benefits and costs of production. Typically, benefits are measured in dollar returns from the crop. The cost of pesticide use is measured as the dollars spent on material and application. No cost is included to account for the potential harmful effects on other people that result from the individual grower's production practices because technological externalities by their nature are not associated with direct monetary costs to the farmer. Therefore, these externalities are not taken into account when choosing among alternative pest control strategies. The cost paid by the farmer is not the same as the cost measured or felt by society.

In recognition of the dilemma, regulations have been introduced by the public sector to modify pest control practices. Pesticide regulations introduce constraints on the farmer's decisionmaking process by limiting the possible pest control alternatives. At the extreme, pesticide regulations decrease health risks to certain segments of society by eliminating profitable farm production practices. However, regulation of pesticide use in order to reduce environmental damage and related health hazards need not result in a reduction in the quality and quantity of agricultural products.

Integrated pest management (IPM) is an approach to crop protection that attempts to reconcile the grower's objectives with society's objectives. This approach relies on ecological principles for the development of pest control strategies that maintain pest populations at tolerably low levels. These strategies include a mix of well-timed chemical applications, biological controls, resistant plant varieties, and cultural practices.

The philosophy of pest management suggests that interdependencies created by pest control strategies, and particularly pesticide use, should be taken into account in pest control decisions. These interdependencies may or may not be accounted for by decentralized markets but should still be part of pest management decisions. It follows that market and nonmarket values should be part of the decisionmaking process.

The actual pest management program followed by the grower will be a subset of the alternative practices known to be available. As research continues and regulations change, the control practices available to growers will change. Market conditions, in particular the prices received for products and the cost of pest control practices, also have their impact. A grower's pest management program should be expected to change with new information. However, although regulation can alter the set of practices available to growers and education can improve the decision process, the collective results of individual decisions will ultimately determine pesticide use. .

Before applying economic theory to the farmer's pest management decisionmaking process, the historical development and philosophy of pest control is described and a definition of pest management is presented. The definition outlines the factors that should be considered in making pest control decisions. Pest management decisions depend on (1) all techniques and methods of control available, (2) all impacts on the associated environment and the pest population, (3) all returns and costs associated with each strategy, and (4) the regulatory constraints faced by the decisionmaker.

This chapter also presents several theoretical models that provide a mathematical framework for choosing a pest control strategy. Each model considers each of the factors listed above. However, models are by definition simplifications of the processes they mirror. Therefore, the models may differ in the control practices, environmental impacts, decision criteria, and regulations included. Clearly, all possible factors cannot be included in any one model. Different specifications of the models can lead to different pest control recommendations. Limitations of these simple models provide insight into the complexity of practical application. For example, from these models it is possible to develop an understanding of how rational decisionmaking by an individual producer can result in damages both to other members of society or even to the producer if such factors as a longer time horizon or secondary effects are not considered.

THE IPM CONCEPT

Integrated pest management is an approach to crop protection where management strategies are developed in the context of an agro-ecosystem. These strategies include an integration of well-timed chemical applications, biological controls, resistant plant varieties, and cultural practices.

The methods used in IPM are not new. Cultural control practices are the earliest form of crop protection used by humankind. The concept of biological control dates from the late nineteenth century while the conscious development of pest-resistant plant varieties began around 1900. Similarly, the use of chemical compounds for crop protection also has a long history. During the eighteenth century various combinations of tobacco, animal manures, soot, dry ashes, seawater, urine, soap, turpentine, and alcohol were recommended for insect and/or disease control.

After World War II, the immense success of chemical controls shifted the emphasis in research away from resistant varieties and other forms of control. The chemical approach dominated applied entomology from the 1920s through the 1960s with some notable exceptions. In the past 15 years, recognition of the negative consequences of dependence on chemical controls revived interest in other control methods.

The idea of integrating control strategies also has a historic base. The term *integrated control* was originally applied in the 1950s to control insects using both biology and chemistry (Smith and Allen, 1954; Stern et al., 1959). The fundamental idea was to attack pest populations at their peak while leaving parasite populations intact. It was later broadened to include all control methods (Smith and Reynolds, 1965). Later the term "pest management" replaced "integrated control" (Geier, 1970). Pest management and IPM are now used interchangeably. The concept of pest management has been broadened to include all classes of pests—diseases, insects, nematodes, and weeds. It implies an integration of disciplines—entomology, plant pathology, agronomy, and economics—as well as an integration of control methods.

As defined by the U.S. Office of Technology Assessment (OTA), IPM is a "comprehensive approach to the use of various control methods that takes into account the role of all kinds of pests in their environment, possible interrelationships among pests, and other factors" (1979).

The Food and Agriculture Organization (FAO) panel of experts on integrated pest control defined integrated pest management as " . . . a pest management system that in the context of the associated environment and the population dynamics of the pest species, utilizes all suitable techniques and methods in as compatible a manner as possible and maintains the pest populations at levels below those causing economic injury" (1967).

Both definitions advocate pest management strategies based on an approach to pest control that incorporates ecological principles into the decision process and looks beyond the short-run production needs of an individual firm.

By taking a broad perspective, the list of control strategies available is increased but so is the complexity of choosing a control strategy. The choice requires knowing the effects of implementation that each available strategy will have on the pest and the environment, and an evaluation of these effects, including interactions among components of each strategy. In other words, the overall impact of each strategy must be predicted from our understanding of the system being managed and compared to alternative strategies using some performance criteria. In order to accomplish this, the characteristics of the system to be analyzed must be identified.

Any definition of pest management is purposefully general and thus vague as to what characteristics should be considered in selecting a pest control strategy and how to evaluate those factors. However, the definitions do serve as general guidelines. Components of the FAO definition of IPM quoted above will be addressed individually to elaborate the ideas presented in the definition.

Associated Environment

Pest management decisions are based on the characteristics of the environment in which the crop is grown. Temperature, precipitation, solar radiation, and wind, directly or indirectly, influence the status of the plant, pest, and natural enemies. For example, the emergence of pests and overwintering behavior are determined by temperature.

The pest problems in a particular field are also related to the physical characteristics of the field and area surrounding the field. The slope of the land, drainage, elevation, and proximity to drainage ditches and natural waterways affect pest levels as well as the entry of any pesticides into the food chain. Wooded areas provide overwintering sites for pests. Weeds bordering a field harbor pests throughout the year.

In turn, pest management decisions have an impact on the associated environment. In this context, pest management decisions are influenced by interdependencies among pesticide users, pesticide producers, and the rest of society.

Important interdependencies related to pest control exist among farmers. Typically, an individual farmer only attempts to control pests in his or her own field. Yet the strategy the farmer follows enters the production function of other growers. Likewise, the management strategies followed by other growers enter the first farmer's production function. For example, pesticide drift becomes a problem when pesticides used to control one crop are damaging to another.

Pesticide use may also result in a secondary pest outbreak. When the primary pest has been controlled another species population may explode because competition for food has been eliminated. This phenomenon may be the result of the individual's actions, a neighbor's actions or both.

Each farmer's application of pesticides decreases the pool of susceptible pests, resulting in a more resistant pest population. As resistant species replace susceptible ones, a recognized consequence of continuous use of a pesticide is a decline in its effectiveness. The value of the pesticide in production is altered by its use. Pesticide producers are also affected because the life of the pesticide is shortened. Unless a replacement compound is introduced, the farmer may find that pest adaptation negates expenditures on control.

Government regulations are another source of interdependencies. Although regulations were originally introduced to protect pesticide users from fraudulent manufacturers, they focus now on environmental and health protection. They are an administrative attempt to force nonmarket values into the pest control decision. Licensing of pesticide applicators, certification of pesticides, and regulation of waste disposal all create costs for the producers and users of pesticides and for society as a whole by way of costs of enforcement.

Certifying a pesticide for use on only a few crops reduces the value of the pesticide to its manufacturer by reducing its potential market. The benefits from using the pesticide to reduce crop damage are also reduced. However, restricting use may prolong the effective life of a pesticide if pest adaptation is slowed. At the extreme, banning a pesticide eliminates the negative consequences of that pesticide, but at the expense of removing all positive effects.

Other interdependencies exist among farmers, farm laborers, beekeepers, hunters and fishermen. Many of these interrelationships cannot be captured by conventional markets because they are difficult to quantify and exclusion costs are high. For example, pesticides used for crop protection may run off into streams and kill fish valued by fishermen. A group of fishermen could pay neighboring farmers to stop spraying pesticides that harm game fish. However, it would be extremely difficult to establish an appropriate price. More importantly, it would be impossible to exclude nonpaying fishermen from benefiting from the increase in game fish. As excluding these free riders is impossible, most fishermen would be unwilling to pay. Consequently, their interests may not be reflected in pest management decisions at the farm level.

Population Dynamics of Pest Species

Pests compete with members of their own species and other species for food. Some insect species will feed at a constant rate until a crop is destroyed while others will adjust their feeding rate to the population density. Pest populations also interact with predators, parasites, and pathogens. Enemies of the pest may compete with each other. When a pest population is reduced, additional food may be available for another species. The problem of a secondary outbreak occurs when an increase in the population of a second species is attributable to control of the target pest.

Techniques and Methods of Control

Pesticides provide an immediate reduction of pest populations and remain an important tool for pest management. However, pesticides need not be applied as a prophylactic. The proper timing of pesticide use, based on the level of pest infestation and plant status can reduce the number of applications necessary without affecting control. In addition, pesticides often harm the natural enemies of the pest. This negative effect can also be diminished by careful timing of applications. Although pesticide use is now the most common method of pest control, several other methods exist including biological controls, resistant plant varieties, and cultural practices.

Biological control is provided by predators, parasites, or pathogens that are natural enemies of the pest. These organisms may be propagated in the laboratory and released into the environment if their natural occurrence is less than the desired level. Because many pests are not native to the areas they infest, the natural enemies of the pest must often be imported. The release of two predators—lady beetle and a fly—imported from Australia in 1888 to control cotton cushion scale on citrus in California is probably the earliest U.S. example of biological control introduced by humans. These two insects eliminated the scale as an economic pest within a year.

Biocontrol agents are very specific and are less likely to produce undesirable side effects than conventional pesticide use. However, biological controls introduced into an ecosystem may not adapt well. The population of the parasite or other control agents may not increase to the levels necessary to significantly reduce the pest population. Also, the cost of a breeding program for biological controls may be far greater than the potential benefits. Therefore, even if a known biological control agent exists, it may not provide a feasible level of control.

Resistant plants have been used effectively in the control of certain nematodes, plant pathogens, and a few insects. Damage is reduced due to some physical characteristics of the plant. Some plants contain chemicals that are toxic to insects feeding on them. Others avoid damage by maturing rapidly. This early maturation allows for early harvesting before extensive damage from pests occurs. Still others do not avoid damage but regenerate lost plant materials quickly.

Cultural or physical practices regulate pests by changing their environment. Cultural control practices, the earliest form of crop protection, were developed mostly by trial and error. Control methods now include removal of crop stubble (sanitation) to reduce overwinter survival of pests, tillage to destroy overwintering pests, removal of alternative hosts, rotation of crops to limit the buildup of pest populations, and the careful timing of planting and harvesting. Other physical practices include pruning, defoliation, isolation from other crops, the use of trap crops, and management of water and fertilizer.

Crop rotation can be used to control insects, weeds, diseases, and nematodes. Crops should not be followed by crops having similar suscep-tibilities if benefits from crop rotation are to be maximized. Some weed problems can be controlled in one crop better than in another. In this case, crop rotation does not directly control weeds but makes it possible for other technologies to provide control.

The increase in narrow row spacing, broadcast seeding, and no-till cultivation resulted in a decrease in the effectiveness of mechanical weed control and an increased reliance on herbicides. Although no-till results in a lower percentage of weed germination, no-till requires greater use of chemicals than conventional tillage because there are no effective cultivation methods available to the farmer. In other words, the farmer controls fewer weeds, but uses herbicides rather than tillage to do so. Additional benefits of minimum tillage practices are reduced soil erosion, the retention of greater levels of organic matter in the soil, and less soil compaction. Thus, heavier herbicide use may be offset by other environmentally desirable effects.

Shifting production to areas where pests are not problems reduces the need for artificial controls. Acreage shifts can also be used to isolate pest-inducing activities from other activities or locate pest-inducing activities in areas where the absorptive capacity of the environment is greatest. Spatial shifts can be encouraged by changes in taxes, subsidies, or acreage allotments.

For example, taxes could be imposed on pesticide use in designated areas to discourage use of pesticides. Taxation would increase the cost to growers in those areas and encourage them to use less pesticides or move production to a tax-free region. Acreage allotments could also limit pesticide use in specified areas by restricting the number of acres that could be sprayed each year.

Other techniques have shown potential for insect control. Among these are traps baited with pheromone attractants. Pheromones are the chemical olfactory stimulants insects use in communication with other individuals of the same species. Sex-attractant pheromones have been the most successful baits. They can be emitted by males or females depending on the insect species but usually female pheromones are used as bait. Traps are baited with synthetically produced pheromones. Flying adult insects are attracted to the trap and are captured on a sticky substance. Pheromones can also be introduced to inhibit mating by making it difficult for the males to find the females. Other control techniques include the release of sterilized males to reduce reproduction and the application of insect growth regulators, pesticides that interfere with insect maturation.

Economic Injury

In defining IPM the FAO stated that a pest management system should "maintain pest populations below those causing economic injury." Entomologists developed the term economic injury in order to determine when pest control is appropriate. The economic injury level is defined as "the lowest population density that will cause economic damage" (Stern et al., 1959). Economic damage is the amount of injury that will justify the cost of artificial control measures. This definition implies crop damage should be tolerated when the cost of control exceeds the value of crop loss due to damage from the pest.

At this point net profit, the difference between returns and costs of pest controls, will be negative. A rational decisionmaker would not implement controls under these conditions.

FIGURE 10.1 Economic Injury Level (EIL) and Economic Threshold (ET) for Hypothetical Pest Situation

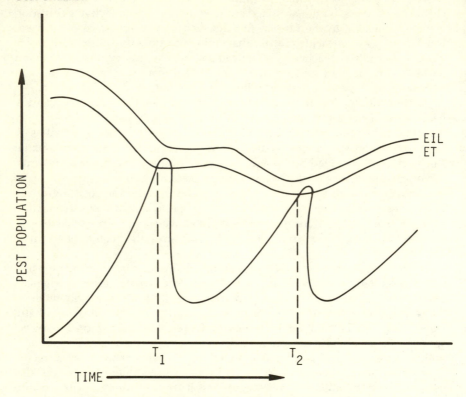

Usually there is a lag between recognition of the need for control and the initiation of control, as well as a second lag before the control takes effect, which complicates the decision process. For this reason it may be necessary to implement controls before the injury level is actually reached.

To capture this distinction, another term was introduced by Vernon Stern and others in their article, "The Integrated Control Concept" (1959). Based on the definitions of economic injury level and economic damage, economic threshold is defined as "the density at which control measures should be applied to prevent an increasing pest population from reaching the economic injury level." The economic threshold is always lower than the economic injury level to allow time for the control to take effect. Edwards and Heath (1964) defined the economic threshold as the population large enough to cause damages valued at the cost of practical control.

Figure 10.1 describes the threshold and injury level concepts graphically. The economic injury level (EIL) at any point in time is always below the economic threshold (ET). Control measures were implemented at times T_1 and T_2 when the population reached the economic threshold.

A distinction is often made between a static and dynamic threshold. The use of the term dynamic and static by entomologists is not synonymous with the use by economists. A static threshold to the entomologist is one that does not change over time. That is, the critical population level does not vary with the status of the plant, the time until harvest, or the weather forecast. Therefore, the only information needed to make a pest control decision using a static threshold level is the threshold level and the pest population in the field. A static threshold may vary with location.

In contrast, a dynamic threshold changes with time. Consequently, the control decision is more complex than for a static threshold. The threshold may change with the accumulated heat units or plant status, as well as with the pest level in the field. For example, a high pest population may be tolerable on a mature plant almost ready for harvest. That same pest population might destroy a crop right at the time the seeds germinate and the crop begins to grow. It follows that the threshold is usually lower early in the season than late in the season.

Figure 10.1 portrays a dynamic threshold because the population level changes over time. A static threshold would be depicted by a straight line. The threshold population level would not change over time.

All of these early definitions focus on the population level at which control should be initiated. A second component of the threshold concept is how much the population should be reduced. Thus, the intensity of pest management is also part of the decisionmaking process. In addition, the decisionmaker must also choose among alternative control methods available. Pest control decisions, then, have three components. First, the method or methods of control must be selected. Second, for each method the grower must decide when controls should be initiated, and third, to what level the population should be reduced. For pesticides this is equivalent to choosing the timing and quantity of the material applied. The questions what, when, and how much—the fundamental resource allocation problems—are precisely those addressed by economic theory.

To summarize, the FAO definition of IPM can be interpreted as a list of characteristics a pest control system should have in order to be consistent with the IPM philosophy. The control system should use methods and techniques that are environmentally sound. The methods and techniques should not work against each other in the long run (to avoid the use of pesticides that may reduce the effectiveness of biological controls over time). A pest management system should be based on ecological principles and draw from control mechanisms found in nature. Finally, the control system should be compatible with producer and user objectives. Thus, it should not tolerate economic damage, but neither should it include control measures that are not economically warranted.

Pest management decisions are made without perfect knowledge of the outcomes associated with alternative strategies. Risk and uncertainty enter the pest management decisionmaking process in several ways, through (1) agricultural biology, (2) technology, and (3) institutions. All three are interrelated. New methods of control, including new pesticides, are continuously introduced, changing the technology available for production. Changing regulation of pest controls contributes to the variation in technology. Organization of the delivery of pest control information is changing rapidly. Economic events change prices. With price changes the value of crop loss and the cost of control vary.

It is often assumed that farmers use pesticides as a form of insurance. That is, pest population levels cannot be predicted with certainty. Large populations are more difficult to control than low populations. Therefore, farmers may spray early in the season regardless of the level of infestation to insure a high crop yield. In this case, some profit is sacrificed to reduce the risk in crop production.

THE ROLE OF REGULATIONS IN PEST MANAGEMENT DECISIONS

Public regulations are usually not included in a list of pest management tactics. They play a critical role in pest management, however. Regulations restrain, encourage, or require the utilization of certain pest control methods. Government regulations take many forms. Most are directed at pesticide use. Restrictions on pesticide use affect farmers' pest control choices.

The first federal law designed to control pesticides was the Federal Insecticide Act of 1910, which pertained only to insecticides and fungicides. Its main purpose was to protect farmers against poor quality or fraudulent products. The 1938 amendment of the Pure Food Law of 1906 set tolerances for certain pesticide residuals in foods. The Federal Insecticide, Fungicide, and Rodenticide Act (FIFRA) was signed into law in 1947. It required that any of these products be registered with U.S. Department of Agriculture (USDA) before they could be marketed in interstate commerce. The main purpose of the law was to make pesticides safe for the user. To this end, the law also required that the label instructions for application be followed by the user.

FIFRA was administered by the Pesticide Regulation Division of USDA until 1970 when responsibility was transferred to the newly established Environmental Protection Agency (EPA). In 1972 FIFRA was amended to include the classification of pesticides and registration of applicators. A more detailed description of the current legislation follows.

To register a pesticide, the applicant must file a statement with the EPA specifying all claims for the product, its complete formula, a copy of the labeling, and any directions for its use. The applicant must furnish any information required by the EPA for registration. Registration will be approved if the pesticide is found to meet the claims made for it and "when considered with any restrictions imposed (under FIFRA) it will perform its intended function without unreasonable adverse effects on the environment; and when used in accordance with widespread and commonly recognized practice it will not generally cause unreasonable adverse effects on the environment."

A major part of the registration process is the Rebuttable Presumption Against Registration Process (RPAR) now known as the Special Review

Process. The RPAR serves as a review process for a particular pesticide that the EPA believes may have potential harmful effects that exceed its benefits. Approximately 45 chemicals or groups of chemicals were subject to the RPAR process in 1980. As of 1980, the registration for six pesticides had been cancelled or suspended by the EPA, and 15 pesticides had been voluntarily cancelled by the registrants.

Federal grades and quality standards set maximum tolerable levels for pest damage to food and insect parts in food. Although some standards are set for health purposes, quite often they reflect a demand for attractive fruit and vegetables. Pesticides have been used extensively for cosmetic purposes. It would be expected that a downward revision of grades and standards would reduce pesticide use while an upward revision would invite increased use (Carlson and Castle, 1972). A change in consumer tastes and preferences could also reduce pesticide use.

Taxes and subsidies can be used to alter pesticide use. Taxes on pesticide use increase the cost of this means of control. Theoretically taxes can be adjusted upward or downward until the "optimal" level of aggregate pesticide use is attained.

Subsidies can be used to make one form of pest control more attractive than another. Subsidies to agricultural chemical companies to develop narrow-spectrum pesticides that kill only a few species make them more profitable to produce. Subsidies to public or private agencies such as the Federal Crop Insurance Corporation encourage the substitution of crop insurance for pesticide application.

Other examples of regulations include the certification of disease-free seeds and plants, a requirement for the removal of abandoned orchards, and ordinances requiring property owners to control weeds. Connecticut and Massachusetts recently passed laws to eradicate the barberry, an alternative host for the stem rust of wheat.

Societal values concerning pest control methods are expressed through the scope and form of regulation. Pest management techniques are chosen at the farm level within the constraints of regulation. The selection process of an individual grower must be consistent with the results of the regulatory process. For example, while society may desire greater use of IPM techniques, the certification of pesticide applicators does not require that specific IPM techniques are used.

DEVELOPING PEST CONTROL GUIDELINES— IMPLEMENTING THE ECONOMIC THRESHOLD

As a science of resource allocation, economic theory can be applied in deciding which combination of available pest management inputs to use, what quantities of each should be used, and when those inputs should be applied. To establish the economic threshold, two questions need to be answered concerning the quantity and timing of a pest management input: (1) To what level should the population be reduced, and (2) at what level should control be initiated? The related questions of how much and when are not necessarily meaningful, however, in all pest control situations.

For certain control programs the decision process includes the number of applications or the amount of material to be applied. Other control strategies involve different assessments of the economic threshold. That is, it is not really meaningful to ask what proportion of a field to plant in a resistant variety or what percentage to harvest early. Similarly, for some strategies the timing of application is not a major concern. For example, a grower might be concerned with whether it pays to construct a deer fence to keep deer from eating a crop but not when to build the fence.

For other pests the threshold concept may be meaningful but extremely difficult to implement. For example, weed seeds may remain viable for up to 20 years. Also, one individual weed produces so many seeds that the concept of a threshold may become meaningless. Finally, the resistance problems that have developed from reliance on insecticides have not occurred yet with herbicides. For these reasons, although the definition of economic threshold refers to all pest control techniques, the threshold concept has been applied primarily to insecticide applications.

Modeling Pest Management Decisions

Any resource allocation problem consists of a description of the production process and a set of criteria for selecting inputs into that process. Mathematical models can be used to simulate biological processes and to compare the system performance under alternate management strategies. Following the FAO definition of pest management, a control strategy should take into account all available methods of control and impacts on the associated environment. In addition, pest populations should not be allowed to exceed a level that could cause economic injury. Models can vary in the complexity of the description of the production process, the environmental impacts included, the possible control strategies, the time frame considered, and/ or the decision criteria for choosing among the control strategies.

These models are, by definition, simplifications of the ecosystems they mirror. For practical purposes a model cannot contain all possible variables or relationships among variables. It is the role of the modeler to decide which variables are important for the description of the system and which can be omitted.

Selecting which attributes are important depends in part on the ultimate use of the modeling effort. This link between the construction and application of a model necessitates judgments by modelers and model users. Yet users of scientific models often ignore or are unaware of the embedded valule judgments or their consequences. Problem definition includes the selection of system components and variables perceived to be significant for the problem at hand. By necessity, certain phenomena are omitted or highly abstracted.

If we restrict the scope of the model to an isolated field, we ignore several environmental relationships important to pest management. The movement of pests and parasites from one field to another, the effect of a neighbor's control program on pest populations, and the development of pest resistance to insecticides are a few examples. It is reasonable to consider the cost of control and the value of the crop as exogenous to the system under this interpretation.

If, on the other hand, the model domain is interpreted as production for a region, ignoring the movement of pest and parasite populations in and out of the system may not be appropriate. The development of resistance to insecticides by the pest over time could be built into the model with some degree of difficulty. The value of allowing a high parasite population also becomes meaningful.

However, this level of aggregation introduces other problems. A single management strategy and yield must be an oversimplification. It is unlikely that all growers in a region will harvest or spray their crops the same number of times in a season let alone on the same day. Different varieties of the same crop produce different quantities and qualities even under the same management practices. On a regional level the cost of control and the value of production will no longer be exogenous to the system.

The model definition determines the alternative control strategies to be compared by the decisionmaker. Many models include only one pest and one crop. Therefore, crop rotation is not a possible control measure. Other constraints on control parameters may reflect societal values. The pesticides available for use are determined, in part, by government regulation. The temporal dimension of the model also limits the control strategies possible. Many crop models only simulate the growing season; therefore, multiyear planning is not an option.

The benefits from reduced insecticide use most commonly cited are (1) slowed development of resistance by the pest; (2) a higher survival rate for predators and parasites of the pest; (3) reduced environmental contamination; and (4) reduced cost of control. Only the last of these is a short-run benefit. The other three can only be realized over several years. Quite often the overwintering habits of pests are poorly understood, making year to year estimates of infestation difficult. Therefore, the benefits of specific control strategies over time may be ignored or inaccurate.

Several theoretical models for determining the economic threshold are presented below. Each has the same problem definition, that is, which pest management strategy is "best." Also, each model uses profit maximization as the decision criteria. The models differ in terms of the variables included, control methods possible, and the time horizon.

Modeling Farm Strategies

The earliest attempt at a systematic approach to determining the economic threshold based on economic theory was developed by Headley (1972). Headley used marginal analysis to derive a rigorous definition for the economic threshold from a simple pest control model. His model has four components: (1) the pest population growth function, (2) the pest damage function, (3) the crop production function, and (4) the pest control cost function.

The pest population increases exponentially over time and can be calculated for any point in time using the pest population function. Once the pest population is determined, the pest damage function calculates the crop lost to the pest.

The crop production function subtracts the crop loss from the maximum possible yield in the absence of pests and calculates the actual yield. In other words, the crop production function describes the relationship between the pest population and yield. As the pest population increases, yield decreases, and when the pest population is decreased by a pesticide, yield increases.

The pest control cost function describes the relationship between the cost of control and the pest population. As the expenditure on pest control increases, the pest population decreases and yield increases.

Finally, the grower is assumed to be a price taker; that is, the level of production does not affect the price received. For any pest population level the total revenue and total cost can be calculated using the model.

Headley used profit maximization as the decision criteria. That is, the manager's objective was to maximize the difference between total revenue and total cost. The optimal level to which the pest population should be reduced is the pest population level that equates marginal revenue and marginal cost. This population level is the economic threshold. The cost of reducing the pest population by one is equal to the resulting increase in the value of the crop produced.

The definition of economic threshold was applied to a single producer considering a single pest for a single season. The only control method considered was a single pesticide application. The timing of the application was assumed to be "entomologically determined." Headley defined the economic threshold as the level to which the population should be reduced and not the level at which controls should be initiated. In other words, Headley's model determined the quantity of the pesticide used and not the timing of the application.

An illustration of this model, using a hypothetical example, is presented in Tables 10.1 and 10.2. Table 10.1 describes the relationship between yield and pest population level. The maximum attainable yield is 200. No damage occurs when the pest population is 2 or less. Damage is a function of the pest population. The realized yield is determined by subtracting the damage from the maximum attainable yield of 200. For example, at a pest population of 6, the attainable yield is 200, the damage is 67, and the actual yield is 133 (200 − 67).

For simplicity, the total cost is the cost of pest control and is a function of pest population. The cost of decreasing the pest population increases at an increasing rate. For example, the cost of reducing the pest population to 1 is $480 while the cost of reducing the population to 6 is $80.

Table 10.2 is a summary of the cost and revenue values at various yield levels. The attainable yield levels are in the first column. The price received

TABLE 10.1: Relationship Between Pest Population, Actual Yield,
             and the Cost of Control

Pest Population	Attainable Yield	Damage	Actual Yield	Total Cost
0	200	0	200	$990
1	200	0	200	480
2	200	0	200	240
3	200	11	190	160
4	200	25	175	120
5	200	44	156	96
6	200	67	133	80
7	200	95	106	67
8	200	126	74	60
9	200	162	38	53
10	200	200	0	48

TABLE 10.2: Summary of a Firm's Pest Management Information

Pest Population	Actual Yield	Marginal Revenue	Marginal Cost
0	200	-----	------
1	200	-----	------
2	200	$2.00	$10.07
3	190	2.00	5.17
4	175	2.00	2.00
5	156	2.00	.98
6	133	2.00	.56
7	106	2.00	.35
8	74	2.00	.23
9	38	2.00	.16
10	0		

is $2.00 per unit of production. The grower is a price taker and does not experience price increases when yield (supply) decreases. Total revenue is the yield multiplied by the price. The cost is transferred from Table 10.1 for each yield level. The total profit is calculated by subtracting the total cost from the total revenue.

The marginal revenue is equal to the price per unit of $2.00 because the grower is a price taker. It could also be calculatd by dividing the change in revenue by the change in production. For example, as yield decreases from 156 to 133, revenue decreases from $312 to $266. The marginal revenue is calculated as follows:

$$(312 - 266) \div (156 - 133) = \$2$$

Similarly, the marginal cost is calculated by dividing the change in cost to the change in yield. For example, as yield decreases from 156 to 133, the cost decreases from \$96 to \$80. The ratio of the change in cost to the change in yield is calculated below:

$$(96 - 80) \div (156 - 133) = \$0.69$$

This means that the marginal cost of increasing yield by one unit over the yield range between 133 and 156 is approximately \$0.69 per unit. With information at more yield levels this calculation would become more precise.

The profit maximizing yield can be determined by inspection of Table 10.2. The maximum profit attainable is \$230 at a yield level of 175. Referring to Table 10.1, a yield of 175 is realized when the pest population is reduced to 4.

From this information, a rational decisionmaker should suppress the pest population to 4 and spend \$120 on pest control. To spend more than that would be unreasonable because it would reduce profits. The cost of increasing the yield exceeds the value of the yield increase. Spending less than \$120 would also be unwise because the decrease in cost is exceeded by the decrease in revenue.

The results are illustrated using the concepts of total cost and total revenue in Figure 10.2a. Total revenue is a straight line with a slope of 2. Total cost is rising at an increasing rate as yield increases. The vertical difference between the total revenue and total cost lines is total profit. It increases and then decreases, reaching the maximum profit at a yield of 175. If the grower were to reduce the pest population to 3 and increase yield to 190, the total cost would be \$160 and the total revenue would be \$380 for a profit of \$220. This is less than the maximum profit of \$230.

An alternative way of reaching the same conclusion is to employ the concepts of marginal revenue and marginal cost. Figure 10.2b illustrates the use of marginal cost and marginal revenue curves. We know that each additional unit of output can be sold for \$2 so marginal revenue is constant at this level. We can define the marginal cost of producing an additional unit of output in terms of the expense for pest control required to reduce damage to the point that yield goes up by one unit. Because all other costs are constant, the marginal cost is solely a function of pest control expenditures.

As might be expected, the marginal cost increases as we try to reduce the pest level further and further in order to increase yield. Table 10.2 illustrates the marginal revenue and marginal cost associated with each additional unit of production. When marginal cost equals marginal revenue at \$2 at a yield of 175, we have reached the optimal degree of expense for pest control. This is the same profit maximizing yield found using total concepts.

Figure 10.3 illustrates the pest population growth function and the damage threshold. From our analysis the economic threshold is 4 and the damage threshold, below which no damage occurs, is 2. Recall that the economic

FIGURE 10.2 Total and Marginal Profit Maximization Concepts

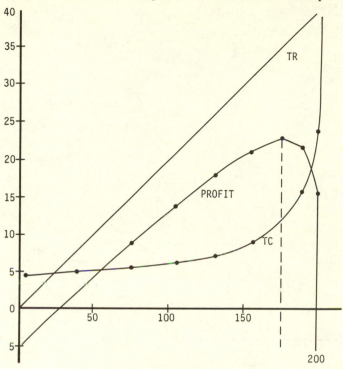

(a) Profit Maximization--Total Concepts

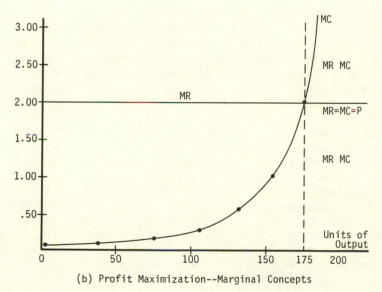

(b) Profit Maximization--Marginal Concepts

FIGURE 10.3 Economic Threshold for Hypothetical Pest Situation—Control Initiated at Time Period 3

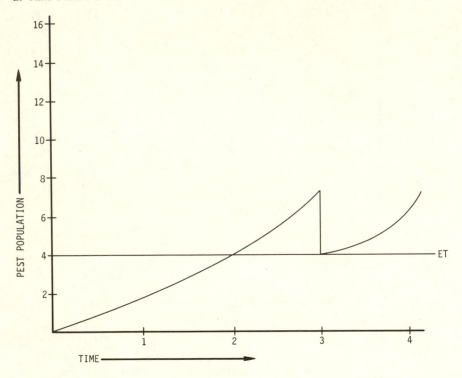

threshold is static. That is, it does not change over time. Also, the decisionmaker is using one application of a pesticide at a specified point in time. The only decision variable is to what level the pest population should be reduced. Adequate spray is applied in time period 3 to reduce the pest population to 4. Notice that in this simple model there is no time lag between the spray application and population response as there was in Figure 10.1.

Reducing pest population below 2 results in no benefits whatsoever. No amount of spending on pest control can increase yields. At pest populations above 4 the marginal revenue exceeds the marginal cost. This means that increasing pest control expenditures results in increased profits because the increase in cost is more than offset by higher revenues from higher yields.

Headley made an important contribution by integrating economic concepts with biological models and refining the definition of economic threshold. Hall and Norgaard (1973) refined the Headley model to allow the timing of application and quantity of pesticide applied to vary. For simplicity, the assumption was made that there is a single optimal time of application that is determined simultaneously with the optimal quantity of pesticide applied. The damage and yield functions have the same form as in the Headley model. The optimum timing and quantity of pesticide application are found by maximizing profit with respect to these two inputs.

Talpaz and Borosh (1974) refined Headley's basic model by allowing for multiple pesticide treatments within a season. This model made it possible to choose among several alternative control practices. The control practices vary by the quantity of pesticides applied for each treatment and the number of applications.

All of these models illustrate the difficulty of integrating the concept of profit maximization with even a simple biological model to determine the optimal timing and application rate for a single pesticide. The Headley model allowed for a single pesticide application at a designated point in time. Only the application rate varied. Hall and Norgaard allowed the timing and quantity of a single pesticide application to vary. Talpaz and Borosh allowed for multiple pesticide treatments where timing and quantity could vary.

Each model considered only one pesticide. However, comparison of alternative pesticide materials could be accomplished by specifying a "kill function" for each pesticide. In other words, the relationship between pest population and pesticide rates would be different for each pesticide.

Pesticide regulations have not been explicitly introduced into these models. The restrictions on pesticide use can be introduced by "constrained maximization": specifying maximum values for pesticide rates, maximum numbers of applications, and minimum time lags between applications. The models described thus far have implicitly considered pesticide regulations by including only pesticides that are registered for use on the crop under consideration.

Modeling Regional Strategies

Hueth and Regev (1974) also used a single crop, single pest, single-year model and relaxed the assumption of a single chemical application. They made an important contribution by including long-run impacts of pest control in their analysis by considering "the dynamic properties of the economic threshold." Specifically, they included increasing pest resistance over time by characterizing pest susceptibility to chemical control as an exhaustible resource. User costs associated with pest resistance were included in the analysis as were monetary costs of control to capture the effects of pest resistance.[1] The user costs considered by Hueth and Regev were "increased future costs of controlling the pest as a result of a decision to apply chemicals today" that resulted in the depletion of the stock of susceptible pests (that is, increased pest resistance).

The economic threshold was determined as follows: "If the marginal value of insecticides in crop production is less than the marginal unit cost of insecticides plus the marginal cost of their use in reducing the stock of susceptibility, none will be used. If any insecticides are used, the level of use will be such that the marginal benefit equals the marginal cost."

Following this analysis, profit maximization that ignores user costs of pesticides results in nonoptimal behavior. However, the activities of an

TABLE 10.3:   Hypothetical Pest Management
               Alternatives

Control Method	Percent Mortality	Cost/Acre
No control	0	$ 0
Combination	75	$ 10
Chemical	90	$ 30

individual grower have essentially no impact on pest resistance. The solution presented was a regional solution for several growers with a multiyear planning horizon that maximized regional profit. Some institutional change was considered necessary before user cost of reducing the stock of susceptibility could be included in an individual's decisionmaking process. The authors suggested that some sort of taxes or subsidies could be put in place "to discourage pesticide use and maximize regional profits."

If growers were taxed for each pesticide application, then the cost of using pesticides would increase. Consequently, pesticide use should decrease as the cost increased. Similarly, a subsidy would compensate growers for crop lost to pest damage. Growers would choose the subsidy over using the pesticide when the value of the subsidy was greater or equal to the value of the crop protected minus the cost of the pesticide.

Hueth and Regev's study is important for at least two reasons. First, they showed that the definition of economic threshold can include future effects of pest management beyond the current season. Second, if interdependencies between growers and time periods are to be considered in developing pest management strategies, profit maximization for a single firm using only market values to measure the benefits and costs of pest control is not adequate criteria for making a decision.

All but the last of the models discussed assumed that pest control decisions are independent of the pest population in subsequent time periods or seasons. When populations are not independent from year to year, combining the optimal strategies for each year independently will not result in an optimal strategy over the entire period. Headley (1975) illustrated this point with a hypothetical management system consisting of three available control methods and a two-year planning horizon. The costs and percent of mortality vary for each control method. He considered the following three control methods: (1) no control, (2) a combination of biological and chemical controls, and (3) chemical control. Table 10.3 depicts the costs and mortality for each.

FIGURE 10.4 Two-Period Pest Control Problems

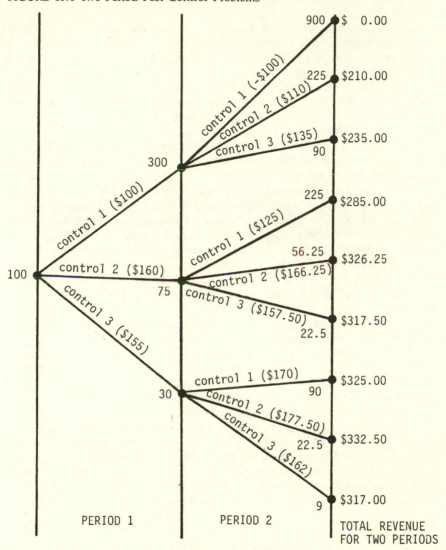

Through this simple example Headley showed that maximization of net income for each time period separately will not lead to the same selection of methods as will maximization of net income over several time periods.

The problem of maximization over two time periods can be solved by constructing a decision tree for each possible combination of controls using the data in Table 10.3 and finding the maximum net income by inspection (Figure 10.4). An initial population of 100 is assumed. The pest populations for each period are shown in Figure 10.4 to the left of each branch of the tree. The net incomes for each control strategy for each time period are in parentheses.

At the beginning of period 1 the grower can choose among the three control strategies. Using control 1, no control, the population grows to 300 by the end of the period, and the net income is $100. Following control 2, a combination of chemical and biological controls, the population at the end of period 1 is reduced 75 percent to 75 and the net income is $160. Using control 3, chemical control, the population is reduced by 90 percent to 30, and the net income is $155. Looking at period 1 only, profit is maximized at $160 by using control 2.

In the second time period the initial pest population is 300, 75, or 30 depending on which strategy was followed in period 1. Again, the grower can choose among the three strategies.

If the grower chose control 1 in period 1, then the initial population in period 2 is 300. Referring to Figure 10.4, if the grower chooses control 1 again, the net profit in period 2 would be a loss of $100. The total revenue for period 2 would be $100 profit from period 1, plus the $100 loss from period 2, for a total of $0. The total revenue for the two time periods is shown in the right column of Figure 10.4.

Similarly, if the grower followed control 1 in period 1, with control 2 in period 2, the net revenue in period 2 would be $115 for a total over the two periods of $210 ($100 + $110). Finally, if the grower followed control 1 with control 3, the net income in the second period would be $135 and the total for the two periods would be $235 ($100 + $135).

The total revenues for the two time periods for each combination of control strategies are listed to the right of the branches of the decision tree. The maximum net revenue is attained by using control 3 in period 1 and control 2 in period 2 for a total of $332.50.

Recall that the profit maximizing solution for period 1 alone was control 2. However, the profit maximizing solution for the two time periods was control 3 followed by control 2. This simple example illustrates that the time horizon under consideration can influence the pest control decision when pest populations are not independent from year to year. Other factors such as resistance to pesticides or secondary pest outbreaks will affect the decision differently, depending on the time horizon under consideration.

SUMMARY AND CONCLUSION

Crop loss occurs despite extensive use of pesticides and other methods of pest control. As the volume of pesticide use has grown, so has the number of species that have developed resistance to pesticides. Other unfavorable consequences of pesticide use include resurgence of target pest populations and outbreaks of secondary pests. Still other negative impacts include health hazards to people and wildlife. These negative results stem from ignoring the adaptive capabilities of the environment and the interrelationship between agro-ecosystems and the broader ecosystem.

Integrated pest management is an approach to crop protection based on ecological principles. Management strategies take into account the role of pests in their environment and interactions among pests. The IPM philosophy also recognizes the interdependencies among members of society resulting from pesticide use. However, the desicions made by growers are governed by rational self-interest, which can result in adverse effects on others. The growers' decisionmaking process may not take into account the long-run and/or regional impacts of their individual actions. Rational decisionmakers will maximize the difference between the benefits and costs of production. Individual growers may not include costs to account for potential harmful effects on other people that may result from their production practices. In other words, costs as measured by the farm business are not the same as those for society. The pest management philosophy encourages judicious use of pesticides and encourages alternative methods of control.

Several theoretical models were presented for selecting among alternative pest control strategies. Each compared the benefits and costs of each alternative so that the "best" management strategy could be selected. Each used profit maximization as the decision criteria. However, each model used a different set of pest control options. One model considered a single pesticide application at a predetermined point in time as the only alternative. In this case, the decision is how much pesticide to apply. Another model looked at various combinations of timing and quantity of a single application. A third model allowed for multiple applications during a season. From these examples it is clear that the specification of the model strongly influences the pest management decision by limiting the set of possible strategies.

In addition, the specification of the costs and benefits determine the choice of management strategies. For example, a decision model may or may not include the long-run costs of increased resistance, parasite mortality, or environmental contamination. It is difficult to quantify these consequences of pest control and still more difficult to encourage individual growers to take long-run regional impacts into account in their pest management decisions. It was also demonstrated that maximizing profit over a one-year period and over a two-year period may not lead to the same choice of pest control. Thus, the time horizon under consideration will also influence pest management decisions.

Limitations of mathematical models due to model specification have been discussed. Specifically, the usefulness of a model is restricted by the problem definition as well as the temporal and spatial parameters selected to direct the modeling process. The limitations become increasingly apparent as innovative approaches to crop protection are developed.

Government regulations restrict and/or disallow the use of pesticides. The registration process requires extensive testing before a new product is allowed on the market. Regulation affects the cost of food production and, to some extent, the value of the food produced. In this way societal values reflected in governmental actions enter the pest management decisionmaking process. Constraints on the decisionmaking process limit the choice of options available to the producer by disallowing certain practices to be included in the set of alternatives.

A negative consequence of a strict regulatory process in the United States has been an increase in imports of agricultural products. Certainly, other cost factors and economic conditions have had a major impact. However, U.S. laws cannot restrict the pesticides applied to food imported into the United States except by placing restrictions on residues. An unfortunate consequence of pesticide regulations may be that traditionally high-pesticide-use crops, particularly fresh market vegetables, will be grown abroad and imported into the United States.

NOTES

1. The term *user cost* was coined by John Maynard Keynes and is used extensively in resource economics. As defined by Scott (1964) user cost is "the present value of the future profit forgone by a decision to produce a unit of output today."

REFERENCES

Carlson, G. A., and E. N. Castle (1972). *Economics of Pest Control.* Journal Paper no. 3456. Raleigh: North Carolina Agricultural Experiment Station.

Edwards, C. A., and G. W. Heath (1964). *The Principles of Agricultural Entomology.* Springfield, Ill.: Thomas Publishers.

Food and Agriculture Organization (1967). *Report of the First Session of FAO Panel of Experts on Integrated Pest Control.* Rome: Food and Agriculture Organization.

Geier, P. W. (1970). "Organizing Large-Scale Projects in Pest Management." *Meeting on Cotton Pests.* Rome: Food and Agriculture Organization, FAO15330-70-WM, pp. 1–8.

Hall, D. C., and R. B. Norgaard (1973). "On the Timing and Application of Pesticides." *American Journal of Agricultural Economics* 55(2):198–201.

Headley, J. C. (1972). "Defining the Economic Threshold," *Pest Control Strategies for the Future.* Washington, D. C.: National Academy of Sciences, pp. 100–108.

Headley, J. C. (1975). "The Economics of Pest Management" in R. L. Metcalf and W. H. Luckman, eds., *Introduction to Insect Pest Management.* New York: John Wiley and Sons.

Hueth, D., and U. Regev (1974). "Optimal Agricultural Pest Management with Increasing Pest Resistance." *American Journal of Agricultural Economics* 56(3):543–552.

Scott, A. (1964). "The Economic Goals of Federal Finance." *Public Finance* 19:241–288.

Smith, R. F., and W. W. Allen (1954). "Insect Control and the Balance of Nature." *Scientific American* 190(6):38–42.

Smith, R. F., and H. T. Reynolds (1965). "Principles, Definitions and Scope of Integrated Pest Control." *Proceedings of the FAO Symposium on Integrated Pest Control,* vol. 1. Rome: Food and Agriculture Organization.

Stern, V. M., R. F. Smith, R. van den Bosch, and K. S. Hagen (1959). "The Integrated Control Concept." *Hilgardia* 29(2):81–101.

Talpaz, H. and I. Borosh (1974). "Strategy for Pesticide Use: Frequency and Applications." *American Journal of Agricultural Economics* 56(4):769–775.

U.S. Office of Technology Assessment (1979). *Pest Management Strategies*. Vols. 1, 2. Washington, D.C.: Office of Technology Assessment.

SUGGESTED READINGS

Bottrell, Dale R. (1979). *Integrated Pest Management*. Washington, D.C.: Council on Environmental Quality, U.S. Government Printing Office.
The philosophical basis for pest management is reviewed. Policy implications are explored.

Carlson, G. A. (1980). "Economic and Biological Variables Affecting Demand for Publicly and Privately Provided Pest Information." *American Journal of Agricultural Economics* 62(5):1001–1006.
The demand for pest management information is estimated. The interaction effects of public and private information delivery are explored.

Flint, Mary Louise, and Robert Van den Bosch (1981). *Introduction to Integrated Pest Management*. New York: Plenum Press.
This text emphasizes the ecosystem management approach to pest control. The basic interactions within the environment are described. Several case studies are presented.

Metcalf, Robert, and William Luckman (1982). *Introduction to Insect Pest Management*, 2d ed. New York: John Wiley and Sons.
This text introduces the fundamental concepts behind the principles, tactics, and strategies of insect pest management. It includes several chapters of real-world applications.

STUDY QUESTIONS

1. Evaluate the possibility for improving markets as a way to adjust the externality effects associated with the use of pesticides. How do the issues in this chapter compare to the problems of controlling acid rain, as discussed in Chapter 6?

2. As a policymaker how might you weigh the benefits of lower-cost disease and blemish-free produce against the hazards to the environment associated with pesticide use?

3. What benefits are there from an analyst's perspective in using simple models, such as Headley's, to evaluate grower behavior?

4. Is economic injury a useful concept in setting up pest management programs? If so, what are its benefits and limitations?

Chapter Eleven

The Greenhouse Effect
and the Canadian Prairies
Simulation of Future Economic Impacts

Louise M. Arthur

Human activities such as the burning of fossil fuels and deforestation are expected to produce profound climate changes in the next century. In this chapter the author examines the economic impact on the Canadian prairies of this climate change—the greenhouse effect. Different forecasting models are presented and their strengths and weaknesses compared. Both linear programming and input-output models are used in order to assess small probability and high-consequence climatic risks for agricultural production.

One of the principal uses of economic models is to estimate the likelihood of future events based on an understanding of earlier events. Economists call this process forecasting. Empirical economic models are developed using data concerning past and current economic phenomena. If the model adequately explains these previous phenomena, the results are extrapolated beyond the data period covered by the model. That is, for forecasting purposes, economists assume the same basic economic relationships revealed by the model will continue into the future.

Even when the economic model is very rigorous and reliable, the forecasts based on the model can be very wrong. Economic relationships may have changed, or events may have occurred that were not anticipated by the modelers and thus not included in the model. Despite these and other sources of forecasting error, empirical models remain the economist's most dependable source for forecasting.

In many of the subdisciplines of economics numerous well-researched models are available for use in forecasting. In the environmental economics field there are few. The quantitative data on environmental processes needed to develop such models are either unavailable, inadequate, or unreliable. In other subdisciplines, models are used to forecast over relatively short time frames, from days to a few years at most. In environmental economics the important environmental conditions often transform very slowly, so measurable changes may occur only decades in the future. Thus, the required forecasts are necessarily for longer terms.

The lack of valid models of environmental processes and the long time frame of many environmental processes create nearly insurmountable problems for economists attempting to estimate the economic impacts of environmental phenomena. Nevertheless, demands for such impact measures exist, and thus attempts will be made to forecast environmental changes and determine their economic effects.

This chapter illustrates some of the difficulties in modeling the economic impact of an environmental change—the greenhouse effect—that may occur a century from now. Obviously, forecasting the economic setting a century from now is impossible. Hence, studies of this type usually involve a simulation of what would happen if the environmental change were to happen *today*, immediately, not gradually. Thus, such simulative "forecasts" do not attempt to provide measures of economic impact that are accurate to the dollar but instead try to reveal the more general nature, pattern, and magnitude of economic effects that can be expected.

PROBLEM BACKGROUND

Climate and weather variability are important factors in planning nearly all aspects of human activity, but it now appears that human activity, in turn, affects climate. In producing heat and energy people burn fossil fuels and thereby release enormous quantities of carbon dioxide (CO_2) and particulate matter into the atmosphere. Other demands for heat, energy, and consumer goods lead us to destroy extensive areas of CO_2-consuming forests, thereby further increasing atmospheric carbon dioxide concentrations.

Most climatologists agree that the documented increases in CO_2 concentrations will bring about profound changes in climate by the next century (Shewchuk, 1984). Numerous other trace gases, both naturally occurring and man-made, have similar climatic effects. These gases include methane from increased bovine populations and rice paddies; nitrous oxide from fertilizers and the burning of coal, oil, and gas; and chlorofluorocarbons from industry and aerosols. The latter two gases may contribute to global warming by decreasing the ozone in the stratosphere, thereby preventing its absorption of infrared radiation. The aggregate climatic influence of these other gases may be approaching the effects of CO_2 and could even surpass these effects, particularly if CO_2 emissions are curtailed (Canadian Climate Centre, 1985; Seidel and Keyes, 1983).

The greenhouse effect generally refers to a gradual climatic warming associated with increased concentrations of these greenhouse gases. The consequent climatic changes are called the greenhouse effect because the mechanism is similar to that in a greenhouse; as the sun's rays heat the earth's surface and energy is radiated back to the atmosphere, some of the energy is trapped by atmospheric CO_2 and other trace gases. Predictions of the eventual effects of this warming trend range from more frequent droughts to a booming arctic economy, northern prairie orchards, and a U.S. midwestern desert. Of course, most of the latter predictions are based on pure, sometimes hopeful, speculation. Nevertheless, scientists believe that the climatic changes will be great enough that we need to develop a strategy for identifying and coping with the issue now.

Currently, much of the research on climate change has focused on identifying the physical relationships between emission and atmospheric retention of greenhouse gases and between changing concentrations of these gases and the consequent climatic effects. Because carbon dioxide represents the single most important greenhouse gas, most climatological research has concentrated on CO_2 emissions and concentrations.

THE NATURE OF THE GREENHOUSE EFFECT OF INCREASING CO_2

No firm consensus exists concerning the cause of the increasing CO_2 concentrations. Some scientists argue that the burning of fossil fuels and extensive harvesting of forests are major contributors, while others claim the recent increasing trend is part of a natural carbon cycle (Shewchuk, 1984).[1] Nevertheless, most predictions are for a doubling of atmospheric CO_2 concentrations in the next 40 to 100 years (Roberts, 1983). Concentrations of CO_2 are generally measured relative to the content of all other gases, in parts per million (ppm) by volume. Since accurate records have become available, average concentrations have risen steadily from 315 ppm in 1958 to 340 ppm in 1980. No systematic records are available for earlier time periods, but preindustrial levels are estimated at 270 to 300 ppm. In the past decade CO_2 concentrations have been increasing at a rate of nearly 0.4 percent per year and are expected to reach 600 ppm or roughly double preindustrial concentrations within the next century. By environmental standards, this would be a major change!

Should this doubling occur, atmospheric models predict a mean global temperature increase of 1.5 to 4 degrees C, with even greater increases predicted in high latitude areas such as Canada and the Soviet Union (Parry and Carter, 1984). The temperature increase could be even greater if the concentrations of trace gases such as methane, nitrogen oxide, and chlorofluoromethanes also increase.

POLICY ISSUES

If human activity is causing the greenhouse effect, can the effect be stopped? Scientists at the U.S. Environmental Protection Agency (EPA) outline the difficulties in doing so; even major efforts to ban coal burning by 2000 A.D. or drastically reduce the use of fossil fuels do not appear to avert a doubling of CO_2 concentrations, and thus will merely postpone the greenhouse effect (Seidel and Keyes, 1983). Furthermore, recent declines in oil prices appear to have induced *increased* use of fossil fuels, and earlier increases in oil prices merely brought about a substitution to less efficient hydrocarbons, that is, coal. The developed world seems intent on a continuing high level of energy use and is using CO_2-producing sources primarily.

Other possible directions for addressing the problem include adapting to the changing climate, technological control of CO_2 emissions, and counteracting the effects of trace gases in the atmosphere. The latter approach is possibly the least promising as it implies global weather modification procedures.

Currently, there are few examples of policy actions stemming directly from expectations of climate change.[2] While there is still considerable ambiguity concerning the actual cause, likelihood, timing, and magnitude of a CO_2-induced greenhouse effect, this uncertainty is only one of the obstacles to government action. Another is the concern governments have out of necessity for short- rather than long-term phenomena. However, longer run changes like the greenhouse effect can be put in the context of the shorter run to facilitate government action (Parry, 1985). The greenhouse effect can be expressed in terms of an increase in the frequencies or probabilities of otherwise anomalous events, such as a 1936 drought, rather than as a totally new climatic regime. Policymakers may then more readily understand the issues, communicate the need for immediate action, and devise adjustment policies to accommodate the increased risk.

The research community has not yet reached a consensus that the uncertain level of CO_2-induced climatic change warrants the drastic action required to alter significantly the rate of CO_2 accumulation; the greenhouse effect would have to be more certain, imminent, and dangerous before we would opt to change our lifestyles considerably or invest substantial sums in technological controls or weather modification. Thus, research continues to emphasize improvements in our ability to forecast the future path of climatic change and its potential impacts, rather than emphasizing a means to averting or adapting to the greenhouse effect.

STUDY OF THE ECONOMIC IMPACTS OF THE GREENHOUSE EFFECT

Study of the economic impacts of climatic problems related to changes in carbon dioxide concentrations is difficult because tremendous uncertainty surrounds projections of expected concentrations and estimates of the resulting climatic changes. Assessing the economic impacts of these ambiguous changes and an appropriate policy response is further complicated by inadequate understanding of *current* socioeconomic sensitivities to climate, as well as by an inability to generate accurate long-term forecasts of the social and economic factors that color responses to climate. Nevertheless, there is now enough scientific support for, and concern over, the magnitude of temperature increase predictions from sophisticated climatic models that economic impact studies and policy analyses are being undertaken throughout the world, despite known errors in the climatic and impact models. These studies are currently at the stage of determining the magnitude and regional distribution of climatic impacts so that effective policies can be designed.

Estimating the economic impacts of future events like a greenhouse effect requires use of simulation models. Simulation modeling is an attempt to reproduce the critical components of a behavioral system. A simulation model for impact analysis, then, requires estimation of both the exogenous stimuli that cause the impact and reproduction of the behavior of impact recipients. To simulate the economic impacts of the greenhouse effect on agriculture, for example, both a model of climate changes and a model of the components of the agricultural sector that are sensitive to climate are needed.

When simulation models are used to estimate the impacts of future events, the usual forecasting errors can be expected. For example, economic impacts of the greenhouse effect on agriculture in the next century will depend in part on successes in plant breeding and other technological improvements, and the future political and socioeconomic environment. Because predictions concerning the future availability of new crop varieties and actions of oil cartels, for example, are even more tenuous than climatic predictions, most economic impact analyses do not attempt to project major technological and sociological changes. If errors in predicting climate were compounded by errors in predicting these latter factors, there would remain no basis on which to judge the meaning or validity of the resulting impact estimates. Instead, most impact models draw on available knowledge of current sensitivities to climatic conditions, for which validity tests are available, to estimate future sensitivities.

The discrepancy between available economic and agronomic impact models and the CO_2-induced climate change issue is illustrated in Figure 11.1. While economic impact models use the time and distance scales of the farm response and regional response boxes in the figure, the climatic impetus is developed using models with dramatically different time and distance parameters, the climate change box in the figure. Agroclimatic models often center on the plant response box, which is even farther from the climatic scenario models. Nevertheless, some linkages between various lower and leftward sections of the figure and regional responses have been made successfully (Arthur and Freshwater, 1986; Carter, Konijn, and Watts, 1984; Jones and Huang, 1983). Only actual attempts to apply current impact assessment techniques to analysis of climatic change will reveal the inadequacies in the interfacing of data and modeling results from very different time and distance scales. Thus, these early attempts at climatic impact assessment will be useful for refining methods of assessment as much as for estimating the precise magnitudes of the impacts before they occur.

The climatic models linking increased carbon dioxide concentrations to climatic effects are generally three-dimensional models of atmospheric circulations, so-called general circulation models (GCMs). Many of these models have been combined with models of oceanic interactions. The GCMs are

FIGURE 11.1 Time and Distance Scales for Climate Models

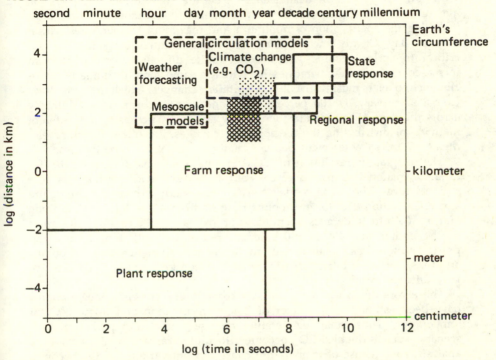

Regional, short-term disruptive event (e.g. UK drought, 1976)

Supraregional, medium-term disruptive event (e.g. El Niño,1982–83)

Source: M. L. Parry and T. R. Carter, eds., "Assessing the Impact of Climate Change in Cold Regions," Summary Report SR-84-1 (Laxenburg, Austria: International Institute for Applied Systems Analysis, 1984).

selected both for their ability to explain current climates and for their relatively fine temporal and spatial resolutions, the latter feature a requirement for regional impact analysis. Despite the resolution advantages of GCMs, the resolution is not sufficient for many economic impact models. Temperature and precipitation predictions from the most commonly used GCMs (those used in the research described below) are provided only as monthly averages. This temporal resolution is extremely fine from a climatological point of view, but crop yield models used in determining economic impacts on agricultural sectors often require daily temperature and moisture conditions, including the specification of minimum and maximum temperatures within a given day. Clearly, increased *minimum* temperatures early in a month critical to spring seeding will produce quite different crop yields from increased *maximum* temperatures later in the same month. Similarly, agroclimatic modelers must distribute precipitation changes, which are sometimes estimated to vary by 100 percent from one month to the next, arbitrarily across the days of the month.[3] Sensitivity analyses, such as trying different methods of distributing the precipitation changes, are often necessary elements of impact assessment because of these model incompatibilities.

The geographic resolution of GCM results is suitable for aggregate (for example, national) impact analyses, but is not adequate for analysis at a regional level. The GCM models used in the study provided temperature and precipitation data for grid points ranging from 4.4 to 8 degrees latitude and from 7.5 to 10 degrees longitude (approximately 300 to 550 miles apart north to south and 400 to 500 miles apart east to west). Temperature and precipitation estimates can vary dramatically across neighboring grid points, and thus, various arbitrary distributions between grid points could produce very different results.

The errors of GCMs for $1 \times CO_2$ (that is, for current concentrations) have been estimated at a factor of 2 for precipitation and up to 5°C for temperature. Thus, small temperature changes under a hypothetical CO_2 scenario, such as doubled CO_2, become difficult to evaluate. Again, sensitivity analysis, such as use of temperature changes from various GCMs, becomes necessary. These various sources of error in the estimates of climatic changes lead to less reliable estimates of the economic impacts of these climatic changes than policymakers would like.

THE GREENHOUSE EFFECT ON THE CANADIAN PRAIRIES: A CASE STUDY

Returns to agricultural production throughout the world have long been subject to the vagaries of weather and climate, particularly on the higher latitude steppes or prairies, where dryland cropping predominates and limited precipitation and heat units are major constraints to crop selection and yields. The extreme sensitivity of the international agricultural sector to weather becomes obvious every time a severe drought strikes one of the world suppliers of major agricultural commodities. Some regions and crops are more vulnerable to drought; some are more critical in ensuring stable world food supplies. One of the most vulnerable and critical areas is the North American plains, which includes the Canadian prairies.

Agricultural sensitivities to climatic variability are most readily observed in areas of geographical or economic marginality, where long-term average returns from production just exceed costs, risks and uncertainty are high, and/or cropping options are few. Producer groups that are considered marginal because they face considerable climatic risk include (1) farmers in the humid tropics with risks of excess precipitation, (2) farmers in the arid and semiarid regions who face risks of insufficient precipitation, (3) farmers in high altitudes and high latitudes who face high intra-annual temperature fluctuations. Farmers in the first group are typically involved in subsistence agriculture, while the latter groups are found in both underdeveloped and developed economies. Although human survival is clearly of critical importance in determining the world agricultural impacts of the greenhouse effect, quantitative impact assessment is more easily undertaken in developed economies with extant databases and models. One of these areas, the Canadian prairies, is of particular interest because it falls within both the high latitude and arid (particularly Saskatchewan and southern Alberta) categories.

The Prairie Setting

The Canadian prairies, comprising the provinces of Alberta, Saskatchewan, and Manitoba (bordering Montana, North Dakota, and Minnesota), are particularly appropriate as case study areas for examining agricultural impacts of climatic change for several reasons. First, while the anticipated changes in climate are worldwide, in the higher latitudes the temperature change is expected to be even greater (Parry and Carter, 1984). Second, the prairies represent a prime example of a high latitude, weather sensitive, agriculturally developed economy. The current climatic conditions, including short growing season and consistent moisture deficits, already severely limit crop production. Prairie crop yields are low relative to those of competitors in the United States and Europe, and prairie farmers have few economically viable varieties from which to select; for example, 80 percent of prairie spring wheat production volumes comprises four varieties, and spring wheat represents over half of prairie crop production (Manitoba Department of Agriculture, 1985). Furthermore, the current climatic regime limits agricultural production to the southern areas of the provinces; global warming could result in substantial increases in arable acreage.[4]

Third, the majority of prairie agricultural production is in the crops sector. In 1983, over 60 percent of the value of Manitoba's farm sales, over 80 percent of Saskatchewan's, and nearly 55 percent of Alberta's farm sales were from the crops sector (Canada Grains Council, 1985). Furthermore, most of the cultivated cropland is entirely dependent on moisture available from annual precipitation, as is much of the pasture and forage land; in Manitoba, for example, only 0.3 percent of the 12 million acres of cropland is irrigated. Consequently, temperature and precipitation changes could severely disrupt prairie agriculture.

Fourth, prairie economies are extremely dependent on agricultural incomes and activities. Primary agricultural production comprises 17 percent of Manitoba's value added for goods producing sectors, 40 percent of Saskatchewan's, and approximately 10 to 15 percent of Alberta's value added. Additional economic activity is directly related to agricultural production by providing inputs to agriculture or transporting, marketing, or processing agricultural products. Therefore, any decline in prairie agricultural production will have substantial impacts on the entire prairie economy.

Finally, the Canadian prairies play a major role in the world grain trade. Over the last decade, Canadian wheat comprised only 5 percent of world production volumes but over 18 percent of total export volumes of wheat. Over 96 percent of this wheat is produced on the prairies, and wheat comprised 71 percent of total grain exports. Prairie barley comprised over 26 percent of world barley exports. Although the prairie region is not the world's major supplier of grains, it supplies sufficient volumes to be considered an important source of supply. Thus, a complete evaluation of the impact of a worldwide greenhouse effect on the Canadian prairies' agricultural sector should include analysis of greenhouse effects on other sellers and buyers in the world grain trade. Clearly, such an analysis would be complex and costly, more costly than warranted by the current accuracies of various estimates of the greenhouse effect. However, the study described below could serve as input into a global study addressing world food balances.

Methods

The objective of this study was to estimate the impacts on the prairie economy of the greenhouse effects from doubled atmospheric carbon dioxide concentrations. The boxes in Figure 11.2 represent the various components of the simulation model developed for the impact analysis. The causal linkages among models are primarily unidirectional and begin with daily weather effects on crop soil moistures, as modeled in the soil moisture simulator. This deterministic, biological model translates the temperature and precipitation of the various climatic scenarios into soil moisture deficits for various crops on various soil types. A series of statistical simulation models determines the yield impact of the moisture deficits. These yield data become the critical factor determining the performance of the aggregate crops sector in each province. For the province of Manitoba, economic models were available to translate these yields into sectoral incomes; these economic models include a linear programming (LP) model of the aggregate crops sector, which requires information from on-farm production simulators, a set of representative farm production and management models (the Farm Models), and a livestock population simulator.[5] Input-output (I-O) models are then used to translate agricultural sector impacts into economic effects on backwardly linked sectors, that is, those providing inputs to primary agriculture, such as the fertilizer and farm machinery industries (Statistics

FIGURE 11.2 Models Used in Impact Analysis

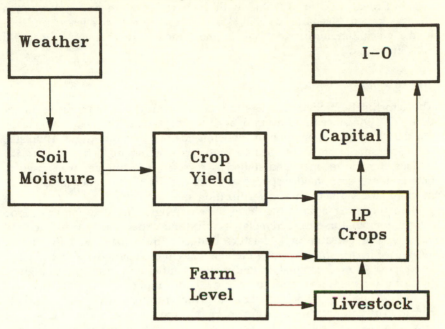

Canada 1981 and 1982). The nature of each of these models is described briefly below.

The Climatic Change Scenarios

All the simulated economic impacts stem from exogenous changes in climate; all other factors such as prices, technologies, and political structure are held constant. Four climatic scenarios were provided by Environment Canada's Atmospheric Environment Service (AES) based on atmospheric models. First, experiments were undertaken for quadrupled CO_2 concentrations, which were then divided by two to obtain temperature and precipitation changes for doubled CO_2; these results are called Scenario A below. For Scenario B, modeling experiments were run for doubled CO_2. Although these scenarios sound identical, the two modeling approaches produce very different climatic results. Both show general warming, but the magnitudes of the warming and the monthly distributions of the temperature and precipitation changes differ.

AES compared the results of these two scenarios to similar experiments for normal CO_2 concentrations to derive *changes* in temperature and precipitation under the new climate. These temperature and precipitation changes were then added to historic, daily temperature and precipitation data for 1961 to 1985.

Scenarios A and B were analyzed with only the temperature changes, called "Scenario A_t or B_t," and with both temperature and precipitation changes, called "Scenario A_{tp} or B_{tp}," as the researchers have less confidence in the precipitation changes than in the temperature changes (Hengeveld and Street, n.d.).

The Agroclimatic Models

The agroclimatic models translate the meteorological events predicted under doubled CO_2 concentrations into agricultural events, that is, crop yields. For this study, a combination of modeling methods was used: deterministic, biological simulators were used to model crop moisture deficits under the various climatic regimes, and statistical regression techniques were used to determine the crop yield response to those deficits and to other factors such as crop variety selection and fertilization rates.

Both modeling approaches have shortcomings. The deterministic, crop moisture simulators are extremely complex and expensive to construct and validate. The Versatile Soil Moisture Budget (VSMB; Baier and Robertson, 1966) used in this study operates daily; it takes into account daily precipitation and runoff, snow accumulation and melt, potential evapotranspiration given the daily temperatures, daily crop growth including rooting patterns, and so forth. Thus, the model simulates a given crop's daily response to daily climate. The data requirements are enormous, the understanding of biological crop responses critical, and the results overwhelming in detail. Nevertheless, the results have been shown to be reliable and generally worth the expense.

However, available biological simulation models account for only the soil and weather factors that affect yields, though it is understood that technological and management factors are also important determinants of crop response to weather. Thus, the results of the VSMB models were used as one input in the statistical regression models of crop yields. Yields were modeled as a function of moisture deficits by growth stage, fertilization rates, crop variety selection, cultivation method, location, and extreme weather events such as excess moisture and killing frosts.

Statistical models also have several shortcomings that should be considered when assessing their results. Statistical models are based on relatively short-run data sets in which factors such as soil properties change so slowly as to be imperceptible. These imperceptible factors must be treated as constants in the model estimation, when in the longer run they may become important determinants of crop yield responses to weather. For example, the decay of organic matter is influenced by moisture and temperature, as are soil erosion and general soil degradation. Thus, under new climatic conditions soil properties may be altered.

Similarly, the natural and bred adaptation of some plant species to new weather stresses in the future cannot be anticipated by models that are based on past observations. While such shortcomings are recognized, they cannot be avoided because some factors cannot be quantified for inclusion in an empirical model.

A third weakness of statistical models relates to difficulties in predicting yield responses to extreme events like droughts and heat waves. Predictions generated from statistical regression equations are most accurate when they fall close to the average of observed values included in the model; success in predicting responses to more rare and extreme circumstances is more difficult to achieve. Yet, under the greenhouse effect, increased severity or frequency of extreme events and accompanying increases in risk may produce the most critical agricultural impacts.

Despite the wide variety of efforts to develop statistical agroclimatic models, one conclusion predominates: Complex climatic effect models seem to be necessary to produce accurate yield predictions. Although no simple aggregate index of weather seems adequate to explain all the complexities of the interactions between weather and plant growth, complicating the yield response function even more are the effects of nonweather factors such as soil textures and organic content, fertilization rates, pesticide use, crop variety selection, and so forth. Thus, a combination of extremely detailed moisture budget simulators (VSMBs) and complex statistical regression models appears to be necessary to model yield responses to new climatic regimes. In this study even this expensive and complex method of simulating yields could explain only half of the historic variation in crop yields. The other half of the yield variation is likely due to other factors: microclimates that are not recorded given the current density of weather stations, variations in farmers' management practices, and pest or soils problems that are unique to small areas.

The yield responses to climate quantified in the VSMB and regression models account for only the temperature and moisture changes due to doubled CO_2. CO_2 also acts as a plant food and has been shown to affect the efficiency of a plant's water use (Kimball, 1982). However, experiments documenting these effects have taken place under optimal greenhouse conditions and do not account for the interaction between water-use enhancement and climatic change from the doubled CO_2. Because yield effects in average field conditions are unknown, this impact of enhanced CO_2 concentrations could not be quantified for inclusion in the statistical yield models.

The Economic Models

The economic models simulate the effects of the predicted crop yields on the agricultural sector (in the LP models, Figure 11.2) and then the effects of the agricultural sector on other economic sectors (I-O models).

LP Models. An LP problem is concerned with the efficient allocation of limited resources to meet a desired objective. The objective is stated in linear mathematical form:

$$a_1x_1 + a_2x_2 + \ldots + a_nx_n$$

where a_i are known coefficients and x_i are unknown variables. In this study the objective is to maximize crop revenues net of variable input costs. The

a_i are the revenue and cost coefficients, and the unknown x_i are the acreages seeded to each crop.

The solution that maximizes the objective function, that is, net revenues, will change every time a coefficient changes. The climatic scenarios described above will change these coefficients; as crop yields change, so do revenues and input costs for harvesting, trucking, machinery repairs, and so forth.

Other constraints affect the model solution. The maximum net revenue that can be achieved is constrained by the size and quality of the resource base, available technology, the transportation system, demands for various crops, etc. For instance, even if grain corn is the highest valued crop under the greenhouse scenario, there is only a limited demand for western Canadian grain corn; corn acreage can increase over 1986 acreages, but the increase is constrained by marketing opportunities.

The solution values in the objective function and constraints indicate several factors: the crops selected for seeding (x_i), the inputs used in growing the crops, the mix of feeds used to meet livestock nutrient requirements (from the livestock simulator, Figure 11.2), the volume of crop sales, and so forth. That is, each solution of the LP models defines the adjustments in aggregate crop production and disposition (sales, storage, seed, or feed) that are predicted to occur under each climatic scenario.

Only one of the climatic change scenarios, Scenario A_{tp}, enhanced crop yields and thus agricultural incomes, and then only in Manitoba and Saskatchewan. In Manitoba this scenario resulted in a $29 million or over 9 percent increase in net crop revenues and a $53 million increase in grain inventories, due to yield increases and seeding of 21,000 additional acres.[6] Based on the yield results alone, the Scenario A_t impacts for Saskatchewan are expected to be similar in percentage terms.

All of the other altered climate scenarios resulted in net income losses in Manitoba and Saskatchewan, with reductions in Manitoba's net crop revenues ranging from $10 million or 3 percent in Scenario B_{tp} to $20 million or 6 percent in Scenario B_t. These results compare to an estimated $69 million, over 20 percent, in expected net revenue losses if a drought of the magnitude experienced in 1961, the most severe on recent record, were to occur under the same economic and technological conditions. The yield results for Saskatchewan indicate similar percentage impacts, with some attenuation of losses in Scenario B_{tp}. Alberta yield results suggest that Scenario B_{tp} may result in slight increases in incomes, but the two scenarios without precipitation suggest decreased incomes would prevail.

I-O Models. Economic effects on other sectors of the provincial economies are related to changes in the farm sectors' expenditures for farm inputs and consumer goods and services. The relationships between the economy beyond the farm gate and the agricultural sector, as represented in the LP models, are simulated using a series of I-O models for the prairie region (based on Statistics Canada, 1982).

I-O models consist of a series of linear, sectoral production functions (the columns of Table 11.1) and linear trading patterns among sectors (the

TABLE 11.1: Technical Coefficients and Multiplier Matrix

From Sector	To	Sectors A	B	C
		(technical coefficients)		
A		.16	.26	.03
B		.08	.07	.18
C		.11	.04	.21
From Sector	To	Sectors A	B	C
		(multipliers)		
A		1.38	.25	.28
B		.45	1.21	.16
C		.27	.38	1.38

rows in Table 11.1). The technical coefficients in the production and trade matrix (top of Table 11.1) provide only information concerning the *direct* purchases of goods from the various sectors in order to satisfy a given sector's production requirements; for example, to produce $1 of output, Sector A purchases $0.16 of its own products (intrasectoral trade among firms), $0.08 of product from Sector B, and $0.11 of Sector C's product. Missing in this "first round" effect is the multiplier effect on other sectors of the economy. For example, Sector B requires inputs from other sectors in order to produce the $0.08 worth of product purchased by Sector A. Sector B's demand for these "intermediate inputs" requires further production, further use of inputs, and so forth, hence the so-called "multiplier effect." Due to this effect, the total (direct and indirect) requirements for Sector B's products to service $1 of production by Sector A rise from $0.08 (top of Table 11.1) to $0.45 (bottom of Table 11.1).

It is the multiplier matrix, as in the bottom of Table 11.1, that is used to conduct economic impact analysis. The multiplier matrix for all endogenous sectors is postmultiplied by the changing demands of exogenous sectors to obtain the change in total industrial output. For this study only the agricultural sector's demands change across climatic scenarios, so the agricultural sector is exogenous, that is, simulated outside the I-O models; it is simulated in the LP models. The endogenous sectors include all producing sectors except agriculture and include all nonfarm household consumption. Farm consumption depends on farm incomes and thus is simulated in the LP models.

Any moneys not spent within the prairie provinces will not stimulate further provincial production. Under normal (baseline) climatic conditions, for example, nearly half of the $1.7 billion in expenditures by Manitoba farmers and farm households is for imported goods and services. Thus, the multiplier effect for agriculture is calculated on this reduced volume of provincial purchases.

Multiplier effects for the entire agricultural sector of each province average around 2.0. That is, for every $1 of provincial output purchased by the agricultural sector another $1 worth of output is produced by other sectors. For the baseline scenario in Manitoba, then, the $1.7 billion in agricultural expenditures becomes $984 million in provincial expenditures after imports are removed; this $984 million in production for agriculture then stimulates another $1 billion in production of other sectors.

Because the multiplier effects merely exaggerate the direct impacts of climate change on agriculture, scenarios that produce positive (negative) agricultural effects will produce positive (negative) effects on other sectors. Therefore, scenario A_{tp} will produce significant positive spin-offs to other sectors, and all other scenarios will produce negative spin-offs of lesser magnitudes. For example, for scenario A_{tp} the output of Manitoba's agriculturally linked sectors will increase approximately 8 percent, while under scenario B_{tp} output will decline by over 5 percent.

CONCLUSIONS OF THE CASE STUDY

Surprisingly, one of the climatic change scenarios enhanced agricultural productivity relative to baseline conditions, though only in Manitoba and Saskatchewan. The other altered-climate scenarios resulted in net income losses in Manitoba and Saskatchewan, but the losses were small relative to losses expected during major, historic droughts. Apparently, compensation for these losses cannot be expected from northward expansion of agriculture, due to the remaining constraints of length of growing season and soil quality. However, this constraint is sensitive to the daily distribution of the monthly average temperature, so as atmospheric modeling results are refined, this conclusion may change. Yields are similarly sensitive to daily distributions of the monthly precipitation and temperature change, so further sensitivity analyses are currently underway using the prairie models.

The results presented here suggest that prairie farmers need not fear an insidious greenhouse effect; they may benefit from the increased temperature and precipitation (Scenario A_{tp}) and at worst will suffer minor losses due to increased drought, which may be offset by the increased water-use efficiencies of the crop under the increased CO_2. The economic implications for prairie farmers of the impact of the greenhouse effect on other major competitors in world markets, particularly the U.S. Midwest, the Soviet Union, and Europe, will likely be as important as the effects on prairie yields, per se. Past studies of U.S., USSR, and European agriculture under the greenhouse effect all predict reduced yields of current crops (Canadian Climate Centre, 1985), which could mean improved markets for Canadian crops. However, most of these studies use only the greenhouse temperature changes, not the precipitation changes that could ameliorate or exacerbate the greenhouse effect.

The results presented here also indicate that speculative projections of the impact of the greenhouse effect may be very misleading. Detailed analysis of the prairie environment did not lead to predictions of prairie orchards or arctic strawberry fields, and similarly detailed analyses in the U.S. Midwest may not reveal expected desertification, particularly if precipitation changes can be included in the analysis. The much less dramatic greenhouse effects revealed in this study suggest that required adaptation strategies, at least for Canadian agriculture, may not be as unprecedented as some policymakers believe. The safest prediction is that "farmers will adapt to a change in climate, exploit it, and, probably, prove the pessimists wrong" (*The Economist*, 1983).

Other impacts of the greenhouse effect have not been considered in the case study. Increased evapotranspiration may reduce already scarce surface and ground water supplies, particularly in the western United States. Increases in global sea levels due to thermal expansion and/or polar ice melt may result in major floods of our highly populated coastal regions and disrupt port operations and aquatic ecosystems. Some of these latter impacts have implications for agriculture, coastal and irrigated, as well as for human survival. However, these other greenhouse effects are even more poorly understood than the direct climatic effects, making it difficult to include them in economic impact models.

While environmental economists must continue to emphasize the uncertainties and generalities of their models, simulation models like those outlined above offer insights into the possible economic consequences of environmental deterioration and change. The estimates of economic impact can alert policymakers and consumers to the long-run economic consequences of their actions and can aid decisionmakers in designing policies that will avert or attenuate these consequences, or at least assist people in accepting and adapting to the consequences.

NOTES

1. Based on paleoclimatic data obtained from tree rings, ice cores, pollen analysis, archeological findings, written histories, and so forth, predictions by other climatologists forecast solar and tidal cycles that suggest global *cooling*. These studies represent an entirely different method of inquiry, which is discussed extensively in Harington (1985) and elsewhere.

2. One example is efforts in the United States to control the use of aerosols.

3. The most conservative approach of an equal distribution across days of the month is used here.

4. With the increased temperatures expected under the greenhouse effect, 3.1 million additional hectares of organic soils and 4 million hectares of mineral soils would become arable in the northern prairies. However, most of this additional area would suggest only marginal crops, such as forages.

5. For Saskatchewan and Alberta the farm income effects were extrapolated from the yield results and the general results from the agricultural sector models for Manitoba.

6. All figures are in 1979 Canadian dollars. Volumes marketed were constrained to reflect the current capacity of the transportation system; hence, much of the increased product remains in inventory. Additional seeded acreage is transferred from summerfallow and pasture land based on increased net revenues from crops.

REFERENCES

Arthur, L. M., and D. Freshwater (1986). *Analysis of the Economic Effects of a Prolonged Agricultural Drought in Manitoba.* Research Bulletin 86-2. Winnipeg: University of Manitoba, Dept. of Agricultural Economics.

Baier, W., and G. W. Robertson (1966). "A New Versatile Soil Moisture Budget." *Canadian Journal of Plant Science* 46:299–315.

Canada Grains Council (1985). *Statistical Handbook.* Winnipeg: Canada Grains Council.

Canadian Climate Centre (1985). "Understanding CO_2 and Climate." Annual Report. Downsview, Ontario: Atmospheric Environment Service.

Carter, T. R., N. T. Konijn, and R. G. Watts (1984). "The Role of Agroclimatic Models in Climate Impact Analysis." Working paper WP-84-98. Laxenburg, Austria: International Institute for Applied Systems Analysis (IIASA).

The Economist (1983). "Life in a Greenhouse." *The Economist* (October 29), 301(7314):43.

Harington, C. R., ed. (1985). *Climatic Change in Canada 5.* Ottawa, Ontario: National Museums of Canada, National Museum of Natural Sciences.

Hengeveld, H. G. and R. B. Street (n.d.). "Development of CO_2 Climate Change Scenarios for Canadian Regions." Mimeograph. Downsview, Ontario: Canadian Climate Centre.

Jones, Clifford D., Jr., and Wen-Yuan Huang (1983). "IO-LP Models for Agricultural Policy Analysis." NRE Staff Report No. AGES830714. Washington, D.C.: U.S. Dept. of Agriculture, Economic Research Service, Natural Resource Economics Division.

Kimball, B. A. (1982). "Carbon Dioxide and Agricultural Yields: An Assemblage and Analysis of 430 Prior Observations." *Agronomy Journal* 75:779–788.

Manitoba Department of Agriculture (1985). *Manitoba Agriculture Yearbook.* Winnipeg.

Parry, M. L., ed. (1985). "The Sensitivity of Natural Ecosystems and Agriculture to Climate Change." Research Report RR-85-1. Laxenburg, Austria: IIASA.

Parry, M. L., and T. R. Carter, eds. (1984). "Assessing the Impact of Climate Change in Cold Regions." Summary Report SR-84-1. Laxenburg, Austria: IIASA.

Roberts, W. O. (1983). "It Is Time to Prepare for Global Climatic Changes." *Conservation Foundation* (April):1–8.

Seidel, S., and D. Keyes (1983). *Can We Delay a Grennhouse Warming?* Washington, D.C.: U.S. Environmental Protection Agency.

Shewchuk, S. R. (1984). "An Atmospheric Carbon Dioxide Review and Consideration of the Mean Annual Temperature Trend at Saskatoon, Saskatchewan." SRC Tech. Rep. 160. Saskatoon: Saskatchewan Research Council.

Statistics Canada (1981). *Census of Agriculture.* Ottawa, Ontario: Ministry of Supply and Services.

Statistics Canada (1982). *The Input-Output Structure of the Canadian Economy, 1971–1978.* Cat. 15-201E. Ottawa, Ontario: Ministry of Supply and Services.

SUGGESTED READINGS

Environment Canada (various issues). *CO₂/Climate Report.* Downsview, Ontario: Climate Program Office, Atmospheric Environment Services.

The CO_2/Climate Report is a quarterly newsletter that includes summaries of recent research in climatic change and the impacts of climate change on all sectors and in all countries.

National Research Council (1976). *Climate and Food: Climatic Fluctuation and U.S. Agricultural Production.* Washington, D.C.: National Academy of Sciences.
The result of an extensive study of the implications of weather and climate fluctuations (both long- and short-term) for U.S. agricultural production, the book covers all potential sources of impact, from plant breeding and pest management, to land and water resources.

Parry, M. L., and T. R. Carter, eds. (1984). *Assessing the Impact of Climate Change in Cold Regions.* Summary Report SR-84-1. Laxenburg, Austria: International Institute of Applied Systems Analysis (IIASA).
This monograph summarizes studies of the impacts of climate change, undertaken throughout the world under the coordination of IIASA. All the studies use simulation approaches to impact estimation, although some applications are more successful than others.

Seidel, S. and D. Keyes (1983). *Can We Delay a Greenhouse Warming?* Washington, D.C.: U.S. Environmental Protection Agency.
Because the greenhouse effect stems from increased CO_2, which, in turn, results from increased use of fossil fuels, this study attempts to determine whether the greenhouse effect could be averted by implementing various energy policies. Simulation models are used to estimate future supplies and demands for alternative fuels as well as the long-term climatic impacts of various fuel-use scenarios.

STUDY QUESTIONS

1. Why is the process of developing a useful mathematical model for economic analysis of environmental issues difficult?

2. Climatic change is an unknown probability/high-consequence event, but one that will not have effects in the near future. Discuss how the use of discount rates for uncertainty and future effects may lead to society ignoring the issue to its peril.

3. Assess the proposition that the critical weakness in formulating public policy for environmental events, such as climatic change, is not the inability of economists to evaluate outcomes and formulate policies but rather the inability of biological and physical scientists to accurately determine outcomes and causes of these events.

4. What adjustments or additions to the models presented in this chapter would be needed to extend the analysis of the greenhouse effect beyond the Canadian Prairie case to consider global economic consequences?

Chapter Twelve

Energy Policy Analysis
Alternative Modeling Approaches

Michael LeBlanc
John Reilly

Energy policy plays a critical role in helping us choose between preservation or consumption of our natural resources, thereby affecting and shaping our present and future environment. The authors discuss the use of models in analyzing three energy issues. The first case study examines the effects of fossil fuel consumption on the levels of CO_2 with a mathematical simulation model. This study complements the analysis in Chapter 11. The second case uses an econometric model to address the impact of natural gas deregulation on agricultural production, costs, and income. The third study uses a multiperiod linear programming model to examine the effects of sulfur dioxide regulations on the production and distribution of coal in the United States, and complements the model presented in Chapter 6. With these three energy modeling case studies, the authors explore the interplay of modeling techniques, specific policy questions, and the roles models play in public decisionmaking.

The case studies examined in this chapter highlight the role that models play as components in public decisionmaking. For a model to be useful in the decision process, it should be constructed in light of the type of policy issue to be addressed, the range and specificity of questions to be asked, and the degree of disaggregation required. For example, with regard to energy issues, one must ask if results at the national level are sufficient, or is disaggregation to census region, state, or county levels required. The modeler must decide if is it sufficient to report an aggregate energy demand figure or determine if it is necessary to disaggregate by major energy carriers such as coal, oil, gas, electricity or by specific petroleum products such as distillate oil, gasoline, or residual oil.

It is fair to say that except in very rare cases decisionmakers involved in a policy issue will have little familiarity with the many models likely to be used to support a set of conclusions. In many cases the decisionmaker is unlikely to even be aware of a particular model's existence. The three energy modeling case studies in this chapter were chosen to illustrate the various roles models can play in the policy process. The chapter reviews the critical economic, physical, and institutional elements typically considered in energy policy research and energy modeling and how these considerations affect the choice of modeling technique. Although the models share common characteristics, the specific approaches differ due to the type of policy question asked.

THE ROLE OF RESEARCH
IN THE ENERGY POLICY PROCESS

Despite the subtle role of models in a final public decision, models do much to help shape qualitative answers to policy questions. A variety of model results may indicate, for example, that coal demand will increase in the future. Such a finding then becomes a force driving numerous resource and environmental concerns ranging from the adequacy of domestic coal resources to effects of sulfur emission on health. Attempts to precisely quantify the demand increase may lead to disagreement due to differing opinions about substitute fuel prices, economic growth, or export demand. For many decisions the information that coal demand will increase, possibly by a significant amount, is sufficient to justify public action. If, however, reputable models widely disagree over whether a particular policy action is beneficial, it may be difficult to develop the political consensus to take a costly action. In this way, models can have powerful effects on decisionmaking even when they disagree. Failure among modeling efforts to broadly agree makes it difficult to reach the political consensus necessary to take action. Disagreement tends to preserve the status quo.

With the recognition that model results may have only subtle effects on policy one can describe at least three roles for energy models and energy policy research. First, energy modeling research may anticipate policy issues. Such anticipatory research uncovers potential problems or issues and develops general expectations about the future level of relevant variables. Anticipatory research provides the policy actor with lead time to consider alternative options and take preventive steps if necessary. Anticipatory research is particularly important for natural resource issues. Some environmental degradations are irreversible by the time physical symptoms manifest themselves. Ecosystems may be able to absorb, without significant damage, low levels of contaminants, but if emissions rise, significant and unacceptable damage may result. For example, precipitation is naturally acidic, and some increase in acid levels from natural levels might be tolerable or even desirable. But significant increases due to coal use have led to acid levels in precipitation that exceed the buffer capabilities of soils in some ecosystems.

The second role of research in the policy process is to aid in the design of policy. In this role a model may be used to examine the implications of a specific policy, determine the optimal level of an effluent tax or other policy instrument, or determine the best mix of policies. Most policy research falls in this category. Generally, this research is reactive or at best somewhat forward-looking and is typically conducted when a policy decision needs to be made quickly. Often, several alternatives are evaluated in an environment where time is a limiting factor. Timing and timeliness are both critical elements if this type of research is to be effective. A typical example is the analysis of the effects of price deregulation of natural gas on commercial, residential, and industrial consumption. The effect of deregulation can be evaluated in terms of a collection of measures such as supply price, production response, or employment effects, or it can be evaluated in terms of a single metric such as social welfare. Supporting models may explicitly optimize a single variable or aggregation of variables (the objective function) or may produce scenarios that report impacts of multiple variables and essentially allow decisionmakers to weight variables as they deem appropriate. The point is, many alternative metrics can be and are used to evaluate policy. The choice of metric and how different metrics are weighted can strongly influence views about the appropriate level and type of policy action. The implicit or explicit weighting of metrics by various actors in the decision process comprises the essence of political debate.

The third role of policy research is to evaluate ongoing policies. Although this role would seem particularly important to policymakers, it is probably the least practiced form of policy research modeling. The reasons are twofold. First, once a decision regarding a particular policy response is achieved, considerable political, intellectual, and institutional capital is set in place. To change this new status quo or "received view" requires a level of evidence that is difficult to achieve and may be far greater than the standard of evidence that originally set the policy. Analysts and decisionmakers recognize this aspect of decisionmaking and allocate their time and money accordingly.

More importantly, perhaps, the agencies responsible for the policy area in question are likely to be the agencies responsible for administering existing policies. And as these agencies potentially fund evaluative research, they are unlikely to be highly motivated to fund research that shows their programs to be poorly designed and implemented. In addition, because research funds are always limited and limiting, it is reasonable to expect resources to be directed elsewhere. Generally, the maintained view is that past policy action has "adequately" addressed a problem. Compromise and imperfection are likely to be present in attempts to amend policy. As a result, the prospect for an actual improvement given the recognition of a potential improvement may be poor, serving as a further disincentive for evaluating policy.

MODELING ENERGY AND RESOURCE ISSUES

Economic models are abstractions of complex and interrelated policy issues. The process of abstracting critical elements of complicated issues requires careful judgment, a working knowledge of the general area, and an understanding of the questions to be asked of the modeling exercise. Most natural resource and energy problems have three distinct though interrelated elements that must be considered, which make these issues the most difficult to meaningfully abstract (that is, model). These elements are physical characteristics and constraints, institutional concerns, and economic behavior.

1. *Physical Characteristics and Constraints*. Resource limits and resource grades, substitute resources and the degree of substitutability, and physical characteristics of resource conversion (from primary energy resources to energy products) must be considered and included as they are judged necessary.

2. *Institutional Concerns*. Industrial market structure, household decision-making considerations, and relevant government regulation must be considered. In almost every case the production or consumption of a particular energy resource is directly regulated by public policy. For example, the production of electricity and the distribution of natural gas are regulated by states as well as the federal government. The consumption of fuels is subject to air pollution limitations promulgated under the Clean Air Act. At a more fundamental level, the production and consumption of all fuels are affected by the allocation of property rights. Tax policy has provided specific credits and exemptions for oil and gas mining while the capital intensive nature of energy production increases the impact of the treatment of depreciation on the energy sector.

3. *Economic Behavior*. How consumers and producers respond to changing energy prices, input prices, output prices, and income and output levels constitutes the principal elements of economic behavior. Economic principles such as intertemporal decisionmaking and exhaustible resource prices, the dual nature of production and cost functions, and the household theory of production are routinely applied in policy models.

What tends to complicate modeling is the high degree of interaction among the physical, institutional, and economic elements of the problem. A pure economic model of oil pricing—the Hotelling model of an exhaustible resource, for example—does not provide reliable price forecasting capability because oil prices are regulated, resources are augmentable through discovery of new deposits and technological advances in extraction, and production is partially controlled by a cartel subject to political instability.

Three case studies are presented below to illustrate the anticipatory, policy design, and evaluative roles models have played in resource issues. The case studies also demonstrate how the questions asked of the model helped shape its design. The first study examines the relationship between the consumption of fossil fuels and the emission of CO_2 which is an important atmospheric trace gas regulating global climate. It is an example of an anticipatory use of energy modeling research. The likelihood, magnitude, timing, and impact of climate change has not been resolved, and therefore a consensus does not exist to take policy action. Modeling and research in the area has focused on improving foresight and thereby providing information necessary to achieve a consensus on what can and should be explicitly done to alter carbon dioxide emissions or plan for a changing climate. Research to date has provided the information necessary to assess the priority that additional research and monitoring should receive in future budgets.

The second case study explores how the proposed deregulation of natural gas would affect agricultural production, costs, and income (LeBlanc, 1985). It is an example of a model specifically used in policy design, in this case deregulation of natural gas. Agriculture is only one small user of natural gas within the United States. Deregulation of natural gas has potentially major effects on residential and industrial gas users, gas pipeline and distribution companies, and gas producers. It is a significant regional issue, with gas-producing states and localities in the Southwest benefiting from higher prices and consumers in the Northeast and North Central sections of the country suffering if prices rose.

The natural gas case study also begins to suggest the broad array of overlapping models brought to bear on an issue of major policy concern; the model presented here was only one of many models used in the decision to alter natural gas pricing regulations. It also indicates the breadth of research required to fully understand the impacts of proposed policies. Direct use of natural gas in agriculture is limited, and, as a result, one might expect natural gas deregulation to have a small impact on agriculture. In the case reported, significant impacts on agriculture are revealed as a result of the indirect effect of natural gas prices on fertilizer costs, an important input to agriculture. Without anticipating and understanding these impacts, policies may have significant unexpected and indirect effects.

The third case examines how sulfur dioxide emission regulations affect the production and distribution of coal in the United States (LeBlanc, Kalter, and Boisvert, 1978). It is an example of research and modeling to evaluate existing policy. Sulfur dioxide emission regulations, as part of the Clean Air Act, have been under scrutiny since their enactment due to the high cost imposed on electric utilities. Observers noted that forcing utilities to limit sulfur from utility stack gases was skewing utility use of coal to low-sulfur and low-Btu coal and thereby increasing electricity production costs and prices. Again, issues of regional equity were a prime consideration. Most high-sulfur and high-Btu coal is mined in the eastern United States, and mining operations are the major source of employment in many localities. Western areas in the proximity of large resources of low-sulfur coal were mixed in their reactions to the economic booms, congestion, and environmental aspects of coal mine development.

The three case studies also provide a survey of alternative methodologies used to explore energy problems. In the CO_2 emissions study, a mathematical simulation model is used to examine the long-term trends in energy supply and demand. Economic and engineering relationships are combined to forecast the interaction of energy availability, price, and demand during the next 70 years on an international scale. Because of the geographical and energy comprehensiveness required of the model, it was necessary to explicitly incorporate key information from different disciplines including geological perspectives on resource availability and engineering perspectives on fuel utilization and conversion technologies. Because of the need to provide very long-term forecasts, a model relying completely on parameters estimated from 10 or 20 years of data (such as would be the case with an econometric model) would have been unreliable.

In the second case study, relationships among costs and prices are derived from underlying relationships among production inputs and outputs. Econometric analysis is used to estimate demands for agricultural inputs, including fertilizer. Economic theory is used, recognizing that demand for inputs is derived from the demand for agricultural output. Unlike the CO_2 model that describes both supply and demand for energy, the derived demand for agricultural inputs model describes only input demand. The latter is a partial equilibrium analysis whereas the CO_2 model explicitly projects market equilibrium. In the model describing the derived demand for agricultural inputs the complexities of numerical solution are avoided through the assumption of profit maximization and application of duality conditions that recognize the correspondence between a firm's production process and its production costs. Economic theory combined with carefully chosen assumptions can therefore simplify a numerical model.

The third case study utilizes a recursive linear programming model to analyze coal distribution and production in the United States. Unlike the CO_2 simulation model the linear programming model is an optimization model. That is, the model explicitly solves an objective function, which is to minimize the costs of production and distribution of coal to meet the exogenously given demand for coal. The model is geographically limited to the United States and does not treat fuels other than coal but provides considerably more detail on coal production and distribution, including detail on individual coal reserves within regions of the United States. These models are further explained in the following sections.

Even with the brief discussion provided above, it is evident that the choice of features in each model is at least partly driven by the issue examined. The following discussion provides additional detail on the models and policy issues involved. The discussion should make evident how the models were designed to fit the question being addressed. A reasonable approach for one problem may be deficient for another. There is by no means, however, an absolute right approach for any problem; a diversity of efforts and approaches to modeling a single issue can aid in determining the extent to which a particular result is sensitive to the modeling technique and set of functional forms and assumptions used to derive the result.

CASE I.
MODELING EMISSIONS OF CARBON DIOXIDE

One of the important by-products of the combustion of fossil fuels is carbon dioxide. CO_2 is naturally present in the atmosphere, playing an important role in the determination of the earth's climate. The presence of CO_2 in the atmosphere produces a greenhouse effect, allowing incoming sunlight to penetrate but trapping heat radiated back from earth, thereby maintaining temperatures in the lower atmosphere. The use of fossil fuels significantly increases CO_2 levels giving rise to the possibility of significant warming and associated changes in climate. Climate change, within the range generally foreseen as resulting from increasing CO_2 concentrations, could cause rising sea levels and coastal flooding, as well as changes in precipitation, soil moisture, and temperature regimes with associated impacts on agriculture and the unmanaged biosphere.

Issue Background

Preindustrial concentrations of carbon dioxide are estimated to have been in the range of 270 to 295 parts per million (ppm). As of 1984, the measured concentration was approximately 345 ppm. At atmospheric concentrations of 600 ppm or higher, global temperature and climate changes would almost certainly become significant and be cause for concern. The 600 ppm level, an approximate doubling from the preindustrial level of CO_2, has become a convenient reference point for policy research. However, climate change significant enough to present problems of adaptation for human societies may well occur at CO_2 concentrations less than 600 ppm. Most recently, research has focused on the role of additional trace gases such as chlorofluorocarbons and methane, which act similarly to CO_2 in the atmosphere. Increases in these gases would exacerbate a CO_2-induced warming trend.

Combustion of fossil fuels is currently the major source of carbon release to the atmosphere. As economic activity expands around the world and energy and fossil fuel use increase, combustion of fossil fuels will become the overwhelming source of CO_2. Forest clearing and cement manufacture are also sources of atmospheric carbon. It is believed that forest clearing has accounted for a significant and possibly predominant share of the increase to date. In the past several decades, however, reforestation has occurred in the Northern Hemisphere, which has served as a carbon sink and has partially offset carbon release from continuing deforestation in the Southern Hemisphere. Cement manufacture currently releases carbon dioxide at a rate on the order of 5 to 10 percent of the fossil fuel emission rate. Because energy use is growing faster than cement production, the share of release from cement production is generally expected to fall in the future.

Carbon emissions and climate change gained the attention of policy research through extrapolations of fossil fuel release rates that were expanding at 4.5 percent per year during the postwar (1950–1973) period. The conclusion was that CO_2 concentrations of 600 ppm would almost certainly be encountered within 50 years. Among the projected consequences of such an increase were inundation of highly populated coastal areas. For example, redrawn maps showed large portions of Florida, Washington, D.C., and the Indian subcontinent underwater.

Policy Research Questions

The issue of CO_2 emissions and climate change has engendered five separate research questions. First, how rapidly will CO_2 emissions grow in the future? Second, what is the natural cycle of carbon deposition among carbon reservoirs, which include the biota, the atmosphere, oceans, and sediment? Third, how do temperature, precipitation, and other measures of climate change in response to changing levels of CO_2? Fourth, how does the unmanaged and managed biosphere (agriculture and forests) respond to climate change and changes in the level of CO_2 directly? And fifth, what effect do climate and biosphere changes have on society? Energy modeling addresses the first of these questions.

The Research Issue and the CO_2 Emissions Model

The model was designed to answer the question how rapidly will CO_2 emissions grow in the future. Its design reflects an assessment of the key elements of the CO_2 issue and policy research questions. These key elements, as defined by the model developers, were as follows:

1. All types of energy were included and energy was disaggregated by fuel type. Although only fossil fuels emit CO_2, fossil and nonfossil energy forms are close substitutes for one another. In addition, CO_2 emissions vary among fossil fuels (see Table 12.1).

2. The model had to be capable of producing reasonable projections 50 to 75 years in the future. Significant accumulation of CO_2 only occurs slowly. A climate change problem may not be evident in a 15- to 20-year forecast.

3. The model had to provide complete global geographical coverage but also provide regional detail. Once in the atmosphere, carbon dioxide mixes rapidly so that concentrations are relatively similar worldwide. Thus, coverage of emission must be all-inclusive. From the standpoint of policy questions, however, it is desirable to assess the impact of emissions limiting controls taken by geographical units smaller than the world as a whole.

4. An equilibrium treatment of energy supply demand was required. Various major energy studies conducted during the 1970s focused on gaps that were likely to occur between supply and demand. Realistic calculation of CO_2 emissions require that a forecasted demand be a realized demand. A demand/supply gap indicates the realized demand will be lower, supply prices will rise encouraging conservation, and the mix of fuels may vary as some previously uneconomic fuels or grades of fuels are supplied at the higher price.

5. The model had to account for CO_2 emissions by regional and fuel sources. To correctly attribute emissions to geographic regions requires an accounting of CO_2 emissions at their source: in the case of shale oil mining, from carbonate rock and gas flaring; at the conversion site, from the production of electricity; or at the point of final consumption.

The CO_2 emissions model can be broadly classified as a market equilibrium, nonoptimizing, parametric simulation model. The market equilibrium feature, discussed above, is distinguished from a purely demand side or purely

TABLE 12.1:   Carbon Release in the Production
and Combustion of Fossil Fuels

Fuel	Carbon
	grams/megajoule
Oil	19.2
Gas	13.7
Coal	23.8
Shale oil mining[a]	27.9
Solar	0.0
Nuclear	0.0
Hydro	0.0

[a]   A Western U.S. shale oil from carbonate rock.

SOURCE: J. A. Edmonds, J. M. Reilly, R. H. Gardner, and A. Brenkert, Uncertainty in Future Global Energy Use and Fossil Fuel CO_2 Emissions 1975 to 2075, No. DOE/NBB-081 (Washington, D.C.: U.S. Dept. of Energy, 1986).

supply side perspective. The structural representation, including separate identification of supply and demand, was judged essential given the need to explicitly account for supply factors such as resource constraints and conversion of coal to liquids and gases, and demand factors such as growth in the level of economic activity and population.

The emissions model is a parametric simulation model in contrast to a model whose parameters are econometrically or statistically estimated within it. Although the functional relationships are identical to those used in some econometric models, the parameters in the model are directly user supplied rather than estimated. This approach was chosen because of the long-term nature of the projection exercise. The validity of estimated parameters for projections 50 to 75 years hence is likely to be poor. Parameters of the model were chosen on the basis of reviews of econometric estimation of historical data but do not necessarily reflect a particular data set or econometric study.

The model is nonoptimizing because individual agents in the model do not explicitly choose the lowest cost energy form. Rather, energy users respond to rising prices by conserving and switching fuels. This response may reflect optimizing behavior but agents need not be at an optimum. In a model that attempts to project the actions of many agents, in this case, all households and industrial users of energy, it is impossible to incorporate the specific circumstances of each agent. For example, geographic availability of fuels or price variability are not incorporated. Optimization with partial or average information on prices or without the full set of constraints provides a poor prediction of behavioral response.

The emissions model is also nonoptimizing in the sense that it does not determine an optimal policy response by maximizing a societal objective function. As previously mentioned, the weighting of elements in an objective function has significant political and equity implications. The model assists the political decisionmaking process through the use of scenario analysis that, together with results of other models and analyses, can be incorporated into the decision.

Model Overview

Figure 12.1 indicates the nine geographic regions in the model. The choice of the number of regions and which areas are included in a particular region is always based on competing goals. In this case, data availability and tractability of the model were arguments for a few regions or for treating the world as a single consuming and producing unit. On the other hand, one could imagine model users asking for information on a specific U.S. state or a specific country in Latin America. Model developers must consider whether the accuracy they could hope to achieve with such detail would be misleading rather than informative even if such a model could be constructed within funding and time limits. Because the model was constructed for the U.S. Department of Energy (DOE) and because the United States produces and consumes large amounts of energy, the United States was treated separately. In considering potential policy questions, it was likely that decisionmakers might ask what would happen if developed market economies cooperated to limit CO_2 emissions. What if the USSR also cooperated but developing countries did not? In addition, the oil-rich Middle East was treated separately from energy-importing regions like Europe. The final nine regions emerged from balancing such considerations.

Figure 12.2 provides a broad overview of the structure of the model. Regional estimates of population, labor force, and labor productivity are combined to provide estimates of gross national product (GNP), a major determinant of energy demand. Technological change leading to more efficient energy-using equipment is also modeled. Changes in these factors shift energy demand over time. Regional energy supply considerations including resource constraints and the new technologies are pictured in the lower left of Figure 12.2. Regional demands and supplies are added together to create a global supply and demand curve for each fuel. The model then uses a numerical search to find the set of fuel prices where fuel demand just equals fuel supply in each region and for each fuel, including imports and exports. Regional taxes and tariffs are introduced as appropriate. For example, Europe

FIGURE 12.1 Regions in the CO$_2$ Emissions Model

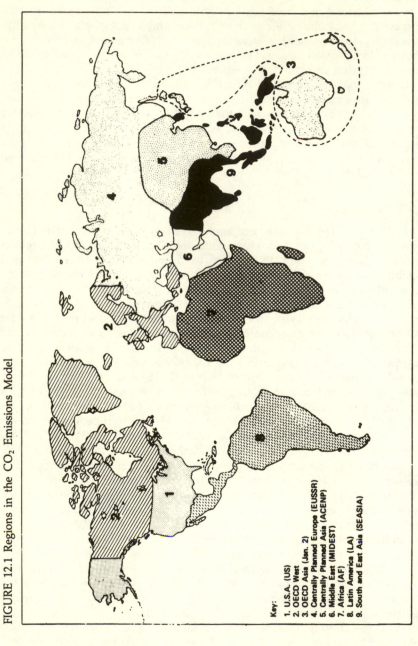

Key:
1. U.S.A. (US)
2. OECD West
3. OECD Asia (Jan. 2)
4. Centrally Planned Europe (EUSSR)
5. Centrally Planned Asia (ACENP)
6. Middle East (MIDEST)
7. Africa (AF)
8. Latin America (LA)
9. South and East Asia (SEASIA)

Source: J. A. Edmonds and J. M. Reilly, *Global Energy: Assessing the Future* (New York: Oxford University Press, 1985).

FIGURE 12.2 Diagram of the CO_2 Emissions Model

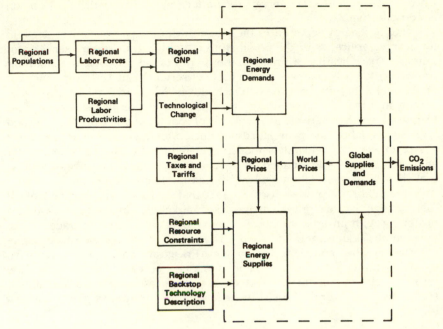

Source: J. A. Edmonds and J. M. Reilly, *Global Energy: Assessing the Future* (New York: Oxford University Press, 1985).

maintains a considerable barrier to coal imports in order to maintain its domestic industry. This trade barrier allows mines in Germany and Great Britain to operate despite production costs that are as much as twice that in low-cost producing areas like Australia, South Africa, and the United States. The final step and the ultimate goal of the exercise, computation of CO_2 emissions, is a straightforward multiplication of CO_2 release coefficients for each fuel by the amount of the fuel used each year.

The detail not captured in Figure 12.2 includes, on the supply side, eight types of primary energy resources: oil, gas, shale oil, coal, biomass, solar electricity, nuclear electricity, and hydroelectricity, all considered to be available at different cost grades. As low-cost grades are exhausted higher prices are required to produce the next grade. Several resource conversion processes are represented, including conversion of shale oil to a petroleum equivalent product and conversion of coal and biomass to a petroleum equivalent or natural gas equivalent fuels. The process of resource conversion results in six primary energy fuels: oils, gases, solids (biomass and coal), hydroelectricity, nuclear electricity, and solar electricity. In addition, conservation and nonelectric solar are included as alternatives that reduce the demands for marketed fuels. From these primary energy fuels, four secondary energy fuels are produced—electricity, gases, solids, and liquids. The primary to secondary conversion allows liquids, gases, and solids to be used with hydro, nuclear, and solar energy to produce electricity if their conversion is cost-effective.

Detail on energy reported in the model includes specification of demand for energy services with the possibility of supplying an energy service (for example, space heating or transportation) with liquid, gaseous, or solid fuels or electricity. Fuels compete on the basis of service costs (including the cost of the fuel), the efficiency with which the fuel is converted to an energy service, and the cost of nonenergy inputs in production of the service. This feature allows the relatively low fuel cost of coal to be offset by its associated high capital, labor, and material costs, which often make it a more expensive source of energy. Demand is modeled hierarchically, that is, demand for aggregate energy is determined on the basis of an aggregate price of energy; fuel shares are then determined on the basis of relative prices.

The equilibrium process uses the fact that demands and supplies of all fuels change as their prices change. The market-clearing price is found by beginning with an arbitrary set of international prices for the traded fuels, for example, liquids, gas, and solids. The initial prices are used to generate a set of supplies and demands by fuel. Prices are adjusted in successive iterations until global supplies and demands for each fuel balance. The result is regional production and consumption, estimates of international trade flows, and world prices consistent with equilibrium in global markets for fuels.

Use of the Model to Support Policy and Policy Research

The emissions model has been used to improve forecasts of future levels of CO_2 emissions and to address the impact of hypothetical policy actions. The forecast activity has proceeded from focusing on a single scenario to attempts to describe the range of likely future scenarios. In recent work, a technique known as Monte Carlo analysis has been used to develop a distribution of model outcomes. To conduct a Monte Carlo analysis, the range and distribution for each exogenous variable is determined, and then a large number of complete sets of variables (400) are sampled from the distributions. The model is then run once with each set of exogenous variables. Characteristics of the model result (in this case CO_2 emissions), so that the mean, variance, and standard deviation can be derived to develop an understanding of the uncertainty associated with a point forecast.

It was important to describe the uncertainty in future forecasts to avoid making "precisely wrong" policy. A highly uncertain forecast suggests that more research and monitoring is needed, especially if catastrophic events indicated within a scenario are to be avoided. The cumulative impact of this work has been to significantly reduce expectations of future levels of emissions. From an expected growth of 4.5 percent per year we can predict with considerable confidence that growth in emissions will be less than 3.0 percent per year, and more likely around 1.0 percent per year. Such results have led to the policy conclusion that there is sufficient time to improve understanding of the climate effects of CO_2 and carefully plan actions to reduce emissions, mitigate climatic impacts, and adapt to a changing climate regime. In addition, the large amount of remaining uncertainty in future emissions has refocused research toward this area in the hope that greater resolution can be achieved.

Policy studies using the model have been conducted by a wide range of organizations. Studies have been conducted by the EPA (Seidel and Keyes, 1983), the Massachusetts Institute of Technology (MIT) Energy Laboratory (Rose, Miller, and Agnew, 1983), and the DOE (Edmonds and Reilly, 1983). These studies include global and regional carbon taxes, bans on producing and exporting coal, policies to subsidize non-CO_2 emitting fuels, and policies to improve technology to better utilize fossil fuels (conservation) and reduce the cost and increase penetration of renewable technologies.

The results of the carbon tax and coal limit studies demonstrate that policy actions taken by a nation or region acting alone have little effect. Restrictions in the use of fossil fuels in one region delay the increase in fuel prices associated with resource exhaustion. The lower prices encourage consumption in regions without consumption constraints. The results are suggestive of the difficulties of achieving the level of cooperation needed to enact global carbon taxes or bans on fuel use. There is an incentive for countries to free ride, taking advantage of the benefits of the restrictions in other countries without paying the cost of limiting fossil fuel use. In fact, the climate change issue provides even greater difficulties for strategies that must rely on cooperative behavior among nations. Countries abstaining from consumption controls may benefit from even lower prices of fossil fuels. In addition, climate change will not be uniformly bad. Some regions may benefit from warmer temperatures—for example, the Soviet Union may obtain ice-free ports and greater access to resources in Siberia. The Sahel in Africa may receive greater rainfall. These regions may have an incentive to accelerate climate change.

The policy studies examining the impact of renewable energy and conservation technology improvements are more optimistic about the ability to change emissions and CO_2 concentrations. It is in the interest of countries and private agents to utilize non-CO_2 emitting technologies if they are cost effective. That is, there is no need to enforce adherence to the policy. Moreover, penetration of the technologies may have benefits beyond the CO_2 problem: Use of conservation and renewable technologies will reduce energy resource demand in general and will limit other environmental problems such as acid rain, particulate pollution, and environmental stresses associated with mining, converting, and consuming fossil fuels. The open question with such policies is how much improvement in the technologies can be purchased with additional research and development expenditures and how substitutable are the new fuels in applications currently using petroleum products, natural gas, or coal.

CASE II.
NATURAL GAS DECONTROL

Government policies have unexpected indirect effects on economic activity. These unexpected effects arise because it is simply too difficult and costly to consider the implications of every nuance of a potential policy action. One example of an indirect effect resulting from a policy action was the effect of the proposed deregulation of natural gas on agriculture. Direct consumption of natural gas in agricultural production is largely limited to crop drying and irrigation. Thus, it would appear that agriculture would be relatively unaffected by policies concerning natural gas. In fact, natural gas is a major feedstock for fertilizer production, and changes in natural gas prices have a direct and significant impact on fertilizer prices. This indirect linkage between proposed natural gas deregulation and the agricultural sector represented an important element in gas price deregulation whether it changed policy directly.

The objective of the agricultural inputs demand model described in this case study was to determine the effects of alternative natural gas prices and consequently alternative fertilizer prices on input demand, production costs, and agricultural income. In this analysis, a variable profit function was used to derive input demand functions and an aggregate supply function for agricultural output. From these relationships the effects of alternative fertilizer prices on input use, production costs, and farm income were determined.

Issue Background

The wellhead price of natural gas has been regulated since the 1954 Supreme Court ruling in the case of *Phillips Petroleum* v. *Wisconsin*. Two separate markets for natural gas developed as a result of that ruling: a regulated interstate market and an unregulated intrastate market. Prices in the unregulated, intrastate markets increased rapidly after 1970, and by 1974, intrastate prices were almost four times greater than prices in the regulated, interstate market. Since 1970 most new gas discoveries have been sold on intrastate markets. Consumers in states without access to intrastate gas supplies have experienced shortages, curtailments, and prohibitions of new gas hookups.

In 1978, Congress passed the Natural Gas Policy Act (NGPA) in an attempt to reduce these supply problems by phasing out the regulation of many categories of natural gas. A price decontrol schedule was established to allow the price on newly discovered natural gas to rise to the oil-equivalent price during the years 1979 through 1985. The deregulation schedule was pegged to 1978 oil prices of $14 per barrel.

Although NGPA initiated phased deregulation of natural gas prices, significant price disparities continued to exist among various categories of gas. In 1981, for example, wellhead prices ranged from $1 per thousand cubic feet (mcf) of gas to $10 per mcf, far exceeding the oil-equivalent price of about $5.50 per mcf. Natural gas resources were not being developed in the most economically efficient manner. High-cost gas was being produced before lower cost gas, and take-or-pay clauses in contracts between gas producers and distributors were contributing to rapid growth in prices despite large excess capacity to produce gas.

Natural gas is an important domestic energy source. On an energy equivalent basis, domestic natural gas production during the early 1980s exceeded domestic crude oil by about 20 percent and coal by about 25 percent. It accounted for over 30 percent of total U.S. energy consumption. The direct use of natural gas in agriculture totaled just under 100 billion cubic feet in 1981 or only about 0.5 percent of total agricultural energy consumption. Natural gas expenditures accounted for 3.5 percent of energy expenditures and less than 0.3 percent of total farm production expenses. About 67 billion cubic feet of natural gas was used to irrigate crops in 1981 and 12.7 billion cubic feet was used to dry crops.

Fertilizer production uses about four times more natural gas than agriculture. Therefore, the major effect of natural gas decontrol on agriculture was likely to take the form of changes in fertilizer prices. Fertilizer use in agriculture has increased dramatically during the last 20 years. From 1967 through 1982 agricultural fertilizer use grew from 14 to 21.5 million nutrient tons. Expenditures during the same period increased over 300 percent. In 1981, as deregulation was being considered, farmers spent about $10 billion on fertilizer, 7 percent of total farm production costs.

Natural gas is the primary feedstock for the production of anhydrous ammonia, the basis for nearly all domestically produced nitrogen fertilizer. One ton of ammonia requires 36,000 to 38,000 cubic feet of natural gas. About 21,000 cubic feet of natural gas is used as raw material from the ammonia, and another 15,000 to 17,000 cubic feet is used to provide heat for the production process.

In 1981 fertilizer producers paid an average price of $2.30 per mcf for natural gas. However, contract prices varied from $0.25 per mcf to $4.60 per mcf. As gas prices were decontrolled, natural gas price increases for fertilizer producers were expected to exceed average increases to other industrial users because fertilizer producers paid less for natural gas. These lower prices resulted from price provisions in long-term contracts between fertilizer producers and gas distributors signed in the 1960s and early 1970s and pricing exemptions granted to agriculturally related firms under the provisions of NGPA. In addition, all fertilizer producers were not affected equally by deregulation because a wide variation in plant efficiency, natural gas prices, and plant location existed.

Substantial uncertainty surrounds the extent to which natural gas price increases are transmitted through the price of fertilizer. The uncertainty is generated by the energy market where the price of natural gas is linked to crude oil prices and by the fertilizer market itself. Domestic fertilizer prices are affected by production costs, the level of agricultural output, and competition from lower cost fertilizer imports.

The presence of lower cost nitrogen imports moderated the ability of fertilizer producers to pass through natural gas price increases to domestic agriculture. During the 1970s the United States was a net exporter of nitrogen fertilizers. By 1982, however, exports and imports were about equal. As low-priced natural gas contracts expired, U.S. nitrogen fertilizer producers were hampered in their competition for international markets. Five billion tons of U.S. ammonia production capacity was closed in 1982, representing 25 percent of total capacity. At the same time, ammonia was imported into the United States at less than $115 per ton, which is $30 to $50 below operating costs for some domestic producers.

Countries with large supplies of low-priced natural gas and rapidly developing nitrogen production capacity (Canada, Mexico, Nigeria, Indonesia, Saudi Arabia, and the USSR) were in a position to increase their share of the U.S. fertilizer market. Their comparative advantage was expected to rise as domestic fertilizer production costs and prices increased in response to higher natural gas prices. Increased ammonia imports contributed to the cost-price squeeze experienced by domestic manufacturers while moderating fertilizer prices paid by farmers.

Policy Research Questions

While the low natural gas prices maintained by regulation benefited those gas consumers, direct and indirect, who obtained low-cost gas, consumers unable to obtain gas were disadvantaged. These inefficiencies in addition to the misallocation of production resources appeared to provide a strong case for a policy of deregulation. Any major change in policy, however, creates a redistribution of income; the benefits and costs of the policy change are not equally shared. As a result, economic justification for policy change must go beyond the concept of a Pareto improvement (no one is worse off, and at least someone is better off) to a Pareto improvement in principle. That is, the total gains could, in principle, be used to compensate the losers in the policy change with enough gains for at least someone to be better off. In practice, direct monetary transfers from gainers to losers rarely occurs. Rather, changes are structured to be implemented gradually; they specifically exempt actions taken prior to the policy change. The need to consider equity generally requires that policy research identify gainers and losers in any policy actions.

Three general policy questions arose in the case of natural gas deregulation: First, what would happen to gas prices after deregulation? Second, who stood to gain from deregulation and what was the overall benefit? Third, who stood to lose from deregulation and what were the extent of the losses?

The modeling case study discussed below addressed agriculture, one of the potential losers. Natural gas, used as a feedstock, accounts for 60 to 70 percent of nitrogenous fertilizer production costs. Increases in fertilizer prices were a particular policy concern because of deteriorating profit conditions in the agricultural sector. From 1970 through 1981 farm production costs increased nearly $100 billion and real income in the agricultural sector decreased 70 percent.

A Model of Farm Profit, Factor Demands, and Capital

The effect of increasing input prices on agricultural production and income depends on the following:

1. How input supply changes as the input's price rises (the elasticity of supply for inputs);
2. How easy it is for the farmer to shift to other inputs when the price of one changes (the elasticity of substitution among inputs), which in turn determines how an input price change affects the output price;
3. And, how much demand for output changes when the output price changes (the elasticity of demand for output).

This analysis modeled the farm's production process and treated input and output prices as exogenous data. An economic model was developed to maximize variable profits subject to the quantity of a quasi-fixed production factor. A quasi-fixed factor of production is one that is fixed in the short-run but varies in the long-run. Buildings and machinery are examples of important farm inputs that cannot be adjusted immediately if input prices change. The existence of such quasi-fixed inputs leads to a supply curve that is more elastic over the long-run than in the short-run. A large increase in fertilizer and energy prices could cause a significant increase in agricultural costs and output prices, adversely affecting farm income in the short-run. One would expect these effects to moderate over time as farmers adjusted farm machinery and other quasi-fixed inputs. The complete set of factor demand functions and an aggregate supply function consistent with economic theory were derived from this simple representation.

Once the equations were derived, it was possible to use econometric techniques to estimate parameters of the equations that directly determined the elasticities of substitution among inputs and output supply. With the fully estimated equations, expected changes in natural gas, other input prices, and in agricultural demand could be entered into the equation to simulate the effects of natural gas deregulation.

Because the focus of the analysis was to evaluate the impact only over the next eight to ten years, econometrically estimated parameters based on recent historical data were not a major limitation as they were judged to be in the CO_2 case study. In effect, the agricultural input demand model assumed that the elasticities estimated from past data would hold in the future and that changes in the structure of production could be captured through the exogenously determined path of quasi-fixed input adjustment. Modeling exercises must seek to describe the major aspects of the structure of the system being modeled or else policy simulations mean very little. The inability of modelers to completely describe the structure of systems means that they can never be sure whether the parameters of the model will remain constant in the future or will, in fact, change with different policies. This handicap plagues all types of models.

Use of the Model in Policy Analysis

Based on the econometric model, natural gas decontrol was predicted to have a small effect on agriculture unless accompanied by renewed growth in crude oil prices and fertilizer import restrictions. Although natural gas prices directly affect agricultural production by increasing costs for crop drying and irrigation, the largest effects were expected to occur through increases in fertilizer prices. Results from this analysis indicated that increases in fertilizer prices caused by natural gas decontrol would be offset by agriculture's ability to substitute other inputs in production. This result contradicted other studies that had not allowed for input substitutions.

The effects on agricultural input demand, production costs, and income were simulated under alternative assumptions about future fertilizer prices, output prices, and capital availability. Fertilizer use was shown to be responsive to changes in fertilizer price. The time path of fertilizer costs reflected the complete interaction of changes in output supply and input substitution. For example, total expenditures on fertilizer do not necessarily increase when fertilizer prices increase. Fertilizer price increases had a small negative effect on energy, but a relatively large positive effect on the demand for labor. Simulations indicated the relative effects of alternative fertilizer price paths on fertilizer demand to be about the same regardless of the output price assumed. Furthermore, the alternative fertilizer price paths generated large differences in profits. Profits, however, varied more between output price assumptions than between fertilizer price assumptions because of the large effects that output price had on output supply and revenue.

The importance of capital suggests that factors that influence investment—interest rates, accelerated depreciation, investment tax credits, and a farmer's access to financial capital—are important determinants of fertilizer demand. When fertilizer prices and output prices were assumed constant, the demand for fertilizer increased by 13 percent as a result of capital investment. Dynamic optimization models, which endogenously determine the level of capital, are needed to more fully evaluate the effects of input price changes.

The absolute magnitude of the effect of natural gas deregulation on farming costs and income depends on the structure of agricultural production and the level of output prices. Although constant and decreasing fertilizer prices were analyzed, it is highly probable that deregulation would result in higher natural gas prices. Without fertilizer import restrictions, fertilizer price increases of 2.5 percent per year imply natural gas price increases of about 12 percent per year. Such a high rate of growth in prices might be difficult to sustain over a decade. However, if real fertilizer price increases averaged only 1 percent per year and output prices are constant, then the model suggests that farm profits could fall by 10 percent.

CASE III.
SULFUR EMISSION REGULATION AND REGIONAL COAL PRODUCTION

Coal is an abundant domestic energy resource that has contributed a significant share of U.S. energy needs in the past. It is currently the major heat source in electricity production and a significant contributor to industrial energy needs. It is also seen as a potentially significant fuel in the future.

There are major coal deposits in both the eastern and western portions of the United States. The bulk of U.S. coal production occurs in eastern mines; most coal is also used in the East. Mining operations in the East are more frequently deep mines, and there are several relatively small, labor intensive operations. Large reserves of coal accessible through low-cost strip mining exist in western states. However, transportation costs are a major consideration limiting exploitation of these reserves. Nevertheless, significant increases in coal production in the United States would be possible through the exploitation of western coal.

Significant negative effects or externalities are associated with coal use. Sulfur emissions from coal combustion are throught to be the major source of sulfur in the atmosphere, which facilitates the formation of sulfuric acid and resultant acid precipitation. Much eastern coal has a sulfur content as much as ten times that of western coal. Limitations on sulfur emissions as a result of the provisions of the Clean Air Act threatened to shift production from the East to the West and cause unemployment and economic contraction in the East.

Issue Background

The U.S. Clean Air Act required major point sources of sulfur emissions to significantly reduce sulfur oxides released from stacks. Coal-burning electric power plants accounted for the majority of such sources; some smelting operations were also affected. At the same time coal became an important source of domestic energy as a result of the Organization of Petroleum Exporting Countries (OPEC) oil embargo in 1972 and 1973 and rising prices for oil and natural gas. Coal also rose in importance because of its versatility (it can be substituted for oil and natural gas in electricity generation), the abundance of domestic coal reserves, and the growing opposition to nuclear power.

The combined impact of these factors on the supply of coal was uncertain. Different regions were affected as production shifted from eastern to western states. This shift affected regional employment and placed significant demands on the coal transportation system. Apart from these specific factors, the rising prices of oil and natural gas and the increasing cost of nuclear power were leading to a hefty increase in the demand for coal. To fully evaluate the effects of specific coal policies required separating policy effects from other changes that were occurring simultaneously and the ability to project effects into the future. This evaluation required improved information on coal shipments, mine development patterns, and resource costs.

Policy Research Questions

Numerous research questions were raised by policies directed at coal production and use. These questions included environmental stresses implied by potential expanding coal use, the interactive effects of sulfur regulation and support of coal use, and the efficiency of sulfur regulations in meeting goals to reduce acid precipitation. A major issue, however, was the regional effects and regional equity of the costs and benefits of the regulations.

The Research Issue and Coal Production Modeling

These regional impacts of changing demand, sulfur dioxide emission regulations, and transportation alternatives were investigated using a multiperiod linear programming model. The following elements were essential to the policy research questions being addressed:

1. A regional representation of coal production to represent local impacts was necessary; at a minimum an East/West distinction was required.
2. Accurate characterization of transportation cost between suppliers and demanders of coal was necessary. This implied significant geographical disaggregation and identification of demand regions and supply regions.
3. The ability to identify mining costs at a level sufficient to represent the variety of mining technologies, operations, and resource deposit characteristics was critical.
4. To examine the impact of the Clean Air Act, the sulfur content and heat value of coal from different production regions had to be determined.
5. Institutional features of long-term contracts that locked in a producer/consumer relationship over 15- to 25-year periods needed to be considered to recognize the inertia in existing supply arrangements. Failure to incorporate this feature would have allowed the model to rapidly switch among supply sources, which was, in reality, severely limited by the long-term contract convention.
6. The ability to estimate the economic pressure for change induced by changing demands and sulfur emission regulation despite the fact that long-term contracts prevented change was necessary.

A multiperiod linear programming model, which allowed production decisions to be made on the basis of cost minimization subject to resource and contract constraints with appropriate regional detail, filled the critical requirements listed above. In particular, the economic pressure for change was represented by the prices derived from the optimization process that would have led to the predicted coal use if long-term contracts had not existed. Such prices are normally called shadow prices and are specifically associated with optimization models.

Model Overview

The multiperiod model included a component that linked coal transportation systems to various supply regions and electrical utility demand centers. Quality differences among supply regions in terms of sulfur and Btu content were recognized as were the different types of coal reserves (surface or deep mine). In total the model consisted of 33 existing or potential production areas and 44 demand regions. Deep mine and surface mining technologies were separately identified, and the different labor requirements and environmental impacts of the two technologies were recognized.

In order to minimize the differences in quality characteristics of the coal, both in terms of Btu and sulfur content within a region, supply regions were determined. Because many air pollution and other environmental policy issues were defined around political jurisdictions, states, excluding those with no current or forecasted consumption, were chosen as demand regions.

The two predominant forms of coal transportation are rail and barge. Coal slurry pipelines have been proposed for long-distance transportation, but their consideration has not led to serious construction plans. Truck transportation is typically used for short-distance hauls. Given these considerations, the model was simplified, without much loss in accuracy concerning the transport of coal among regions, by representing only rail and barge transportation. The model was designed to allow combinations of these modes including both rail-to-barge activities using the interior river system and rail-to-barge activities using the Great Lakes. Generation of electricity at the mine mouth was allowed. Thus, electricity transmission could, if economically competitive, substitute for coal shipments. Generating facilities for this mode were assumed to exist in the corresponding supply regions.

To account for many of the long-run decisions involved in the allocation of coal resources, the model was also modified to enable solution through time. Recursive programing techniques allowed optimal solutions for future years to be constrained by decisions made in the past. A primary reason for using a recursive rather than a multiperiod approach was to incorporate long-term contracts. Historically, nearly 75 percent of all coal deliveries have been made under contracts lasting from 15 to 25 years. The remaining 25 percent is supplied by the spot market characterized by marginal mines moving in and out of the market depending upon the price of coal and the supply constraints on mines having contract obligations. In the model, contracts were assumed to be a standard 20 years. As a result, the reallocation of coal production in any given year was constrained by decisions made as much as 20 years earlier.

Within this framework, the explicit objective function in the allocation model was to find the shipping and production patterns that minimized the combined transportation and production costs of moving coal resources from the supply regions to the numerous demand points. In the short-run, contract coal shipments were not altered; only spot shipments or new production were decision variables. The resulting output identified how much coal was produced in each supply region and the demand region(s) to which the coal was shipped. Because the heat content and sulfur content of each coal supply region were known, the characteristics of coal burned in each demand region were known. The model was completed by describing the physical and institutional constraints imposed on the cost minimization objective function.

Specifics of the fuel and policy question directly determined several details in the model. First, heating value was incorporated because the demands were for the energy in coal rather than its raw tonnage. That is, a utility needing to raise a given amount of steam to drive electricity-generating turbines would require 10 percent more tons of coal if the coal had a 10 percent lower heating value.

Second, sulfur content was included because of the nature of the policy question addressed. National sulfur dioxide regulations prohibited emissions of more than 1.2 pounds of SO_2 per million Btu (Public Law 88-206). Because the sulfur restriction applied only to burning and not to delivery, one way to meet emission standards was to mix high- and low-sulfur coal when it was burned.

Third, incorporation of regional coal reserves was necessary to represent production limits; cumulative production could not exceed the coal existing in the supply region. These constraints prevented a region from establishing supply contracts in excess of the identified coal reserves in the region.

Fourth, constraints beyond coal reserve limits were necessary to represent transportation capacity limitations. In general these constraints could include route constraints (existing rail lines and waterways) and rolling stock constraints (available barge and rail cars). Only route constraints were modeled explicitly because physical stocks in the initial time period were adequate and could be expanded to meet needs.

To begin the analysis, a solution to the linear programming model described above was obtained for production and demand conditions prevailing in 1973. As this solution was to provide the starting point for the multiperiod analysis, no initial contract or sulfur constraints were assumed. The proportions of spot and contract coal were allowed to vary from the historical levels (in subsequent multiperiod solutions) by permitting contracts on new development. Contracts in effect as of the 1973 solution were decaying at a constant rate (5 percent per year). Demand not bound by a contract could move on the spot market or new development could be solicited by negotiating a new contract.

Use of the Model to Support Policy and Policy Research

Two alternatives, one with and one without sulfur regulations, were used for the 1975 through 1990 scenarios. In addition, each of these alternatives was run assuming a high and a low demand level for the years 1985 and 1990. Contracts signed prior to, or in, 1973 were not subject to the sulfur regulations; however, shipments from new development and the spot market were forced to conform to emission standards. Consequently, for the 1990 demand alternatives, only 5 out of 44 regions met the actual per ton air quality standards; but with all original contracts due to expire by 1993, compliance was nearly complete in all regions.

The most effective way of deriving the policy implications of imposing restrictions on the amount of sulfur emissions was to compare the model's results with those assuming no sulfur restrictions. One comparison of interest was the added production and transportation costs associated with imposing emission restrictions of 1.2 pounds of sulfur dioxide per million Btu. To meet 1975 demand levels, the combined cost of production and transportation was 11.0 percent higher when sulfur restrictions were imposed. The costs were only 8.3 percent higher in 1980. For 1985 (1990) the costs were 13.0 percent (16.3 percent) and 14.1 percent (18.2 percent) higher, assuming low and high demand, respectively, as a result of the added restrictions.

The other significant implications (and the reasons for higher costs) of implementing sulfur restrictions began with the production and new development patterns in 1975. As a result of the restrictions, only 67.2 percent of the coal production originated in eastern supply regions, compared with 83.5 percent without the restrictions. Western regions dominated new development from the outset. Only 19.0 percent of the new development occurred east of the Mississippi River in 1975.

When compared with the 1973 and 1975 solutions without sulfur constraints, there was a significant reversal in the East to West shipping patterns. The northern Great Plains and the western regions began shipments of 74.3 million tons to areas east of the Mississippi, including Illinois, Indiana, Michigan and Ohio. Closer analysis reveals that many of the new West to East linkages (approximately 81 percent or 60 million tons) originated in southern Montana and northern Wyoming. Large differences also occurred in tonnage shipped from other supply regions, except Texas and the northeastern Great Plains. The lower sulfur content and per mile transport costs of these western coal reserves more than compensated for the lower Btu content and longer distances. These reversed trends (when compared to the situations with no sulfur constraints) were accentuated in future years as the long-term contracts decayed.

The analysis of shadow prices provided interesting insights into the changes in the objective function to marginal changes in constraint levels. Regional shadow prices for solutions containing sulfur constraints indicated that New England, the Middle Atlantic, the South Atlantic, and East South Central regions were the areas most severely affected by sulfur regulation. The average price increase for these areas from 1973 to 1975 was $7.65 per ton. Comparisons with the solution not constrained by sulfur restrictions showed the average price increase for these areas to be $0.20. Analysis through time showed that the greatest differences between delivered prices for solutions with and without sulfur constraints occurred in 1975. For example, the average difference in 1975 was $7.87 while a 1985 solution showed a difference of only $5.11 per ton.

In addition to information concerning delivered prices, preliminary insights into the impact of stack-gas scrubbers was examined by inspecting the shadow prices associated with the sulfur constraints. That is, the effect of installing scrubbers was approximated by allowing higher sulfur emission levels (relaxing sulfur constraints). Regional variation in sulfur constraint shadow values followed a pattern similar to one found for demand constraints. Regional variation was generally higher in the East and Northeast than the West (a pattern generated in large part by the location of low-sulfur coal supplies). Thus it appeared that the use of stack-gas scrubbers would be considered most seriously in the East. Moreover, a comparison of sulfur constraint shadow price magnitude with the amortized cost of scrubbers suggested that investment in stack scrubbers between 1980 and 1985 was a viable alternative to the use of low-sulfur coal for meeting emission standards.

Examination of the shadow prices associated with the demand constraints also provided some indication of expected changes in coal prices. Because of the inability of eastern supply regions to adequately supply low-sulfur coal, large regional price differentials among the supply regions could arise. The long distances over which western coal is shipped, and the rising demand for low-sulfur coal, would have precipitated coal price increases in the East significantly higher than those in the West. In the absence of sulfur restrictions, even in the face of higher future demand, price differentials would have remained much lower. Undoubtedly, much of this price increase would have been passed through to eastern consumers.

The strict enforcement of national ambient air standards for sulfur dioxide emissions was predicted to cause extremely large flows of investment into the northern Great Plains with associated congestion, changes in the general social climate, and environmental degradation. Severance taxes imposed by western states in an attempt to slow development or add to state revenues could increase costs and conflict with national policy objectives.

CONCLUSIONS

In order to relate energy and resource models to policy decisionmaking, three case studies were used to illustrate the roles models play in policy decisions. The general roles described for models included anticipatory research, alerting decisionmakers to potential problems in time to act; aids to policy design; and evaluative research, determining whether existing policy is meeting its original objectives.

The case studies also illustrated the types of decisions made in constructing and using a model. It is not possible to assemble a list of criteria a model must meet before it is acceptable, or a list of criteria, that if met, will ensure the model will be useful in guiding policymakers. This observation has led many model users familiar with both the modeling and the policy process to refer to modeling as an art rather than a science.

A model from which one can consistently extract useful advice is more highly valued among model users or policymakers than a theoretically elegant but impractical model. The usefulness of a model is linked to the quality of judgments made by the modeler. In addition, users tend not to believe results just because they come from a model; an intuitive explanation is required as well. Therefore, the modeler plays a critical role in explaining and applying the model. Assumptions in and results out without a clear explanation of what happens inside the model has been referred to as the problem of the "black box." Models even more than statistics can be made to show any result.

These views of policymakers suggest that they have become disenchanted with the use of models in the policy process. The disenchantment probably reflects the high expectations created for models in the wake of expanding databases and ever-greater computing power more than the actual contribution made by models themselves. A contributing factor, however, is the difficulty or impossibility of verifying a claim that a specific model result led to a particularly good decision. When the decision is bad, of course, there is plenty of blame for all participants. However, modelers, as a group, must share the blame for disenchantment with models. Too often modelers retreat from the decision process with excuses: "The results were only scenarios and not meant to be a prediction of what was likely to happen," or "Of course we did not consdier the possibility of an OPEC boycott, an economic recession, or safety concerns with nuclear power."

Despite the disenchantment and what some would term the poor record of models, decisionmakers continue to fund modeling and model development. Models can be improved if they are constructed with an awareness of the physical, institutional, and economic considerations important to the issue at hand. What is important depends, to a large extent, on the way the model will be used. The modeling choices highlighted here include:

1. The type of model—is it optimizing, econometric, simulation, market equilibrium, or partial equilibrium in nature;
2. Geographic disaggregation and coverage—does the model cover the world, world regions, a nation or a state, and should multiple geographic regions be included;
3. Other disaggregation issues—in the case of energy, should fossil versus nonfossil fuels, coal/oil/gas, or individual petroleum products be identified separately.

In presenting the cases some general modeling principles were apparent. Any model is a highly simplified characterization of a complex system. As a result, models suffer, to a greater or lesser degree, from problems associated with aggregation, uncertain parameters, uncertain exogenous changes in the economic environment, and the transfer of information among actors. The users of modeling techniques, models, and model results need to be constantly aware of the limits and constraints of the results. In the most general sense, any policy decision necessarily involves taking an action in the present that will impact the future. As such, it is always the case that a decision to act is associated with a set of expectations about the future environment the present action will shape and the various outcomes different actions will have. These expectations may be implicit and may be very different for different participants in the decision process. The purpose of policy research, in general, and energy modeling and forecasting, specifically, should be to improve the expectations on which policy decisions are based. Forecast scenarios must be created that are coherent and founded on accepted methodology and a solid understanding of the physical, economic, and institutional aspects of the issues.

Much of the discussion in this chapter on the role of models in policy decisions applies equally to the analysis and discussion of the eleven previous chapters. The generality of the recommendations should not be surprising; the formal models of this chapter are merely attempts to provide mathematical rigor and quantification to discussions of factors affecting natural resource issues. A graphical representation of supply and demand curves is a model. The concept of the CO_2 model is an elaboration of such a simple model. An observation by decisionmakers that increasing population puts pressure on the environment is a rudimentary model where an increase in the population increases the demand for the natural resources and the environment. Natural resources policy analysis and policy modeling are extensions of the decisionmaking process. As such, the aim is to make better decisions through a careful and thorough consideration of all aspects of the issue bringing whatever information and data are available to bear on the issue.

REFERENCES

Edmonds, J. A., and J. M. Reilly (1985). *Global Energy: Assessing the Future.* New York: Oxford University Press.

———— (1983). "A Long-Term, Global, Energy-Economic Model of Carbon Dioxide Release from Fossil Fuel Use." *Energy Economics* 5(2):74–88.

Edmonds, J. A., J. M. Reilly, R. H. Gardner, and A. Brenkert (1986). *Uncertainty in Future Global Energy Use and Fossil Fuel CO_2 Emissions 1975 to 2075*, DOE/NBB-081. Washington, D.C.: U.S. Dept. of Energy.

LeBlanc, M. R. (1985). "The Effects of Natural Gas Decontrol on Fertilizer Demand, Production Costs, and Income in Agriculture." *The Energy Journal* 6(1):117–135.

LeBlanc, M. R., R. J. Kalter, and R. N. Boisvert (1978). "Allocation of United States Coal Production to Meet Future Energy Needs." *Land Economics* 54(3):316–336.

Rose, David, Marvin Miller, and Carson Agnew (1983). "Global Energy Futures and CO_2-Induced Climate Change." Report No. MITEL 83-015. Cambridge, Mass.: MIT Energy Laboratory.

Seidel, Stephen, and Dale Keyes (1983). "Can We Delay a Greenhouse Warming?" Washington, D.C.: U.S. Environmental Protection Agency.

SUGGESTED READINGS

Chapman, Duane (1983). *Energy Resources and Energy Corporations.* Ithaca: Cornell University Press.

An unconventional examination of energy problems. This book begins with a theoretical discussion of growth, monopoly, and social costs in the energy industry. The author concludes with recommendations for achieving lower social costs with no decrease in living standards. The work is an excellent counterpoint to Gordon's neoclassical treatment.

Darmstaedter, Joel, Hans Landsberg, and Herbert C. Morton (1983). *Energy Today and Tomorrow: Living With Uncertainty.* New York: Prentice-Hall, for Resources for the Future.

This book provides an excellent, comprehensive overview of energy resource issues for the undergraduate student. It includes a discussion of environmental, national security, and resource issues associated with energy production and use. The authors emphasize the dilemma of making choices in an uncertain environment where all options have negative as well as positive aspects.

Edmonds, Jae, and John Reilly (1985). *Global Energy: Assessing the Future*. New York: Oxford University Press.
This work is an assessment of global energy resources, both conventional and exotic, and of factors affecting future energy demand. The book provides projections of fossil energy use to the year 2050, predicting the impact of fossil fuel use on atmospheric CO_2 levels. Much of the book is accessible to a general audience with some background in resource economics or related disciplines. The model used for developing projections is available in various magnetic formats, including a personal computer version. The model has been used in classrooms.

Gordon, Richard (1981). *An Economic Analysis of World Energy Problems*. Cambridge, Mass.: MIT Press.
As a neoclassical economics treatment of energy issues, the main text presents material accessible to an undergraduate economics major. The focus is on the economic analysis of energy problems rather than the institutional, social, and political nuances of energy issues.

Intrilligator, Michael (1971). *Mathematical Optimization and Economic Theory*. Englewood Cliffs, N.J.: Prentice-Hall.
This work is a self-contained introduction to and summary of static and dynamic optimization techniques and their application to economic theory. The level of mathematics background required is kept as elementary as possible. Key mathematical results are summarized in the appendices.

Varian, Hal (1978). *Microeconomic Analysis*. New York: W. W. Norton & Company.
This book is a microeconomic theory text for first-year graduate students and advanced undergraduates with a strong mathematics background. It is an excellent reference text particularly for neoclassical economic models of consumer and producer behavior. It provides a complete treatment of the principles and application of the theory of duality between physical production, price, and cost relationships.

STUDY QUESTIONS

1. Identify the major characteristics of the three types of models—simulation, optimizing, and econometric—described in this chapter. How is each type of model useful for analysis of resource and environmental problems?

2. Use the discussion in this chapter on the role of research and a case study from one of the previous ten chapters to discuss how economic concepts can play a useful role in applied policy formulation.

3. On the basis of the information provided in this chapter and in Chapter 5 on nuclear waste disposal, Chapter 6 on acid rain, Chapter 9 on the Columbia River, and Chapter 11 on global climatic effects, evaluate the proposition that the United States should expand its sources of electricity primarily through coal-fired thermal power plants.

4. Provide an example, from this or previous chapters, of how the reluctance to use prices to allocate resources among individuals and over time resulted in resource misallocation; show also by example how reliance on prices to allocate resources can lead to a socially undesirable outcome.

Acronyms

AES	Atmospheric Environment Service
BMPs	Best Management Practices
BPA	Bonneville Power Administration
DNR	Department of Natural Resources
EFSEC	Energy Facility Site Evaluation Council
EIL	Economic Injury Level
EIS	Environmental Impact Statement
EPA	Environmental Protection Agency
ET	Economic Threshold
FAO	Food and Agriculture Organization
FERC	Federal Energy Regulatory Commission
FIFRA	Federal Insecticide, Fungicide, and Rodenticide Act
FPL	Farmland Preservation Law
GAO	General Accounting Office
GCMs	General Circulation Models
GNP	Gross National Product
HLNW	High-Level Nuclear Waste
I-O	Input-Output
IDAs	Intensely Developed Areas
IPM	Integrated Pest Management
LDAs	Limited Development Areas
LP	Linear Programming
LRTAP	Long-Range Transport of Atmospheric Pollutants
LWVEF	League of Women Voters Education Fund
MEY	Maximum Economic Yield
MFCMA	Magnuson Fisheries Conservation and Management Act
MRS	Monitored Retrievable Storage
MSY	Maximum Sustainable Yield
NEPA	National Environmental Protection Act
NFMA	National Forest Management Act
NGPA	Natural Gas Policy Act
NRC	Nuclear Regulatory Commission
OECD	Organization for Economic Cooperation and Development
OPEC	Organization of Petroleum Exporting Countries
OTA	Office of Technology Assessment
OY	Optimum Yield
PCM	Perfectly Competitive Market
PNUCC	Pacific Northwest Utilities Conference Committee

RARE II   Roadless Area Review and Evaluation
RCAs   Resource Conversation Areas
RPAR   Rebuttable Presumption Against Registration Process
USGS   U.S. Geological Survey
USDA   U.S. Department of Agriculture
USDOE   U.S. Department of Energy
USNRC   U.S. National Research Council
VSMB   Versatile Soil Moisture Budget
WPPSS   Washington Public Power Supply System

Index